Anti-Poverty and Rural Development

Prof. K. Venu Gopal Rao

MANGLAM PUBLICATIONS
DELHI-110053 (INDIA)

Published by :
MANGLAM PUBLICATIONS
L-21/1, Street No. 5, Shivaji Marg, Near Kali Mandir,
J.P. Nagar, Kartar Nagar, West Ghonda, Delhi-110053
Phone : 011-22945677, (M.) 9968367559, 9868572512
E-mail: manglam.books2007@rediffmail.com
manglam.publications2007@rediffmail.com

Anti-Poverty and Rural Development

First Edition 2010

ISBN 978-93-80013-45-9

PRINTED IN INDIA

Published by Ravindra Kumar Yadav for Manglam Publications, Delhi-110053 Laser Typeset by M.K. Graphics, Delhi- 53, Printed at Sachin Printers, Moujpur Delhi- 53

Preface

It has often been said that there is an'urban bias' in development, due to the assumption that economic growth and modernization naturally occurs in cities and has as its ultimate destination development by urbanization. This has meant that problem oriented interventions are typically focused on excluded rural people and built around rural paradigms. Even in development practice that is explicitly urban, stakeholders are often viewed through a rural lens. This has often left development practice with what amounts to a rural bias. Nowhere has this urban bias in development policy and rural bias in development practice been more clearly manifest than in the developmentalist states of Asia. Drawing on contemporary empirical data from the Urban Poverty Project (UPP), an ongoing World Bank/Indonesian government urban anti-poverty initiative in Northern Java, we discuss some of the ways in which this rural bias has weakened the conceptual tools for imagining development in urban environments. It will be our argument that the dominant rural/village development trope and its corresponding scalar dichotomies between local and global and social dichotomies between traditional and modern have formed the basis of much of the way we think about and practice development. This has often obscured, rather than clarified what people actually want and need and how it can best be delivered.

—*Author*

Contents

1

Introduction

POVERTY IN INDIA

Poverty is one of the main problems which have attracted attention of sociologists and economists. It indicates a condition in which a person fails to maintain a living standard adequate for his physical and mental efficiency. It is a situation people want to escape. It gives rise to a feeling of a discrepancy between what one has and what one should have. The term poverty is a relative concept. It is very difficult to draw a demarcation line between affluence and poverty. According to Adam Smith - Man is rich or poor according to the degree in which he can afford to enjoy the necessaries, the conveniences and the amusements of human life.

Even after more than 50 years of Independence India still has the world's largest number of poor people in a single country. Of its nearly 1 billion inhabitants, an estimated 260.3 million are below the poverty line, of which 193.2 million are in the rural areas and 67.1 million are in urban areas. More than 75% of poor people reside in villages. Poverty level is not uniform across India. The poverty level is below 10% in states like Delhi, Goa, and Punjab etc whereas it is below 50% in Bihar (43) and Orissa (47). It is between 30-40% in Northeastern states of Assam, Tripura, and Mehgalaya and in Southern states of TamilNadu and Uttar Pradesh.

Poverty has many dimensions changing from place to place and across time. There are two inter-related aspects of poverty-

Urban and rural poverty. The main causes of urban poverty are predominantly due to impoverishment of rural peasantry that forces them to move out of villages to seek some subsistence living in the towns and cities. In this process, they even lose the open space or habitat they had in villages albeit without food and other basic amenities. When they come to the cities, they get access to some food though other sanitary facilities including clean water supply still elude them.

And they have to stay in the habitats that place them under sub-human conditions. While a select few have standards of living comparable to the richest in the world, the majority fails to get two meals a day. The causes of rural poverty are manifold including inadequate and ineffective implementation of anti-poverty programmes.The overdependence on monsoon with non-availability of irrigational facilities often result in crop-failure and low agricultural productivity forcing farmers in the debt-traps. The rural communities tend to spend large percentage of annual earnings on social ceremonies like marriage; feast etc.Our economic development since Independence has been lopsided .There has been increase in unemployment creating poverty like situations for many. Population is growing at an alarming rate. The size of the Indian family is relatively bigger averaging at 4.2.The other causes include dominance of caste system which forces the individual to stick to the traditional and hereditary occupations.

Since the 1970s the Indian government has made poverty reduction a priority in its development planning. Policies have focused on improving the poor standard of living by ensuring food security, promoting self-employment through greater access to assets, increasing wage employment and improving access to basic social services. Launched in 1965, India's Public Distribution System has helped meet people's basic food needs by providing rations at subsidized prices. Although it has affected less than 20% of the Poor's food purchases, the system has been important in sustaining people's consumption of cereals, especially in periods of drought. It has provided women and girls with better access to food and helped overcome the widespread discrimination against female consumption within households. It has also reduced the burden of women, who are responsible for providing food for the household. The largest credit-based government poverty reduction programme in the world, the Integrated Rural Development Programme provides rural households below the poverty line with credit to purchase income-generating assets. Launched in 1979, the programme has supplied subsidized credit to such groups as small and marginalized farmers, agricultural laborers, rural artisans, the physically handicapped, scheduled castes and scheduled tribes. Within this target population, 40% of the beneficiaries are supposed to be women. Although the programme has reached 51 million families, only 27% of the borrowers have been women. The programme has significantly increased the income of 57% of assisted families.

Rural poverty is largely a result of low productivity and unemployment. The Jawahar Rozgar Yojana, a national public works scheme launched in 1989 with financing from the central and state governments, provides more than 700 million person days of work a year about 1% of total employment for people with few opportunities for employment. The scheme has two components: a programme to provide low-cost housing and one to supply free irrigation wells to poor and marginalized farmers. The public works scheme is self-targeting. Since it offers employment at the statutory minimum wage for unskilled manual labor, only those willing to accept very low wages the poor are likely to enroll in the scheme. By providing regular employment and thereby increasing the bargaining power of all rural workers, the public works scheme has had a significant effect in reducing poverty. It has also contributed to the construction of rural infrastructure (irrigation works, a soil conservation project, drinking water supply). Evaluations show that 82% of available funds have been channeled to community development projects. Targeting was improved in 1996 when the housing and irrigation well components were delinked and focused exclusively on people below the poverty line.

TRYSEM (Training rural youth for self employment) was started to provide technical skills to the rural youth and to help them to get employment in fields such as agriculture, industry, services and business activities. Youth of the poor families belonging to the age-group of 18-35 are entitled to avail the benefits of the scheme. Priority is given to persons belonging to ST/SC and ex-servicemen and about 1/3 seats are reserved for women. Minimum Needs Programme was taken up as an integral part of the 5th Five Year Plan and it was intended to cater to the minimum needs of the people such as rural water supply, rural health, road building, adult education, primary education, rural electrification and improvement of the urban slums etc.With the intention of removing urban unemployment some schemes such as SEPUP (Self-employment programme for the urban poor); SEEUY (Scheme for self-employment of the educated urban youths) .These schemes gives loans and subsidies for the urban unemployed youths to create or to find for themselves some jobs. The SEPUP had provided financial help for about 1.19 urban unemployed youths in the year 190-91.

The participation of civil society organizations in poverty reduction efforts, especially those directed to women, has increased social awareness and encouraged governments to provide better services. Cooperatives such as the Self-Employed Women's Association provide credit to women at market rates of interest but do not require collateral; they also allow flexibility in the use of loans and the timing of repayments. These civil society organizations have not only contributed to women's material well being; they have also helped empower them socially and politically. Such credit initiatives, by bringing women out of the confines of the household, are changing their status within the family and within village hierarchies. The demands of civil society organizations for better social services have spurred the government to launch campaigns to increase literacy and improve public infrastructure. And their calls for greater accountablllty and real devolution of power are increasing the likelihood that expenditures for poverty reduction will reach the needy, especially women.

The Indian state has undoubtedly failed in its responsibilities towards its citizens over the last 50 odd years. There is a need for the state to move out of many areas and the process has been started with economic liberalization. The process of decentralization should devolute lot more powers, both functional and financial, to panchayats. The lack of transparency and accountability has hampered our economic development at all levels. The problem of poverty persists because of a number of leakages in the system. New laws have to be evolved to ensure more accountability. Bodies like the Planning Commission should be modified into new constitutional bodies that can hold governments accountable for their failure to implement development programmes. A strong system of incentives and disincentives also needs to be introduced. The encouragement of non-governmental organizations and private sector individuals in tackling poverty is imperative, as the state cannot do everything.

The government has initiated, sustained, and refined many programs since independence to help the poor attain self sufficiency in food production. Probably the most important initiative has been the supply of basic commodities, particularly food at controlled prices, available throughout the country. The poor spend about 80 percent of their income on food while the rest of the population spends more than 60 percent. The price of food is a major determinant of wage scales. Often when food prices rise sharply, rioting and looting follow. Until the late 1970s, the government frequently had difficulty obtaining adequate grain supplies in years of poor harvests. During those times, states with surpluses of grain were cordoned off to force partial sales to public agencies and to keep private traders from shipping grain to deficit areas to secure very high prices; state governments in surplus-grain areas were often less than cooperative. After the late 1970s, the central government, by holding reserve stocks and importing grain adequately and early, maintained sufficient supplies to meet the increased demand during drought years. It also provided more remunerative prices to farmers.

India Poverty: In rural areas, the government has undertaken programs to mitigate the worst effects of adverse monsoon rainfall, which affects not only farmers but village artisans and traders when the price of grain rises. The government has supplied water by financing well digging and, since the early 1980s, by power-assisted well drilling; rescinded land taxes for drought areas; tried to maintain stable food prices; and provided food through a food-for-work program. The actual work accomplished through food-for-work programs is often a secondary consideration, but useful projects sometimes result. Employment is offered at a low daily wage, usually paid in grain, the rationale being that only the truly needy will take jobs at such low pay.

In the 1980s and early 1990s, Indian government programs attempted to provide basic needs at stable, low prices; to increase income through pricing and regulations, such as supplying water from irrigation works, fertilizer, and other inputs; to foster location of industry in backward areas; to increase access to basic social services, such as education, health, and potable water supply; and to help needy groups and deprived areas. The total money spent on such programs for the poor was not discernible from the budget data, but probably exceeded 10 percent of planned budget outlays.

India has had a number of antipoverty programs since the early 1960s. These include, among others, the National Rural Employment Programme and the Rural Landless Employment Guarantee Programme. The National Rural Employment Programme evolved in FY 1980 from the earlier Food for Work Programme to use unemployed and underemployed workers to build productive community assets. The Rural Landless Employment Guarantee Programme was instituted in FY 1983 to address the plight of the hard-core rural poor by expanding employment opportunities and building the rural infrastructure as a means of encouraging rapid economic growth. There were many problems with the implementation of these and otherschemes, but observers credit them with helping reduce poverty. To improve the effectiveness of the National Rural Employment Programme, in 1989 it was combined with the Rural Landless Employment Guarantee Programme and renamed Jawahar Rozgar Yojana, or Jawahar Employment Plan.

State governments are important participants in antipoverty programs. The constitution assigns responsibility to the states in a number of matters, including ownership, redistribution, improvement, and taxation of land. State governments implement most central government programs concerned with land reform and the situation of small landless farmers. The central government tries to establish programs and norms among the states and union territories, but implementation has often remained at the lower bureaucratic levels. In some matters concerning subsoil rights and irrigation projects, the central government exerts political and financial leverage to obtain its objectives, but the states sometimes modify or retard the impact of central government policies and programs.

DEVELOPMENT PLANNING

Planning in India dates back to the 1930s. Even before independence, the colonial government had established a planning board that lasted from 1944 to 1946. Private industrialists and economists published three development plans in 1944. India's leaders adopted the principle of formal economic planning soon after independence as an effective way to intervene in the economy to foster growth and social justice.

The Planning Commission was established in 1950. Responsible only to the prime minister, the commission is independent of the cabinet. The prime minister is chairperson of the commission, and the minister of state with independent charge for planning and program implementation serves as deputy chairperson. A staff drafts national plans under the guidance of the commission; draft plans are presented for approval to the National Development Council, which consists of the Planning Commission and the chief ministers of the states. The council can make changes in the draft plan. After council approval, the draft is presented to the cabinet and subsequently to Parliament, whose approval makes the plan an operating document for central and state governments (see The Legislature; Local Government, ch. 8).

The First Five-Year Plan (FY 1951-55) attempted to stimulate balanced economic development while correcting imbalances caused by World War II and partition. Agriculture, including projects that combined irrigation and power generation, received priority. By contrast, the Second Five-Year Plan (FY 1956-60) emphasized industrialization, particularly basic, heavy industries in the public sector, and improvement of the economic infrastructure. The plan also stressed social goals, such as more equal distribution of income and extension of the benefits of economic development to the large number of disadvantaged people. The Third Five-Year Plan (FY 1961-65) aimed at a substantial rise in national and per capita income while expanding the industrial base and rectifying the neglect of agriculture in the previous plan. The third plan called for national income to grow at a rate of more than 5 percent a year; self-sufficiency in food grains was anticipated in the mid-1960s.

Economic difficulties disrupted the planning process in the mid-1960s. In 1962, when a brief war was fought with China on the Himalayan frontier, agricultural output was stagnating, industrial production was considerably below expectations, and the economy was growing at about half of the planned rate. Defense expenditures increased sharply, and the increased foreign aid needed to maintain development expenditures eventually provided 28 percent of public development spending. Midway through the third plan, it was clear that its goals could not be achieved.

Food prices rose in 1963, causing rioting and looting of grain warehouses in 1964. War with Pakistan in 1965 sharply reduced the foreign aid available. Successive severe droughts in 1965 and 1966 further disrupted the economy and planning. Three annual plans guided development between FY 1966 and FY 1968 while plan policies and strategies were reevaluated. Immediate attention centered on increasing agricultural growth, stimulating exports, and searching for efficient uses of industrial assets. Agriculture was to be expanded, largely through the supply of inputs to take advantage of new high-yield seeds becoming available for food grains. The rupee was substantially devalued in 1966, and export incentives were adjusted to promote exports. Controls affecting industry were simplified, and greater reliance was placed on the price mechanism to achieve industrial efficiency.

The Fourth Five-Year Plan (FY 1969-73) called for a 24 percent increase over the third plan in real terms of public development expenditures. The public sector accounted for 60 percent of plan expenditures, and foreign aid contributed 13 percent of plan financing. Agriculture, including irrigation, received 23 percent of public outlays; the rest was mostly spent on electric power, industry, and transportation. Although the plan projected national income growth at 5.7 percent a year, the realized rate was only 3.3 percent.

The Fifth Five-Year Plan (FY 1974-78) was drafted in late 1973 when crude oil prices were rising rapidly; the rising prices quickly forced a series of revisions.

The plan was subsequently approved in late 1976 but was terminated at the end of FY 1977 because a new government wanted different priorities and programs. The fifth plan was in effect only one year, although it provided some guidance to investments throughout the five-year period. The economy operated under annual plans in FY 1978 and FY 1979.

The Sixth Five-Year Plan (FY 1980-84) was intended to be flexible and was based on the principle of annual "rolling" plans. It called for development expenditures of nearly Rs1.9 trillion (in FY 1979 prices), of which 90 percent would be financed from domestic sources, 57 percent of which would come from the public sector. Public-sector development spending would be concentrated in energy (29 percent); agriculture and irrigation (24 percent); industry including mining (16 percent); transportation (16 percent); and social services (14 percent). In practice, slightly more was spent on social services at the expense of transportation and energy. The plan called for GDP growth to increase by 5.1 percent a year, a target that was surpassed by 0.3 percent. A major objective of the plan was to increase employment, especially in rural areas, in order to reduce the level of poverty. Poor people were given cows, bullock carts, and handlooms; however, subsequent studies indicated that the income of only about 10 percent of the poor rose above the poverty level.

The Seventh Five-Year Plan (FY 1985-89) envisioned a greater emphasis on the allocation of resources to energy and social spending at the expense of industry and agriculture. In practice, the main increase was in transportation and communications, which took up 17 percent of public-sector expenditure during this period. Total spending was targeted at nearly Rs3.9 trillion, of which 94 percent would be financed from domestic resources, including 48 percent from the public sector. The planners assumed that public savings would increase and help finance government spending. In practice that increase did not occur; instead, the government relied on foreign borrowing for a greater share of resources than expected.

The schedule for the Eighth Five-Year Plan (FY 1992-96) was affected by changes of government and by growing uncertainty over what role planning could usefully perform in a more liberal economy. Two annual plans were in effect in FY 1990 and FY 1991. The eighth plan was finally launched in April 1992 and emphasized market-based policy reform rather than quantitative targets. Total spending was planned at Rs 8.7 trillion, of which 94 percent would be financed from domestic resources, 45 percent of which would come from the public sector. The eighth plan included three general goals. First, it sought to cut back the public sector by selling off failing and inessential industries while encouraging private investment in such sectors as power, steel, and transport. Second, it proposed that agriculture and rural development have priority. Third, it sought to renew the assault on illiteracy and improve other aspects of social infrastructure, such as the provision of fresh drinking water. Government documents issued in 1992 indicated that GDP growth was expected to increase from around 5 percent a year during the seventh plan to 5.6 percent a year during the eighth plan. However, in 1994 economists expected annual growth to be around 4 percent during the period of the eighth plan.

Four decades of planning show that India's economy, a mix of public and private enterprise, is too large and diverse to be wholly predictable or responsive to directions of the planning authorities. Actual results usually differ in important respects from plan targets. Major shortcomings include insufficient improvement in income distribution and alleviation of poverty, delayed completions and cost overruns on many public-sector projects, and far too small a return on many public-sector investments. Even though the plans have turned out to be less effective than expected, they help guide investment priorities, policy recommendations, and financial mobilization.

MINISTRY OF RURAL DEVELOPMENT

India has been a welfare state ever since her Independence and the primary objective of all governmental endeavors has been the welfare of its millions. Planning has been one of the pillars of the Indian policy since independence and the country's strength is derived from the achievement of planning. The policies and programmes have been designed with the aim of alleviation of rural poverty which has been one of the primary objectives of planned development in India. It was realized that a sustainable strategy of poverty alleviation has to be based on increasing the productive employment opportunities in the process of growth itself. Elimination of poverty, ignorance, diseases and inequality of opportunities and providing a better and higher quality of life were the basic premises upon which all the plans and blue-prints of development were built.

Rural development implies both the economic betterment of people as well as greater social transformation. In order to provide the rural people with better prospects for economic development, increased participation of people in the rural development programmes, decentralization of planning, better enforcement of land reforms and greater access to credit are envisaged.

Initially, main thrust for development was laid on agriculture industry, communication, education, health and allied sectors but later on it was realized that accelerated development can be provided only if governmental efforts are adequately supplemented by direct and indirect involvement of people at the grass root level. Accordingly, on 31st March 1952, an organization known as Community Projects Administration was set up under the Planning Commission to administer the programmes relating to community development. The community development programme inaugurated on October 2, 1952, was an important landmark in the history of the rural development. This programme underwent many changes and was handled by different Ministries.

In October 1974, the Department of Rural Development came into existence as a part of Ministry of Food and Agriculture. On 18th August 1979, the Department of Rural Development was elevated to the status of a new Ministry of Rural Reconstruction. That Ministry was renamed as Ministry of Rural Development on 23rd January 1982. In January 1985, the Ministry of Rural Development was again converted into a Department under the Ministry of Agriculture and Rural Development which was later rechristened as Ministry of Agriculture in September 1985. On July 5, 1991 the Department was upgraded as Ministry of Rural

Development. Another Department viz. Department of Wasteland Development was created under this Ministry on 2nd July 1992. In March 1995, the Ministry was renamed as the Ministry of Rural Areas and Employment with three departments namely Department of Rural Employment and Poverty Alleviation, Rural Development and Wasteland Development.

Again, in 1999 Ministry of Rural Areas and Employment was renamed as Ministry of Rural Development. This Ministry has been acting as a catalyst effecting the change in rural areas through the implementation of wide spectrum of programmes which are aimed at poverty alleviation, employment generation, infrastructure development and social security. Over the years, with the experience gained, in the implementation of the programmes and in response to the felt needs of the poor, several programmes have been modified and new programmes have been introduced. This Ministry's main objective is to alleviate rural poverty and ensure improved quality of life for the rural population especially those below the poverty line. These objectives are achieved through formulation, development and implementation of programmes relating to various spheres of rural life and activities, from income generation to environmental replenishment.

In order to ensure that the fruits of economic reform are shared by all sections of societies five elements of social and economic infrastructure, critical to the quality of life in rural areas, were identified. These are health education drinking water, housing and roads. To impart greater momentum to the efforts in these sectors the Government had launched the Pradhan Mantri Gramdoya Yojana (PMGY) and the ministry of rural development was entrusted with the responsibility of implementing drinking water, housing and rural roads component of PMGY

During the Ninth Plan period, several anti-poverty Programmes have been restructured to enhance the efficiency of the Programmes for providing increased benefits to the rural poor. Self Employment Programmes have been revamped by merging the Integrated Rural Development Programme (IRDP), the Development of Women and Children in Rural Areas (DWCRA), the Supply of Improved Tool-Kits to Rural Artisans

(SITRA), the Training of Rural Youth for Self Employment (TRYSEM), the Ganga Kalyan Yojana (GKY) and the Million Wells Scheme (MWS) into a holistic self-employment scheme called Swarnjayanti Gram Swarozgar Yojana (SGSY).

Keeping in view the needs and aspirations of the local people, Panchayati Raj Institutions have been involved in the programme implementation and these institutions constitute the core of decentralized development of planning and its implementations. The Ministry is also vigorously pursuing with the State Governments for expeditious devolution of requisite administrative and financial powers to PRI's as envisaged under 73rd amendment act of the Constitution of India. On 25th December 2002, under Drinking Water Sector, a new initiative'Swajal Dhara' empowering the Panchayats to formulate, implement, operate and maintain Drinking Water Projects has been launched. In order to further involve PRIs in the development process, a new initiative'Hariyali' has been launched by Hon'ble Prime Minister on 27th January, 2003. Hariyali has been launched to strengthen and involve Panchayati Raj Institutions in the implementation of Watershed Development Programmes namely IWDP, DPAP and DDP.

The empowerment of rural women is crucial for the development of rural India. Bringing women into the mainstream of development is a major concern for the Government of India. Therefore, the programmes for poverty alleviation have a women's component to ensure flow of adequate funds to this section. The Constitutional (73rd) Amendment, Act 1992 provides for reservation of selective posts for women. The Constitution has placed enormous responsibility on the Panchayats to formulate and execute various programmes of economic development and social justice, and a number of Centrally Sponsored Schemes are being implemented through Panchayats. Thus, women Members and Chairpersons of Panchayats, who are basically new entrants in Panchayats, have to acquire the required skill and be given appropriate orientation to assume their rightful roles as leaders and decision makers. To impart training for elected representatives of PRIs is primarily the responsibility of the State Governments/ Union Territory Administrations. Ministry of Rural Development also extends some financial assistance to the States/UTs with a view to improve the quality of training programmes and to catalyze capacity building initiatives for the PRI elected members and functionaries.

This Ministry is a nodal department for the two international organizations viz., the Centre on Integrated Rural Development of Asia and the Pacific (CIRDAP) and the Afro-Asian Rural Development Organization (AARDO).

The Ministry consists of the following three Departments:

1. Department of Rural Development
2. Department of Land Resources
3. Department of Drinking Water Supply

The Department of Rural Development implements schemes for generation of self employment and wage employment, provision of housing and minor irrigation assets to rural poor, social assistance to the destitute and Rural Roads. Apart from this, the Department provides the support services and other quality inputs such as assistance for strengthening of DRDA Administration, Panchayati raj institutions, training & research, human resource development, development of voluntary action etc. for the proper implementation of the programmes. The major programmes of the Department of Rural Development are Pradhan Mantri Gram Sadak Yojana, (PMGSY), Rural Housing (RH) Sampoorna Gramin Rozgar Yojana (SGRY) and Swaranjayanti Gram Swarozgar Yojana (SGSY).

Department of Land Resources implements schemes to increase the bio-mass production by developing wastelands in the country. Department also provides the support services and other quality inputs such as land reforms, betterment of revenue system and land records. It also undertakes development of desert areas and drought prone areas in the country. The major programmes of the Department of Land Resources are Drought Prone Area Programme (DPAP) The Desert Development Programme (DDP) the Integrated Wasteland Development Programme (IWDP) and Land Reforms (LR). These aim at increasing the soil and moisture conservation and productivity of the wasteland of the degraded lands thereby increase the income of the people. The provision of Drinking Water Supply and extension of Sanitation facilities to the rural poor are the main components of the activities of the Department of Drinking Water Supply. The major programmes of the Drinking Water Supply Department are The Swajaldhara, the Accelerated Rural Water Supply Programme (ARWSP) and the Total Sanitation Programme (TSP).

THE DISTRICT RURAL DEVELOPMENT AGENCY

Role and Functions

If effective programme design is critical to successful implementation of rural development programmes, so is an effective delivery agency. None of the anti- poverty programmes can have impact unless they are implemented with a clarity of purpose and a commitment to the task. It is here that the DRDAs play a critical role. The DRDAs are not be implementing agencies, but can be very effective in enhancing the quality of implementation through overseeing the implementation of different programmes and ensuring that necessary linkages are provided. To this extent the DRDA is a supporting and a facilitating organisation and needs to play a very effective role as a catalyst in development process.

The District Rural Development Agency is visualised as a specialised and a professional agency capable of managing the anti- poverty programmes of the Ministry of Rural Development on the one hand and to effectively relate these to the overall effort of poverty eradication in the District. In other words, while the DRDA will continue to watch over and ensure effective utilisation of the funds intended for anit-poverty programmes, it will need to develop a far greater understanding of the processes necessary for poverty alleviation/ eradication. It will also need to develop the capacity to build synergies among different agencies involved for the most effective results. It will therefore need to develop distinctive capabilities rather than perform tasks that are legitimately in the domain of the PRIs or the line departments. The role of the DRDA will therefore be distinct from all the other agencies including the Zilla Parishad.

DRDAs must themselves be more professional and should be able to interact effectively with various other agencies. They are expected to coordinate with the line departments, the Panchayati

Raj Institutions, the banks and other financial institutions, the NGOs as well as the technical institutions, with a view to gathering the support and resources required for poverty reduction effort in the district. It shall be their endeavor and objective to secure inter-sectoral and inter- departmental coordination and cooperation for reducing poverty in the district. It is their ability to coordinate and bring about a convergence of approach among different agencies for poverty alleviation that would set them apart.

The DRDAs are expected to coordinate effectively with the Panchayati Raj The institutions. Under no circumstances will they perform the functions of PRIs.

The DRDAs are expected to oversee the implementation of different anti-poverty programmes of the Ministry of Rural Development in the district. This is not to be confused with actual implementation, which will be by the Panchayati Raj and other Institutions. The DRDAs will monitor closely the implementation through obtaining of periodic reports as well as frequent field visits. The purpose of the visit should be to facilitate the implementing agencies in improving implementation process, besides ensuring that the quality of implementation of programmes is high. This would include overseeing whether the intended beneficiaries are receiving the benefits under the different programmes.

The DRDAs shall keep the Zilla Parishad, the State and the Central Government duly informed of the progress of the implementation of the programmes through periodic reports in the prescribed formats. Special report, as and when called for, shall be provided.

It shall be the duty of the DRDAs to oversee and ensure that the benefits specifically earmarked for certain target groups (SC/ST, women and disabled) reach them. They shall take all necessary steps to achieve the prescribed norms.

The DRDAs shall take necessary step to improve the awareness regarding rural development and poverty alleviation particularly among the rural poor. This would involve issues of poverty, the opportunities available to the rural poor and generally infusing a sense of confidence in their ability to overcome poverty. It would also involve sensitizing the different functionaries in the district to the different aspects of poverty and poverty alleviation programmes.

The DRDAs will strive to promote transparency in the implementation of different anti- poverty programmes. Towards this end, they shall publish periodically, the details of the different programmes and their implementation.

Keeping in view, the substantial investment that are being made in poverty alleviation programmes, the DRDAs shall ensure financial discipline in respect of the funds received by them, whether from Central or State Governments. They shall also ensure that the accounts are properly maintained including in respect of the funds allocated to banks or implementing agencies in accordance with the guidelines of different programmes.

Thus the role of the DRDA is in terms of planning for effective implementation of anti-poverty programmes; coordinating with other agencies- Governmental, non-Governmental, technical and financial for successful programme implementation; enabling the community and the rural poor to participate in the decision making process, overseeing the implementation to ensure adherence to guidelines, quality, equity and efficiently; reporting to the prescribed authorities on the implementation; and promoting transparency in decision making and implementation.

In addition the DRDAs shall coordinate and oversee the conduct of the BPL Census and such other surveys that are required from time to time.

The DRDAs shall also carry out/ aid in carring out action research/ or evaluation studies that are initiated by the Central/ State Governments.

The DRDAs should deal only with the anti-poverty programmes of the Ministry of Rural Development. If DRDAs are to be entrusted with programmes of other ministries or those of the State Governments, it should be ensured that these have a definite anti-poverty focus. Entrusting of any programme to the DRDAs, other than anti- poverty programmes of the Ministry, be it of any other Ministry of Government of India or the respective State Government will have to be done with the approval of the

Secretary, Rural Development of the respective State(s), who should examine such request in consultation with the Ministry of Rural Development, Government of India, In such cases, it must be ensured that adequate provision is made for requisite staffing needed for proper implementation of the programme.

Organizational Structure

In order to be effective, the DRDA must have an appropriate staffing structure as well as suitable personnel policy. Keeping in view the role and functions of the DRDA listed in the previous chapter, the staffing structure of DRDA must include positions for Planning for poverty alleviation, Project formulation, Social organisation and Capacity building, Gender concerns, Engineering supervision and Quality control, Project monitoring, Accountancy and Audit functions as well as Evaluation and Impact studies. An indicative staffing structure is given in Annexure and is also detailed below. The State Government may modify the structure suitably, but without altering the basic design, to take care of the needs of individual districts keeping in view their size as well as specificity. However, this will also be subject to the overall ceiling of administrative costs admissible to the DRDAs in the State. By and large the staff appointed should be dedicated to DRDA-related works and should not be frequently transferred.

2

Centrally Sponsored Schemes

INDIRA AWAAS YOJANA (IAY)

Indira Awaas Yojana, which used to be a component of Jawahar Rozgar Yojana, became an independent scheme from 1997-98 onwards. Its objective is construction of free houses to members of the Scheduled Castes/Scheduled Tribes, freed bonded labourers in rural areas and also to non SC/ST Rural poor people living below the poverty line.

Beneficiaries are selected from the Below-the-Poverty-Line (BPL) list approved by the Grama Sabha. At least 60% of the total IAY allocation during a financial year should be utilized for construction/upgradation of dwelling units for SC/ST BPL households. A maximum 40% of allocation is for non-SC/ST BPL rural households. 3% of the above categories should be allocated for physically and mentally challenged persons. Government of India has also asked the States to earmark 15% of the beneficiaries from amongst the minorities. New houses as well as upgradation of kutcha houses are being taken up under the scheme. It is funded by the Centre and the State in the ratio of 75:25.

New housesFrom 01.04.2005 onwards, the unit cost of a new house has been fixed at Rs. 25,000 for ordinary soil and Rs.27,500 for difficult soil.

Based on the budget announcement of the Union Finance Minister in February, 2008, this amount is likely to be increased by Rs.10, 000/- and the unit cost raised to Rs.35, 000/- for ordinary soil and Rs.37, 500/- for difficult soil. Moreover, the State

Government provides an additional amount for RCC roofing cost in addition to its matching share. With effect from 2006-07, the above RCC roofing cost has been raised from Rs.9, 000 to Rs.12, 000 per house.

The minimum plinth area of a house should be 20 square metres. All new houses are provided with the toilets and smokeless chulhas.

Beneficiaries undertake the construction with locally available materials employing low cost technologies. As the cost of construction of new houses has increased substantially, it has been decided to raise the RCC roofing cost from the existing Rs.12, 000 to Rs.20, 000 per house.

This along with the increase in unit cost as announced by the Central Government will raise the total cost of an IAY house from existing Rs.37,000 and Rs.39,500 to Rs.55,000 and Rs.58,500 for ordinary soil and difficult soil respectively.

A further subsidy of Rs.1,200 out of Total Sanitation Funds is dovetailed to enable each beneficiary construct a toilet in the IAY house.

Table : Indira Awaas Yojana (IAY) New Houses

Sl. No.	Year	Financial Allocation (Rs.in crores)	Physical Allocation
1	2000 - 01	108.02	32,064
2	2001 - 02	104.64	31,285
3	2002 - 03	124.82	40,786
4	2003 - 04	100.42	41,022
5	2004 - 05	151.68	42,625
6	2005 - 06	152.33	42,195
7	2006 - 07	189.19	49,850
8	2007 - 08	255.32	69,239
9	2008 - 09	380.78	69,233

District-wise breakup of Physical and Financial Allocation under IAY New Houses for year 2008-09 is given below:

Table : District-wise Physical and Financial Allocation under IAY New Houses 2008-09

Sl. No	Name of the District	Total (Rs. in lakhs)	No.of New houses
1	Coimbatore	1593.387	4553
2	Cuddalore	1020.672	2916
3	Dharmapuri	635.409	1815
4	Dindigul	1071.729	3062
5	Erode	1002.357	2864
6	Kancheepuram	951.237	2718
7	Kanniyakumari	381.987	1091
8	Karur	647.919	1851
9	Krishnagiri	753.516	2153
10	Madurai	679.932	1943
11	Nagapattinam	846.495	2419
12	Namakkal	741.321	2118
13	Perambalur	986.247	2818
14	Pudukottai	663.912	1897
15	Ramanathapuram	592.209	1692
16	Salem	958.527	2739
17	Sivagangai	618.012	1766
18	Thanjavur	751.347	2147
19	The Nilgiris	179.379	513
20	Theni	446.040	1274
21	Tiruchirappalli	813.096	2323
22	Tirunelveli	996.093	2846
23	Tiruvallur	1301.319	3718
24	Tiruvannamalai	1011.528	2890
25	Tiruvarur	512.307	1464
26	Tuticorin	831.411	2375
27	Vellore	1738.503	4967
28	Villupuram	999.909	2857
29	Virudhunagar	505.737	1445
	Total	**24231.537**	**69233**

SAMPOORNA GRAMEEN ROZGAR YOJANA (SGRY)

The primary objective of the scheme has been to give supplementary wage employment to rural labour, thereby providing food security and improving the nutritional levels in rural areas.

The secondary objective of the scheme is the creation of durable community assets and development of rural infrastructure. The district allocation is apportioned in the ratio 20:30:50 among the District Panchayat, Panchayat Unions and Village Panchayats.

NATIONAL RURAL EMPLOYMENT GUARANTEE SCHEME-TAMIL NADU

The National Rural Employment Guarantee Act was enacted in September 2005. The National Rural Employment Guarantee Scheme was launched on 02.02.2006 and is being implemented in ten districts, viz., Cuddalore, Dindigul, Nagapattinam, Sivagangai, Tiruvannamalai and Villupuram from 02.02.2006 onwards and in four more districts viz. Thanjavur, Tiruvarur, Tirunelveli and Karur from 01.04.2007 onwards. From 01.04.2008 onwards, the scheme is being extended to the remaining twenty districts of the State which are; 1. Ariyalur, 2. Dharmapuri, 3. Perambalur, 4. Pudukottai, 5. Ramanathapuram, 6. Namakkal, 7. Vellore, 8. Thoothu kudi, 9. Virudhunar 10. Salem, 11.Erode, 12. Tiruchirapalli, 13. Kanchee puram 14. Theni, 15. Tiruvallur, 16. Madurai, 17. Nilgiris, 18. Kanniyakumari, 19. Coimbatore and 20. Krishnagiri.

Objectives of the Scheme

The National Rural Employment Guarantee Act, 2005 (NREGA) guarantees 100 days of employment in a financial year to any rural household whose adult members are willing to do unskilled manual work. This Act is an important step towards the realization of the right to work. It is also expected to enhance people's livelihoods on a sustained basis, by developing the economic and social infrastructure in rural areas. The Village Panchayat will issue job cards to every registered individual. Payment of the statutory minimum wage and equal wages for men and women are the notable features of the scheme. National Rural Employment Guarantee Scheme - TN under National Rural Employment Guarantee Act was formulated in G.O M.S No. 89, RD & PR (CGS1) dt 2.8.2006 and published in Tamil Nadu Govervement Gazette Extraordinary No.181 dt 2.8.2006.

Funding Pattern

The cost of the scheme is shared between the Centre and the State in the ratio of 90:10. The Central Government will bear the following costs:a) The entire cost of wages for unskilled manual workers. 75 percent of the cost of material and wages for skilled and semi-skilled workers. Administrative expenses, which will include, inter alia, the salary and allowances of Programme Officers and their support staff and work site facilities. Administrative expenses of the Central Employment guarantee Council.The State Government will bear the following costs: 25 percent of the cost of material and wages for skilled and semi-skilled workers.Unemployment allowance payable in case the State Government cannot provide wage employment within 15 days of application. Administrative expenses of the State Employment Guarantee Council.

Priority of Works

Taking into account the field conditions in Tamil Nadu, the works are being taken up in Tamil Nadu in the following priority: Formation of new ponds. Renovation of existing Ponds, Kuttais, Kulams, Ooranies, Temple tanks etc. Desilting of channels. Desilting and strengthening of bunds of irrigation tanks. Formation of new roads. Other water conservation/soil conservation measures/flood protection measures.

Special Steps Taken to Ensure Successful Implementation of NREGS

On assumption of office in the month of May 2006, this Government noticed that the scheme had not taken off properly. This was evident from the fact that the expenditure made up to 31.03.2006 was only Rs. 3 crores and that works had been taken up only in 924 Village Panchayats out of a total of 3,830 Village Panchayats in the six Districts.This Government was quick to identify the issues and bottlenecks that were responsible for the poor progress in the implementation of the programme and came out with a series of initiatives to address those issues and to remove the implementation bottlenecks.As a result of the concerted efforts taken by this Government, a sum of Rs.619 crores has been utilized and over 800 lakh mandays of employment have been generated up to 31.03.2008.

About 82% of the work force comprises women and 56% are Scheduled Castes. A notable feature of the scheme is that it has had a buoyant effect on rural wages.

The following special steps were initiated to streamline and expedite the implementation of the scheme:

1. A separate Rural Schedule of Rates was approved exclusively for this scheme in the G.O.Ms. No. 77, RD & PR (CGS-1) Department dated 14.07.2006, thereby removing a major hurdle in getting the statutory minimum wage of Rs.80 per day for seven hours of prescribed work. Rates for working on laterite rock, which is common in Sivaganga district, were added to the Schedule vide G.O M.S No 35 RD & PR Department dated 12.3.2007. The Rural Schedule of rates under National Rural Employment Guarantee Scheme for the year 2007-08 was ordered in G.O.No.101 RD & PR (CGS-I) Department dated 13.06.2007.
2. A minimum of 30% registrations has been insisted upon in each Village Panchayat. The average percentage of registration in the Phase-I districts is over 65%. In the Phase-II districts, the average registration has crossed 50%, which indicates that there is widespread awareness about the scheme.
3. The existing formats of Job Cards and Nominal Muster Rolls have been revised to make these documents more transparent informative and difficult to manipulate in the process of scheme implementation.
4. Since the scheme requires intensive touring, the Government have sanctioned additional fuel of 50 litres per month for each of the vehicles in the Panchayat Unions. The Government have also sanctioned additional fuel of 75 litres for the vehicles of the Assistant Executive Engineers (RD) vide G.O.Ms.No.27 RD&PR (CGS-I) Department, dated 20.02.2008.
5. Makkal Nala Paniyalars (MNPs) have also been made responsible for the implementation of the scheme at the field level.
6. Additional ministerial, technical and computer staff have been sanctioned at District, Division, Block and Village levels in order to ensure proper implementation and close supervision of the scheme. Due to the extension of this scheme to the remaining 20 districts of Tamil Nadu with effect from 1.4.2008, the Government has sanctioned

additional administrative staff, additional fuel for block vehicles for 20 Phase - III National Rural Employement Guarantee Scheme districts vide G.O. Ms. No. 27, RD & PR (CGS-1) Department, dated 20.2.2008.

7. Only 100% labour intensive works have been taken up in order to prevent the entry of contractors who are strictly banned as per the NREG Act.
8. Only bigger works not less than Rs. 3 lakhs in value have been taken up in order to ensure that i) adequate numbers of workers get sustained employment at a work site for at least 30 days, ii) the assets created are visible, durable and genuinely beneficial to the community, iii) resources are not wasted by being spread too thinly, iv) the works are monitored closely and leakages are minimised.
9. In order to ensure greater transparency and fair play, it has been ordered to disburse the wages to the workers in the presence of at least four members of the following committee:
   (a) President of the Village Panchayat.
   (b) Vice–President of the Village Panchayat
   (c) Ward Member of the area where the work is executed
   (d) An SC/ST Ward Member, if none of the persons in Sl.Nos. 1, 2 and 3 belongs to SC/ST Community.
   (e) Two animators of graded Self Help Groups.
   (f) A representative of the Panchayat Level federation.
10. A 25-member Tamil Nadu State Employment Guarantee council has been constituted vide the G.O Ms No. 117, RD & PR (CGS-I) Department, dated 14.09.2006 to monitor and review the implementation of the scheme. The first, second and third meetings of this council were held on 25.11.2006, 11.06.2007 and 03.03.2008 respectively.
11. In order to ensure efficient monitoring of the scheme through Management Information System (MIS), three computers and a printer have been sanctioned to each of the 141 block offices of Phase-I and II NREGS districts. In 2008-09, computers, printers and computer room facilities will also be provided for the block offices of Phase-III NREGS districts.

12. In order to ensure a total transparency in the implementation of the Scheme, the Government ordered for the conduct of Social Audit of the Scheme in all Village Panchayats of NREGS districts along with the conduct of Grama Sabha meeting on 15th August, 2nd October and 26th January in 2007-08. Likewise, the conduct of Social Audit of the scheme will be conducted along with Grama Sabha meetings in the year 2008-09 also.

SWARNA JAYANTI GRAM SWAROZGAR YOJANA (SGSY)

SGSY is being implemented since April 1999 as a major anti-poverty scheme for the rural poor, by organizing them into Self Help Groups (SHGs), providing them with skill development training and helping them to get credit linkage with financial institutions and providing infrastructure and marketing support for the products produced by them. Government of India and the State Government are sharing the costs in the ratio of 75:25.The SGSY fund is used to provide subsidy for the Revolving fund and Economic assistance to Self Help Groups. Part of the Scheme component is also utilised for formation of groups and conduct of training for their basic orientation and skill upgradation. Upto 20% of the total allocation can also be spent on putting up of Infrastructure required for promotion of activities of SHGs. The SHGs, after the first grading, are provided with a revolving fund of Rs.25,000 (bank loan of Rs.15,000 and Rs.10,000 as subsidy). After the second grading, the successful groups are provided with economic assistance, the maximum eligible subsidy being 50% of the project cost with a ceiling of Rs.1.25 lakhs. In 2008-09 a sum of Rs.125.16 crores has been allocated for the implementation of this scheme with a credit target of Rs.174.69 crores.

In order to implement the scheme in a more purposeful manner, the following initiatives will be taken in 2008-09:

(i) A major portion of the Scheme component will be utilised for the disbursement of the subsidy component of Revolving fund to the eligible SHGs formed under Mahalir Thittam.

(ii) To encourage the marketing of products produced by SHGs, Calendar of Exhibitions of SHG products for the Districts are being prepared and arrange the exhibitions will be accordingly conducted as per the schedule charted out in the Calendar.

(iii) The implementation of SGSY scheme was so far monitored by Director of Rural Development and Panchayat Raj, whereas, the Mahalir Thittam and Vazhundhu Kattuvom Project that also focus on the empowerment of women, are monitored by the Managing Director of Tamil Nadu Corporation for Development of Women.

In order to ensure that there is a convergence of activities taken up under SGSY scheme, Mahalir Thittam and the Vazhundhu Kattuvom Project, the monitoring of SGSY scheme has now been ordered to be transferred to the Managing Director, Tamil Nadu Corporation for Development of Women.

TOTAL SANITATION CAMPAIGN (TSC)

The Government of India have restructured the Comprehensive Rural Sanitation Programme with effect from 1.4.1999 and launched the Total Sanitation Campaign (TSC).

Table : Sharing pattern under TCS

Category	Government of India Share	Government of Tamil Nadu share	Beneficiary contribution
IHHL	60%	20%	20%
School Toilet	70%	30%	0
Anganwadi Toilet	70%	30%	0
Sanitary Complex	60%	20%	20%

The main objectives of the TSC are to bring about an improvement in the general quality of life in the rural areas and to accelerate sanitation coverage in rural areas to access to toilets to all by 2012 by motivating communities and Panchayati Raj Institutions in promoting sustainable sanitation facilities through awareness creation and health education.Individual Household Latrines, School Toilets, Anganwaadi Toilets, Sanitary Complexes and Rural Sanitary Marts are taken up under the scheme. The project envisages a demand-driven approach with increased stress on awareness building and meeting the demand with alternate delivery mechanisms. With effect from 1.4.2006, the sharing pattern between the Centre and the State is as follows:

The unit cost for different types of toilets is as follows:

Table : Unit cost under TSC (Amount in crores)

Category	Government of India Share	Government of Tamil Nadu share	Beneficiary contribution
IHHL -Model-1: Unit cost up to Rs.1500/- (including superstructure)	900	300	300
Model 2 : Unit cost Rs.1500/- to Rs.2000/-	600	600	800
Above Rs.2000/-	Nil	Nil	2,000
School Toilet	14,000	6,000	0
Anganwadi Toilet	3,500	1,500	0
Sanitary Complex	1,20,000	40,000	40,000

The allocation of funds for TSC is :

Government of India	Rs.454.37 crores
Government of Tamil Nadu	Rs.185.43 crores
Beneficiaries	Rs.157.24 croe
Total	**Rs.797.04 crores**

The physical and financial performance of the State under TSC as on 31.3.2008 are as follows:

Table : Physical Performance

Category	Target	Achievement
IHHL - BPL	42,14,089	27,19,101
APL	40,30,794	23,14,993
School Toilets	40,418	34,347
Anganwadi Toilets	25,470	22,171
Sanitary Complex	1,295	1,295
Sanitary Marts	244	192
Total	**83,12,310**	**50,92,099**

Funds received so far are :Rs.479.06 crores (GoI: Rs.258.89 crores; GoTN: Rs.138.87 crores; and beneficiaries: Rs.90.58 crores)

The expenditure as on 31.3.2008 is Rs. 387.81 crores.

The maintenance of sanitation and hygiene in the villages are the mandatory duties of Village Panchayats as envisaged under Sec.110 (d) of the Tamil Nadu Panchayats Act, 1994. The disposal of solid waste and sewage water is becoming a major problem for many Village Panchayats especially those situated in the vicinity of the Corporation and bigger Municipalities and individual Village Panchayats may not be a viable unit for contracting out solid waste management and sewage disposal. Hence it is proposed to group several suburban Village Panchayats into clusters so as to form a viable unit for contracting out or allow Village Panchayats to enter into partnership with the neighbouring Corporations or Municipalities in this regard.

It is proposed to launch a State level Multi-Media campaign this year in order to change the mind-set of the rural public regarding sanitation practices and generate demand for individual household toilets.

Member of Parliament Local Area Development Scheme (MPLADS)

The objective of this Scheme is to fill the gaps existing in the provision of infrastructure through various Central and State schemes thereby enabling wholesome development. A sum of Rs.2 crore is allotted per Member of Parliament (Lok Sabha and Rajya Sabha) per year for taking up developmental works identified by the concerned M.P. In the case of Lok Sabha, the scheme is implemented in the districts falling within the constituency of the concerned MP. In the case of Rajya Sabha, the MP can suggest works in one or more districts within the State from which he is elected. As far as the nominated MPs are concerned, they can suggest works anywhere in India.

The District Collector gives administrative sanction for the works. The guidelines contain a'negative list' of works not permitted under this scheme and also an illustrative list of works that may be taken up. Under the scheme, all maintenance works of any type are prohibited. Desilting of ponds, rivers, tanks, canals etc. are also treated as maintenance activities and cannot be taken up under MPLADS.

Illustrative List of Works that can be taken up under MPLADS:

1. Construction of buildings for schools, hostels, libraries and other buildings of educational institutions belonging to Government or local bodies. Such buildings belonging to aided institutions and unaided but recognised institutions can also be constructed provided, however, that the institution be in existence for not less than two years.
2. Construction of tube-wells and water tanks for providing water to the people in villages, towns or cities, or execution of other works, which may help in this respect. Water tankers can also be purchased for providing drinking water.
3. Construction of roads including part roads, approach roads, link roads etc. in villages and towns and cities. Very selectively kutcha roads can also be constructed where the MP concerned and the District Head agree to meet the locally felt need.
4. Construction of culverts/bridges on the roads of above description and of open cut or tube wells.
5. Construction of common shelters for the old or handicapped.
6. Construction of buildings for local bodies for recognised District or State Sports Associations and for cultural and sports activities or for hospitals. Provision of multi-gym facilities in gymnastic centres, sports associations, physical education training institutions etc. is also permissible.
7. Special forestry, farm forestry, horticulture, pastures, parks and gardens in Government and community lands or other surrendered lands.
8. Desilting of ponds in villages, towns and cities.
9. Construction of public irrigation and public drainage facilities.
10. Construction of common gobar gas plants, non-conventional energy systems/devices for community use and related activities.

11. Construction of irrigation embankments, or lift irrigation or water table recharging facilities.
12. Construction of public libraries and reading rooms.
13. Construction of creches and anganwadis.
14. Construction of public health care buildings, including family welfare sub-centres together with the ANM residential quarters. Such buildings belonging to aided institutions also can be constructed.
15. Construction of crematoriums and structures on burial/ cremation grounds.
16. Construction of public toilets and bathrooms.
17. Construction of drains and gutters.
18. Construction of footpaths, pathways and footbridges.
19. Provision of civic amenities like electricity, water, pathways, public toilets etc. in slum areas of cities, town and villages and in SC/ST habitations, provision of common work-sheds in slums and for artisans.
20. Construction of residential schools in tribal areas.
21. Construction of bus-sheds/stops for public transport passengers.
22. Construction of veterinary aid centres, artificial insemination centres and breeding centres.
23. Procurement of hospital equipment like X-Ray machines, ambulances for Government Hospitals and setting up of mobile dispensaries in rural areas by Government Panchayati Institutions. Ambulances can be provided to reputed service organisations like Red Cross, Ramakrishna Mission etc.
24. Electronic Projects:
    (i) Computer in education project of High school/College
    (ii) Information footpath
    (iii) Ham Club in high schools
    (iv) Citizen band radio
    (v) Bibliographic data-base projects.
25. Construction of Level Crossing at unmanned Railway crossing.

26. Purchase of Audio-Visual Aids of educational nature for Government, Government-aided and also unaided but Government recognised educational institutions provided there is proper place and proper provision for safe custody of these aids.
27. Purchase of Night Soil Disposal System for local bodies.
28. Purchase of motor boats for flood and cyclone affected areas.
29. "Works related to animal care/ welfare like construction of buildings / shelters, provision of ambulances, medical equipment and development of infrastructure facilities like provision of drinking water, drainage etc."
30. Purchase of motor boats for flood and cyclone affected areas.
31. "Works related to animal care/ welfare like construction of buildings / shelters, provision of ambulances, medical equipment and development of infrastructure facilities like provision of drinking water, drainage etc."

List of works not permissible under MPLADS :

1. Office buildings, residential buildings, and other buildings relating to Central or State Governments, Departments, Agencies or Organisations.
2. Works belonging to commercial organisations, private institutions or co-operative institutions.
3. Repair and maintenance works of any type other than special repairs for restoration/up-gradation of any durable asset.
4. Grant and loans.
5. Memorials or memorial buildings.
6. Purchase of inventory or stock of any type.
7. Acquisition of land or any compensation for land acquired.
8. Assets for all individual benefit, except those which are part of approved schemes.
9. Places for religious worship.

PRADHAN MANTRI GRAM SADAK YOJANA (PMGSY)

The Government of India launched PMGSY on 25th December 2000 to provide all weather roads to all rural habitations with population more than 1000 in the first phase and to all habitations with population between 500 and 1000 in the second phase. This is a 100% Centrally assisted scheme. In the first three Phases, Rural Development and Panchayat Raj Department has taken up 3370.97 Kms at an estimated cost of Rs. 434.08 Crores. So far 3299.95 Km road works have been completed with an expenditure of Rs. 385.21 Crores. Under Phase IV, 820.46 Km road works at an estimated cost of Rs. 117.27 crores were entrusted to Highways Department for implementation. Rural Development and Panchayat Raj Department is implementing the Scheme under Phase V and road works to a length of 849.25 Km at an estimated cost of Rs. 182.05 Crores have been taken up. 405.91 Km road works have been completed with an expenditure of Rs. 74.96 crores so far.

Table : Pradhan Mantri Gram Sadak Yojana - (PMGSY)

Sl. No.	Phase	Financial Allocation (Rs. in crores)	Physical Allocation Nos.	Physical Allocation Km.
1	Phase 1	153.49	866	1,448.47
2	Phase 2	115.81	450	808.58
3	Phase 3	164.78	498	1,113.92
4	Phase 4	117.27	412	820.46
5	Phase 5	182.05	379	849.25
	Total	733.40	2605	5,040.68

Bharat Nirman was launched by Government of India in April 2005 as a time bound business plan of Government of India for building rural infrastructure in the areas of irrigation, roads, housing, water supply, electrification and telecommunication connectivity. Under the roads component of Bharat Nirman: Every habitation of over 1000 population and above (and above 500 in hilly and tribal areas) would be provided all-weather road connectivity. 'Through routes' in the Core Network connecting farm to market are to be upgraded. Funds under PMGSY (for new connectivity and Upgradation) and from State Government (for renewal) are being used to achieve the targets of the road components of Bharat Nirman. Status of connectivity of habitations is determined as per the Core Network. Core Network was revised in December 2007 and as per the revised core network status of connectivity is as follows:

Table : Status of Connectivity as per the Revised Core Network

	1000+	500-999	250-499	Less Than 250	Total
Total No. of habitations	10,783	16,513	17,104	18,519	62,919
Total no. connected habitations	10,764	16,234	16,574	17,439	61,011
Balance unconnected habitations	**19**	**279**	**530**	**1,080**	**1,908**

19 uncovered habitations (96 eligible, 77 covered, leaving a balance of 19 uncovered) will be covered in the forthcoming phases. The detailed project reports (DPRs) for the 19 habitations are being prepared under Bharat Nirman Phase II and will be sent to MoRD, GOI shortly.

Table : Length Coverage (Upgradation and Renewal) under Bharat Nirman

SL. No	Target (2005-2009)	Cumulative achievement up to April' 2008	Cumulative achievement in %
1	11,115 Km	6,343.50	57.10

Out of the proposals (DPR) for 1700 Km cleared by GoI, 1328 Kms have been completed till date. The works for the remaining 372 Kms of roads will be completed by June' 2008.

A proposal from Rural Development and Panchayat Raj Department to a length of 797 Kms to a tune of Rs. 195 crores and a proposal from Highways Department to a length of 1,286 Kms to a tune of Rs. 232 crores totally, the proposal of 2,083 Kms to a tune of Rs. 427 crores have been cleared by MoRD during May' 2008 as PMGSY Phase VI (or Bharat Nirman Phase I) scheme. These works will be implemented shortly.

Phase wise achievement is as follows:

Table : Progress under Bharat Nirman

Category	Target Length (in Km)	Achievement (in Km) PMGSY Phase	Length (in Km)	Balance	Source of Funds
Upgradation	6,670	II	27.2	5348.2	PMGSY
		III	267.9		
		IV	642.9		
		V	383.8		
		Total	**1,321.8**		
Renewal	4,445	5021.70		0	State Govt. (12th Finance Comm. and CRIDP)
Total	11,115	6343.50		5342.7	

National Project on Biogas Development

This is a 100% Centrally sponsored scheme envisaging a subsidy of Rs.2,100 for general category and Rs. 2,800 for SC/ST and small farmers and Rs.3, 500 for hilly areas.

Rajiv Gandhi Rehabilitation Package (RGRP) funded by Government of India

The Rajiv Gandhi Rehabilitation Package (Reconstruction component) forms-part of Tsunami Rehabilitation Programme (TRP) drawn by the Government of India for reconstruction of damaged physical and social infrastructure and for revival of impaired livelihoods due to the Tsunami on 26.12.2004. The programme emphasizes on improving quality of life using replacement and upgradation of assets as means to achieve it.

Schemes which are implemented

(a) In sites where NGOs constructed houses, certain basic facilities like cement concrete roads, provision of street lights, sanitation arrangements, land filling, etc. have not been provided by these NGOs and these facilities are being provided under the Project, as ordered in G.O.Ms.No.215 Revenue (NCIII(1) dept dated:23.4.07 and G.O. Ms.No.248 Revenue (NCIII(2) dept dated: 11.5.07.

(b) Houses which have originally been agreed to be constructed by NGOs but subsequently backed out by them are being constructed with necessary basic amenities, as per G.O. Ms.No.625 Revenue NC IV(2) dept dated:20.9.06 and G.O.Ms.No.161 Revenue (NC-III) dept dated: 26.3.07.

(c) Vulnerable houses within 200 meters from High Tide Line (HTL) and also government built houses which are 10 years old as on 01.01.2006, within 1000 meters from the HTL are being reconstructed and required basic amenities in these housing sites are also being provided, as ordered in G.O. Ms.No.60 Revenue (NC-IV(2) dated:29.1.07.

Provision of basic amenities in NGOs built sites

(i) Cement Concrete roads to a length of 138 Kms. at a cost of Rs.40.62 crores have been taken up in 128 sites. About 100 Kms. long roads have already been completed at an expenditure of Rs.24.06 crores and rest of the roads are programmed to be completed by May, 2008.

Table : Provision of internal C.C. Roads in the NGO constructed housing sites under RGRP

S.No	District	works	Length in Km	Tendered cost (Rs in Lakhs)
1	Tiruvallur	5	6.20	37.14
2	Kancheepuram	19	15.23	380.91
3	Villupuram	8	15.83	456.07
4	Cuddalore	15	7.13	232.40
5	Nagapattinam	61	71.16	2487.38
6	Tirunelveli	8	9.99	234.96
7	Thoothukudi	8	6.25	154.15
8	Kanniyakumari	9	5.59	78.84
	Total	**133**	**137.38**	**4061.85**

(ii) Out of 3019 street lights to be provided at a cost of Rs.266.31 lakhs, 2696 street lights have already been erected, incurring an expenditure of Rs.251.10 lakhs.

(iii) Sanitation arrangement by way of septic tanks and soak pits are being provided to 4262 houses built by NGOs without these facilities and 495 stand alone toilets are also being constructed, at a total cost of Rs.4.54 crores. Out of this, 3200 houses have already been provided with sanitation facilities at a cost of Rs.1.56 crores.

(iv) In 9 sites in Nagapattinam district where NGOs have constructed houses in low lying areas, land filling has been taken up in order to prevent flooding of the houses during rainy seasons at a cost of Rs.2.76 crores, in order to prevent inundation during rains. About 92% of filling has been completed at an expenditure of Rs.2.27 crores.

Construction of houses and provision of basic amenities in NGOs backed out sites

Some of the NGOs initially agreed to take up the construction of tsunami damaged houses, subsequently backed out after two years of tsunami occurrence. This department was requested to take up the construction of these houses and also the provision of basic amenities in these sites. Under this,

- o every house to be built will be of 325 sq.ft. plinth area,
- o every house will be built with the disaster resistance features,
- o basic amenities like cement concrete roads, street lights, and necessary Public Buildings etc. will be provided to these sites.

Table : Details of NGO backed out houses taken up under RGRP

S.No	Name of District	No. of houses taken up	Agreement value (Rs in Lakhs)
1	Tiruvallur	314	771.26
2	Kancheepuram	556	1258.55
3	Villupuram	450	1023.63
4	Nagapattinam	1085	2423.49
5	Thoothukudi	224	547.03
	Grand Total	**2629**	**6023.96**

Accordingly, 2629 houses in Nagapatinam, Thoothukudi, Villupuram, Kancheepuram and Tiruvallur districts are being constructed in 20 N.G.Os backed out sites. The construction is in various stages and bulk of these houses are programmed to be completed by July, 2008.

Works to provide basic amenities in the form of CC Roads, Community Halls, Child Welfare Centres and Storm Water Drain etc. are also taken up at a cost of about Rs.10.52 Crores. Most of these works are in progress and will be completed by June, 2008.

Table : Reconstruction of Vulnerable houses under RGRP

Sl. No	Name of the District	No.of houses taken up			Tendered Cost (Rs in Lakhs)
		Insitu	Relocation	Total	
1	Kancheepuram	426	0	**426**	1082.04
2	Villupuram	314	0	**314**	772.44
3	Cuddalore	1504	115	**1619**	4436.06
4	Nagapattinam	49	38	**87**	222.72
5	Thanjavur	1084	210	**1294**	3131.48
6	Pudukottai	2343	0	**2343**	5904.36
7	Ramanathapuram	3417	698	**4115**	10987.05
8	Thoothukudi	687	28	**715**	1744.60
9	Tirunelveli	2021	0	**2021**	5092.92
10	Kanniyakumari Phase - I	1026	24	**1050**	2205.00
	Total	**12871**	**1113**	**13984**	**35578.67**
1	Tiruvallur	3056		**3056**	7273.28
2	Kanniyakumari Phase - II)	1393	-	**1393**	3315.34
	Grand Total	**17320**	**1113**	**18433**	**46167.29**

Reconstruction of vulnerable houses

With the object of relocating the people who are living in vulnerable houses within 1000 metres from the HTL, a decision was taken up by the State Government to reconstruct these vulnerable houses as multi hazard resistant structures. As a first step, vulnerable houses located within 200 metres from the HTL and the houses built by the Government under different schemes like Indira Awaaz Yojana and Singaravelar Fishermen Housing Scheme, within 1000 metres from HTL, but 10 years old as on 01.01.06 have been taken up for reconstruction under the project. About 20,000 such houses have been taken up for reconstruction in coastal districts. All these constructions are programmed to be completed within the financial year 2008-09.

Basic amenities such as Cement Concrete Roads, Street Lights, Burial Ground / Cremation Sheds, Village Ponds, necessary Public Buildings etc. are also proposed for the entire coastal stretch of 1000 metres from the HTL in these coastal Panchayat Villages by utilising funds allocated at the rate of Rs.40,000 per house. The tender process for this purpose is under progress to carry out works at an estimated cost of Rs.80 crores.

3

Eco-friendly Energy Resources for Rural Development

GENERAL INTRODUCTION

The electrical energy demand is increasing every day. In order to meet with increasing electricity demand. Govt. of India is planning and installing various type of generating stations.

So we see that what is mean by power station? An electric power station is factory in which energy is converted from one form or another to electrical energy for example in thermal. The energy is first in the form of heat in the fuel, which may be coal gas or oil. This heat is liberated by combustion in the boiler furnace and is then used to convert water into steam.

The energy in the steam used to convert mechanical energy into electrical energy. There are two types energy sources one is non conventional energy source and another is conventional energy source.

NON - CONVENTIONAL ENERGY SOURCES

In this system following energy plant are observed ,

1. Solar energy plant
2. Solar cells
3. Tidal energy
4. Geo thermal energy
5. Wind energy

6. Bio-gas plant
7. Bio-mass plant.

SOLAR ENERGY PLANT

The thermo-nuclear fusion take place in the interior of sun at 45 x 106 degree farenheight. Thus a tremendous amount of hot energy constantly released by sun.

In solar energy plant solar collector absorb the maximum amount of solar radiation and convert it into heat energy water is used as flit it will absorb heat and convert in to steam in boiler. Then steam is passed to the turbine to drive generator.

TIDAL ENERGY

There is a tremendous energy in the tides of ocean catching soc water at high tide in an ocean and releasing it through turbine to low tide and turbine brine generator and electrical energy is generated.

GEOTHERMAL ENERGY

Geothermal energy means the heat which is in the interior of the earth is extracted and used for power generation. In side the earth about 100 km radio active materials one present large amount of heat is produced because of nuclear fission. Due to which molten is mass is produced by melting surrounding area this moten moss trees to come towards earth surface. It can not reach surface the water which penetrated in this area gets heated and steam is take place.

WIND ENERGY

The wind is having very large energy because of pressure and temp difference in the regions. A conversion of wind energy to electrical energy useful in areas where strong wind for sufficient and long period of year present sent.

CONVENTIONAL - ENERGY SOURCES

(1) Thermal power station.
(2) Hydro electric power station.
(3) Nuclear power station

(4) Diesel power station

(5) Gas turbine dine plant

THERMAL POWER STATION

The thermal power station working is based on the Ranking cycle the basic idea is that steam is generated in a boiler and is used for driving turbine.

HYDRO - ELECTRIC POWER STATION

The basic requirement of hydropower project is that geo graphical situation must be convenient for contraction for construction dam, reservoir etc. Dam is constructed to storage the water and it is built at the toper than powerhouse and from dam through pen stock water is forced on turbine and electrical energy is achieved.

NUCLEAR POWER - STATION

Due to nuclear-reaction tremendous heat is produced. By using heat steam is produced which is released on turbine and electrical energy is generated.

DIESEL POWER - STATION

The electric power generation by diesel plants is becoming costly because of increasing sing fuel cost. The diesel engine works on four stroke i.e.

(1) Suction

(2) Compression

(3) Ignition

(4) Exhaust

As seen from demand of rural area above power station are not economical space required above plant is very large so eco friendly energy sources for rural development are very important.

THE GENERAL ENERGY NEEDS IN RURAL SECTIOR

BASIC NEEDS

(1) Potable drinking water supply.

(2) Cooking

(3) Domestic and street lightening.

AGRICULTURAL NEEDS

(i) Water pumping for irrigation

(ii) Storage and drying agricultural crops.

(iii) Fuel to operate form machinery.

INDUSTRIALS NEEDS

(1) Rural industries manufacture of soap, bricks, charcoal, metal products, leather and agroindustrial products, printing, hand loom industry.

(2) Operating agricultural implements. For over come above needs solar cells, and various eco-friendly energy sources are used which are as discussed below.

INTRODUCTION TO ECO-NOMICAL, ECO-FRIENDLY ENERGY SOURCES

As the fulfilled need of rural sector some non-conventional energy sources are helpful. The decentralized energy system based on solar, wind, bio-mass, minihydel etc. Hold a great promise and have shown isolated packets where reaching electricity by the conventional method is being.

BIOGAS PLANT AND THEIR APPLICATION

Organic waste available in rural areas in agricultural waste, human waste, piggery waste etc this waste is anaerobically fermented with oxygen, it gives rise to a gas which is 60% methane. This is an efficient and versatile fuel. The left over sludge can be used as fertilizer it takes 3 to 5 animals to run a biogas plant for family of 5 to 6. Therefore, 0.5 cattle per on is required to provide energy for substance and fertilizers. In India, the cost of family size biogas plant for 5 persons is about 4000/- on large size. Village biogas plant may also be used for dairies, hospitals etc.

Biogas is very simple. A pond with cement concrete walls is constructed first. The shape of pond can be circular or square. Agriculture waste, animal waste, human waste etc are poured in above pond. A. P. V.C coated cylindrical with dome shape at the top, is placed in the pond. The galvanized or P. V. C. piping connections are done at the top of the bank. Animal or human waste in the tank will get fermented and during fermentation process 65% gas is liberated. This gas can be directly used for cooking or heating purpose. In case of large size gas plants gas can be supplied to hospital, dairies etc.

1. Aquatic wastes
2. Forest wastes like coconut husk.
3. Industrial wastes.

The made is generated periodically and can be converted into useful biogas the problem of waste disposal is also solved as the sludge is used is manure.

DUNG FROM ANIMALS

The animals douter the exreta (dung) which is used as manure fuel and in feed to biogas plant. 1 kg of cattle dung about 45 lit. of biogas during winter and about 55 lit. biogas during summer.

SIGNIFICANCE OF BIOGAS PLANTS IN INDIA'S ENERGY STRATEGY

Up to 1971 end about 15,00,000 numer family sing biogas plants have been installed in India. About 415 numbers of biogas tired internal combustion engines at rated capacity of 5 mm have been installed. By 2000 A.D. 1,50,00,000 biogas plants may be operation in India.

Biogas plants have a very significant role in India's rural development and energy development.

The fuel used for biogas plant is desired from renewable animal waste and agricultural waste. The biogas produced by the biogas is used in rural areas for the following :

(i) As fuel for cooking
(ii) As fuel for driving engines for pumps
(iii) As a fuel for engine drives generating plants for supplying electrical energy to the community.
(iv) Residue from biogas plants is used as manure.
(v) Energy conservation of fossil fuels and obtrical energy from conventional power plants.

(vi) Conservation of trees and plants which would be used as fuel if biogas not available.

AVERAGE COMPOSITION OF BIOGAS

The raw biogas obtained, raw the biogas plants by the process of anaerobic digestion is methane rich fuel gas.

1)	Methane	55 to 60 %
2)	Carbon dioxide	35 to 40 %
3)	Hydrogen (H2)	5%

ANAEROBIC FERMENTATION (DIGESTION) PROCESS USED IN BIOGAS PLANTS

During the anaerobic digestion, the organic matters under goes fermentation and the biogas is liberated.

The anaerobic digestion as following stages :

Stage 1. Formation of acids and chemicals. The micro organism of anaerobic and facultatine groups produce fermentation and hydrolysis to form acids.

Stage 2. Production of methane (CH_4) in this stage the organic acids and chemicals formed in the 2nd stage are decomposed by the anaerobic to reduce methane (CH_4) and carbon dioxide gases.

ADVANTAGES

(1) The left over sludge in the pond can be used as fertilizer.

(2) The animals are essentials in rural area, so animal waste, or other wastes are easily available.

(3) This plant is very economical in rural areas.

JANTA AND DEENBANDHU BIOGAS PLANTS

Deenbandhu biogas plant is a low cost design for family requirement. Basically to reduce the cost of popular design of fixed dome biogas plant called Janta biogas plant.

JANTA BIG - GAS PLANT

This plant has cylindrical digester with flat bottom and dome shaped roof. Upper position of cylinder acts as gas storage chamber with production of gas the slurry from the gas storage chamber is displaced into inlet and outlet displacement chamber which are connected with digester through inlet and outlet chutes respectively.

DEENBANDHU BIO - GAS PLANT

Unlike J.B.P. this design has curved bottom and a hemi-spherical top jointed their bases with no - cylindrical portion in bottom. The digester, gas storage chamber and the empty space above the slurry are all provided within this shape. All slurry displaced out of the gas storage chamber is stored in the outlet displacement chamber as there is no displacement spaces on the inlet side. The inlet is in the form of a pipe which connects the digester with slurry mixing tank.

Deenbandhu bio-gas plants, despite their lower retention time are equally efficient in terms of total gas yield per unit of feed out they are more efficient in terms of total gas production per unit volume of digester. From this we conclude the D.B.P. is more efficient than J.B.P.

BIOMASS PLANT AND THEIR APPLICATION

Photosynthesis is at the base at all biomass production and food-chains. It converts physical energy into chemical energy and generates oxygen, the life sustaining gas. Various type of bio-mass and or bio-fuels available are firewood, agricultural alcohol, vegetable oil hydro carbon plants, particularly those yielding rubber and petroleum like-materials fresh weeds, sewage grown algae, algal hydro carbons and biological production of hydrogen using halo bacteria algae azolla and even higher plants.

In the face of increasing population and industrialization India face acute problem of energy supply and demand. Since the area of culturable land has increased many fold brones especially of agricultural of origin is available in plenty in interated approach suggesting a proportionate use of this waste removable source base would go a long way in solving resources confixt for the production of fuel fodder and fertilizer.

Pressure on land caused by increasing population supplemented by agriculturization and industrialization is resulting in ruthless exploitation of natural resources to meet the fuel requirement. This has led to the air pollution and many other problems until now we were using the natural resources the coal, diesel, petrol etc. But these resources are going to be extinguished one day, therefore we have to think of new way energy.

Energy is varying uniform. It may be in electrical form or any other electrical energy is the backbone of the industry. No industry can work without electrical energy.

BIOMASS - FOR ENERGY

Bio-mass for energy denotes that portion of bio-mass used for combustion purpose. In agriculture energy saving and substitution became necessary through a better use of bio-mass. At present the crop residues are usually used for heating purpose, animal residues also for methanisation Bio-mass accounts for about 440 percent of total energy consumed at national level and forms the bulk of rural energy foe cooking purposes bio-mass is the chief fuel in the hape of fire wood and non fire wood bio-mass. Dry, stream, stalks, coconut shelf, dung etc. obtained through crop and animal residues are used as fuel in addition to fire wood and fuel stick obtained from other sources. The problem with the non fire wood bio-mass is that it's thermal efficiency may be lower. Modern chulas complemented with bio-mass and energy plantations may prove to integrate energy resources towards augmentation. Because bio-mass is the major source of energy for rural people.

The larger proportion of bio-mass is available for fuel purpose. In the case of garden crops, the crop residues suitable for fuel purpose.

BIO-MASS - COMPETITION FOR FUEL, FOODAR AND FERTILIZES.

In the face of increasing population and industrialization, India faces a cute problem of energy sources demand since the area of cultivable land has increase many foid, bio-mass especially of agricultural origin is available in plenty.

The rural population in the developing countries is mainly dependent upon fire-wood. The world consumption of fire-wood is estimated at around 5% - 10% of total energy consumption, but it is about 6% in the developing countries where approximately 80% of the total fuel is employed for cooking.

Thus sustainable development would essentially need to be an appropriate energy mix to meet the basic needs of food and fuel for the human, fooder for the line stocks and at same time maintains of the soil fertility. In this context the role of biomass as a non conventional renewable source is of paramount importance.

There is a presently enormous amount of bio-mass on the globe which refers to all forms of organic matter including crop residues agro-industrial byproducts, urban waste, animal dung and poultry waste.

In addition the fermented residues get enriched in nitrogen as a result of growth of these fungi besides increasing the biological value of these residues which can use as the fertilizers supplemented in the soil to improve it's fertility.

CONCLUSION

So we seen that, what do you mean by power station and energy source like bio-gas and bio-mass those are Eco-friendly and those mostly used in Ruler needs in Ruler sector domestic purpose like portable water supply, cooling, drinking and also utilized this system used in Agriculture needs and as well as industrial needs without any pollution. So these sources much better and much eco-friendly for Ruler development and domestic purpose.

4

Potentials of Village and Small Enterprise Sector in the North Eastern Region of India

The Village and Small Enterprise sector (VSE) has not only a tremendous potentiality of development in the North-Eastern Region (NER) of India, it also suits most to this region's natural endowment, human resources and sociological conditions. This sector also provides a great scope to women empowerment and thus reduction in gender-based inequalities in the society. This paper examines the prospects and constraints of development of the VSE sector in the NER with a special reference to social, technological and infrastructural aspects.

The Village and Small Enterprises in the Indian Economy: Village and small enterprises in India have an age-old history. Artisans in different trades were needed to provide implements to farming operations; furniture and fixture needed to build houses; clothes to wear; ornaments, jewellery and footwear to put on; and a plethora of other articles.

They also supplied those articles to the town-dwellers and the rich. Side by side there were persons who provided various services to the people in rural as well as urban areas. When Mahatma Gandhi pleaded for a thrust to be given to these trades and spoke of village-based tiny productive activities, he had, in fact, many things in mind. However, the planned development of India was inclined to large and heavy industries.

Table-1 : Year-wise Value Of Plant & Machinery (Vpm In Rs. Lakh) Installed By Operating Regd. Ssi Units

Year	VPM	Units	Year	VPM	Units	Year	VPM	Units	Year	VPM	Units	Year	VPM	Units
1901	320	180	1921	146	90	1941	448	235	1961	8045	1196	1981	44864	22464
1902	262	203	1922	310	154	1942	497	356	1962	4432	1771	1982	54950	30994
1903	204	187	1923	296	124	1943	662	312	1963	3432	1163	1983	48679	27767
1904	294	226	1924	184	142	1944	570	335	1964	5607	1375	1984	60141	35086
1905	487	306	1925	443	229	1945	2035	451	1965	5913	2897	1985	84045	49056
1906	242	250	1926	130	129	1946	1627	398	1966	3860	1489	1986	76148	41746
1907	463	263	1927	232	186	1947	1810	439	1967	5579	2021	1987	79482	45980
1908	282	236	1928	553	153	1948	1031	432	1968	7227	2904	1988	82287	49258
1909	713	310	1929	231	166	1949	1005	317	1969	7871	2937	1989	95525	49602
1910	252	83	1930	453	315	1950	1780	683	1970	18794	10009	1990	130800	81071
1911	39	42	1931	159	174	1951	1244	223	1971	9700	4344	1991	97216	54554
1912	141	52	1932	462	271	1952	1264	487	1972	16194	7510	1992	132197	70846
1913	93	41	1933	293	297	1953	687	270	1973	13663	6866	1993	121802	60208
1914	145	48	1934	305	240	1954	604	326	1974	17138	7708	1994	149086	66005
1915	118	66	1935	632	360	1955	1056	571	1975	20541	11848	1995	191714	85080
1916	51	58	1936	260	287	1956	1225	452	1976	26628	10287	1996	194591	85700
1917	214	57	1937	616	345	1957	1914	558	1977	25872	10388	1997	199852	85446
1918	567	72	1938	666	351	1958	1493	573	1978	33027	15525	1998	231529	86124
1919	175	57	1939	424	283	1959	1634	527	1979	33492	15728	1999	205248	72376
1920	318	145	1940	1159	381	1960	5549	2409	1980	63252	37381	2000	150406	56736

Yet, although with a concern of lesser order, village and small industries flourished and complemented the industrial economy of India. A synoptic view of growth of small-scale enterprises may be obtained through Table-1. Its growth accelerated in the 1960's and continued unabated since then to cross 86 thousand units (firms) in 1998.

The Case of North-Eastern Region of India: The predicaments of the North-Eastern Region (NER) of India are well known. A very large part of this region is hilly - not much suitable to a gainful agriculture. Farming can of course sustain the people, but cannot generate any appreciable surplus. This is one of the reasons why in the pre-British rule this region was neglected by the then centers of power. In the last hundred years of the British rule in India, this region attracted the missionaries (as well as the government) who did a lot to improve the socio-economic condition of the local people who were largely cut off from the main stream of civilization. After India won freedom, the larger part of the region and the inhabitants therein were given help and assistance of various nature. However, since those areas did not have much prospects to be chosen for location of large manufacturing enterprises, partly due to their location at the frontiers, the industrial development of this region lagged behind other parts of the country.

The North-Eastern Region of India comprises eight states; Arunachal Pradesh, Assam, Manipur, Meghalaya, Mizoram, Nagaland, Tripura, and (now), Sikkim. Among these, Arunachal Pradesh, Meghalaya, Mizoram, Nagaland and Sikkim are largely hilly and sparsely populated. Other states are only partly hilly in various proportions to the plain land, and relatively thickly populated. Among these latter states, Assam and Tripura have more arable land in proportion to the hilly area.

Accordingly, the economic activities in the secondary and the tertiary sectors have grown in proportion to the primary sector in the different states (Table-2). Manipur, with a long tradition in weaving, sericulture, handicrafts, etc has engaged much larger proportion of workers in the secondary sector, followed by Assam that vies closely with the national figure. On the other end, Arunachal Pradesh, Mizoram and Sikkim have slender engagement of workers in the secondary sector. Nagaland has a poor performance in the tertiary sector. Meghalaya performs slightly better than Nagaland but stands far behind the national figure. Arunachal Pradesh, Manipur and Mizoram are more or less at par with India. It may, however, be noted that the tertiary sector in the NER is largely based on the activities generate through external assistance and not by the primary and secondary activities in the states within.

Table-2 : Occupational Distribution of Workers Population in the North-Eastern Region

State Household Industry Workers	**Total Percent Workers**	**Cultivators Other Workers**	**Percent Percent**	**Agricultural Labourers**	**Percent**
Sikkim					
Persons	263043	131258	49.90	17000	6.46
4219	1.60	110566	42.03		
Males	165716	70107	42.31	8762	5.29
2849	1.72	83998	50.69		
Females	97327	61151	62.83	8238	8.46
1370	1.41	26568	27.30		
Arunachal Pradesh					
Persons	482902	279300	57.84	18840	3.90
6043	1.25	178719	37.01		
Males	293612	136336	46.43	10329	3.52
3177	1.08	143770	48.97		
Females	189290	142964	75.53	8511	4.50
2866	1.51	34949	18.46		
Nagaland					
Persons	847796	548845	64.74	30907	3.65
21873	2.58	246171	29.04		
Males	488968	270927	55.41	15985	3.27
9193	1.88	192863	39.44		
Females	358828	277918	77.45	14922	4.16
12680	3.53	53308	14.86		
Manipur					
Persons	945213	379705	40.17	113630	12.02

96920	10.25	354958	37.55		
Males	527216	214282	40.64	49928	9.47
20547	3.90	242459	45.99		
Females	417997	165423	39.58	63702	15.24
76373	18.27	112499	26.91		
Mizoram					
Persons	467159	256332	54.87	26783	5.73
7100	1.52	176944	37.88		
Males	263008	130497	49.62	12775	4.86
3476	1.32	116260	44.20		
Females	204151	125835	61.64	14008	6.86
3624	1.78	60684	29.73		
Tripura					
Persons	1159561	313300	27.02	276132	23.81
35292	3.04	534837	46.12		
Males	831346	220962	26.58	162640	19.56
14830	1.78	432914	52.07		
Females	328215	92338	28.13	113492	34.58
20462	6.23	101923	31.05		
Meghalaya					
Persons	970146	467010	48.14	171694	17.70
21225	2.19	310217	31.98		
Males	568491	255018	44.86	90888	15.99
9358	1.65	213227	37.51		
Females	401655	211992	52.78	80806	20.12
11867	2.95	96990	24.15		
Assam					
Persons	9538591	3730773	39.11	1263532	13.25
344912	3.62	4199374	44.03		
Males	6870960	2634068	38.34	832508	12.12
133902	1.95	3270482	47.60		
Females	2667631	1096705	41.11	431024	16.16
211010	7.91	928892	34.82		
India					
Persons	402234724	127312851	31.65	106775330	26.55
16956942	4.22	151189601	37.59		
Males	275014476	85416498	31.06	57329100	20.85
8744183	3.18	123524695	44.92		
Females	127220248	41896353	32.93	49446230	38.87
8212759	6.46	27664906	21.75		

Source: http://www.censusindia.net/t_00_009.html

Table-3(A): Distribution Of No. Of Reg.units By Year Of Permanent Registration

State	Up to 1957	58	59	60-65	66-74	75-76	77-79	1980-84	1985-90	1991-96	1997-98	1999 & +	NR	Total
SK	2	0	0	0	0	1	0	5	42	65	13	19	0	147
AR	0	0	0	0	7	6	43	40	78	49	13	16	2	254
NG	3	0	1	0	13	14	34	12	31	81	26	318	1	534
MN	52	0	0	0	77	27	50	318	2287	1132	245	365	6	4559
MZ	5	0	0	0	4	7	21	181	1033	639	344	466	18	2718
TR	40	0	0	7	66	12	31	101	193	315	87	76	10	938
MG	7	0	0	0	8	6	11	119	324	527	326	609	1	1938
AS	63	1	0	5	170	53	211	1155	3278	5592	1780	1963	118	14389
NE	172	1	1	12	345	126	401	1931	7266	8400	2834	3832	156	25477
IN	11525	232	244	5807	33006	14513	36981	135929	288827	423707	183682	193093	20905	1348451

Table-3(B): Trends in Number of Small-Scale Enterprises in the North-Eastern Region

Year	Sikkim	Arunachal	Nagaland	Manipur	Mizoram	Tripura	Meghalaya	Assam	NER
1991	NA	525	615	4059	2478	4967	1368	12802	26814
1992	NA	689	644	4308	2592	5661	1569	14354	29817
1993	NA	896	675	4571	2633	6604	1660	15814	32853
1994	NA	1121	704	4797	2693	7224	1765	17103	35407
1995	NA	1200	731	5034	2880	7311	1977	18637	37770
1996	NA	2280	749	5188	3466	7512	2079	20035	41309
1997-98	294	4456	712	5322	3907	1798	2982	34258	53729
1998-99	306	4546	982	5447	4313	1867	3247	36482	57190
1999-2K	322	4694	1276	5587	4490	1931	3505	38303	60108
2000-01	333	4750	1600	5778	4610	1967	3778	40419	63235
2001-02	341	4797	1969	5868	4970	2000	4044	42947	66936
2002-03	351	5022	2513	5974	5293	2020	4213	45193	70579

Source: Basic Statistics of NER 2000, NEC, Shillong; Basic Statistics of NER 2006 : NER DATABANK NEDFi

Note: For some States (e.g. Arunachal, Trpura and Meghalaya) data from the two sources appear to be inconsistent

Rural and Small-Scale Industries in the North-Eastern Region: The 3rd Census of Small-Scale Industries conducted in 2002-03 (Govt. of India, 2003) revealed that the number of registered small-scale enterprises in the NER exceeded 25.4 thousand (Table-3(A)). The year of registration of those enterprises indicates the growth of SSI in different states. Assam, Manipur and Tripura have many enterprises that were registered in the 1950's or before. In other states such enterprises were only a few and far between. However, since the 1960's most of the states experienced a fillip in the establishment and registration of small-scale enterprises. Trends in SSI are also revealed by Table-3(B).

Much like living beings enterprises too are subject to the laws of life epitomized in birth, growth, maturity and persistence, decline and finally death or extinction. Closure of an enterprise, especially in the small-scale industries sector, is very common. The Census found that a little over 35 percent of rural enterprises in the nation are closed due to various reasons, internal and external (Table-4). In Manipur, however, only 27 percent of the rural enterprises recorded closure. The incidence of closure was more in Sikkim (50 percent) and Meghalaya (47 percent). In the urban sector, the incidence of closure was the highest in Tripura against the lowest in Manipur as well as Nagaland.

Table-4: Percentage Distribution Of Working/ Closed Units In The Regd. Ssi Sector

State	Rural Working	Urban Closed	Working	Closed
INDIA	64.39	35.61	58.18	41.82
MIZORAM	58.01	41.99	68.78	31.22
SIKKIM	50.00	50.00	54.77	45.23
TRIPURA	58.21	41.79	37.84	62.16
ARUNACHAL	44.17	55.83	62.71	37.29
MEGHALAYA	52.98	47.02	45.72	54.28
NAGALAND	66.28	33.72	86.48	13.52
ASSAM	60.14	39.86	56.67	43.33
MANIPUR	73.10	26.90	86.87	13.13

Source: Third Census of SSI, Govt. of India, 2003

Table-5(a): Duration Of Oper. Of Working Regd. Ssi Units In Rural Areas Of Ne Region

State	Duration of Operation in number of months [Percentage of Units] NR = Not Reported												Total
	< 1	1-2	2-3	3-4	4-5	5-6	6-7	7-8	8-9	9-10	10-11	11-12	NR	Units
Sik	0.00	0.00	4.62	7.69	6.15	15.38	4.62	9.23	3.08	4.62	0.00	35.38	9.23	65
Aru	0.69	0.00	10.42	11.81	11.11	8.33	2.78	2.78	7.64	11.11	10.42	22.22	0.69	144
Nag	0.00	0.00	0.00	3.51	3.51	3.51	9.65	7.89	14.04	21.05	27.19	5.26	4.39	114
Man	0.69	0.33	1.47	2.69	2.74	5.88	10.04	11.47	10.98	23.40	11.19	18.13	0.98	2449
Miz	0.00	0.00	0.75	0.37	1.87	2.24	2.61	5.60	4.48	4.10	7.09	70.52	0.37	268
Tri	0.00	1.11	1.11	1.30	0.19	3.90	3.71	6.12	6.86	22.26	15.96	33.95	3.53	539
Meg	0.00	1.52	0.08	0.15	0.99	10.05	1.75	4.41	11.87	12.40	4.11	52.59	0.08	1314
Ass	0.19	0.33	0.72	0.97	0.57	2.95	2.76	3.53	5.91	24.71	25.45	31.44	0.47	6990
Ind	0.19	0.47	0.74	1.14	1.14	3.01	2.37	3.78	4.76	12.30	14.55	54.71	0.86	608422

Table-5(b): Duration Of Oper. Of Working Regd. Ssi Units In Rural Areas Of Ne Region

State	Cumulative Duration of Operation in number of months [Percentage of Units] NR = Not Reported													Total
	< 1	< 2	< 3	< 4	< 5	< 6	< 7	< 8	< 9	< 10	< 11	< 12	NR	Units
Sik	0.00	0.00	4.62	12.31	18.47	33.85	38.47	47.69	50.78	55.39	55.39	90.78	9.22	65
Aru	0.00	0.00	0.00	3.51	7.02	10.53	20.18	28.07	42.11	63.16	90.35	95.61	4.39	144
Nag	0.69	1.02	2.49	5.19	7.92	13.80	23.85	35.32	46.30	69.70	80.89	99.02	0.98	114
Man	0.00	0.00	0.75	1.12	2.99	5.22	7.84	13.43	17.91	22.01	29.10	99.63	0.37	2449
Miz	0.00	1.11	2.23	3.53	3.71	7.61	11.32	17.44	24.30	46.57	62.52	96.47	3.53	268
Tri	0.00	1.52	1.60	1.75	2.74	12.79	14.54	18.95	30.82	43.23	47.34	99.92	0.08	539
Meg	0.19	0.52	1.23	2.20	2.78	5.72	8.48	12.02	17.93	42.63	68.08	99.53	0.47	1314
Ass	0.19	0.66	1.40	2.54	3.68	6.68	9.05	12.83	17.60	29.89	44.44	99.14	0.86	6990
Ind	0.69	0.69	11.11	22.92	34.03	42.36	45.14	47.92	55.56	66.67	77.08	99.31	0.69	608422

Rural enterprises often do not run for all months during a year. It was found that at the national level some 42.36 percent fo the total number of enterprises ran less that 6 months. For Manipur, this figure was 5.22 percent, the least in NER against 33.85 percent in Sikkim that was the largest. Meghalaya, Assam and Mizoram had less than 10 percent rural enterprises that ran for six months or less (Table-5(a), (b)). Enterprises that do not run throughout the year naturally incur higher costs due to fixed capital remaining idle. Organizational Aspects of Small Enterprises in the NER: Small-scale enterprises in India are mostly (about 85.9 percent) proprietary. The second largest category is that of the partnership, followed by cooperative management. Small-scale enterprises are usually not organized on the principles of a private company. However, in Nagaland, only 76.58 percent enterprises are proprietary and 7.22 percent are under the cooperative management. Sikkim and Assam come next in management of enterprises under the cooperative management. On the other hand, rarely we find enterprises in the other states run under the cooperative management (Table-6).

Table -6: State-wise Percentage Distribution Of No. Of Registered Units By Type Of Organisation

State	No. Of Units Having Type of Organization					Total
	Proprietary	Partnership	Cooperative	Pvt. Company	Others	
SIKKIM	93.10	2.30	4.02	0.57	0.00	100.00
ARUNACHAL	97.25	0.00	0.39	0.00	2.35	100.00
NAGALAND	76.58	1.94	7.22	1.76	12.50	100.00
MANIPUR	98.96	0.50	0.07	0.30	0.17	100.00
MIZORAM	97.44	1.02	0.44	0.15	0.95	100.00
TRIPURA	89.78	6.15	1.88	0.63	1.56	100.00
MEGHALAYA	98.92	0.21	0.36	0.41	0.10	100.00
ASSAM	92.69	3.27	3.57	0.25	0.21	100.00
INDIA	88.85	7.21	2.42	0.34	1.17	100.00

The gender-wise distribution of entrepreneurs in the NER, first of all, indicates that the percentage of male entrepreneurs is far more than the female entrepreneurs in all states and both sectors, rural and urban (Table-7).

Table-7: Gender And Social Class Wise Entrepreneurship Profile

State	Percentage No. Of Units in rural areas Managed by												
	Male		Female		SC		ST		OBC		Others		Total
	R	U	R	U	R	U	R	U	R	U	R	U	
SIKKIM	34.48	48.28	5.75	11.49	2.87	6.90	12.07	19.54	3.45	9.77	22.41	24.14	100
ARUNACHAL	49.41	30.59	7.06	12.94	0.39	0.39	49.41	32.55	0.00	0.39	6.67	10.20	100
NAGALAND	18.52	68.08	2.12	11.29	1.06	7.05	18.87	68.61	0.00	0.35	0.71	3.35	100
MANIPUR	41.77	42.27	11.24	4.72	0.67	0.33	22.72	1.22	3.63	4.22	25.96	41.25	100
MIZORAM	7.69	65.63	2.12	24.56	0.07	0.33	9.55	87.74	0.04	0.18	0.18	1.94	100
TRIPURA	52.45	41.92	2.92	2.71	6.05	2.61	1.46	0.42	10.53	5.84	37.33	35.77	100
MEGHALAYA	44.01	22.96	23.74	9.29	0.26	0.77	66.10	28.74	0.05	0.10	1.39	2.63	100
ASSAM	40.46	46.07	7.85	5.63	4.01	4.11	3.85	1.85	8.86	6.03	31.58	39.69	100
INDIA	39.83	51.85	4.50	3.82	4.94	2.91	2.06	1.48	19.24	19.27	39.83	32.02	100

In Meghalaya, which is inhabited mostly by the tribes that are matrilineal and perhaps matrifocal too, the male entrepreneurship far exceeds the female entrepreneurship, although the latter is more prominent there than elsewhere in the NER (Mishra, 2007). In the urban areas of Sikkim, Arunachal Pradesh, Nagaland and Mizoram, female entrepreneurs are more in proportion than those in the rural areas, which indicates that in these states urbanization and economic development have worked in favour of gender equality in economic spheres. In Arunachal Pradesh, Manipur, Tripura and Meghalaya rural entrepreneurship is more vivid, indicating the spread of industrial development beyond urban areas. Particularly in Mizoram and Nagaland, urban entrepreneurship dominates the scene and it appears that the rural areas have remained unattractive.

Table-8: Participation of Women in SSI Sector

State	Unregistered		Registered	
	Enterprises Managed by Women	Women Enter-prises	Enterprises Managed by Women	Women Enter-prises
INDIA	880780	926187	114361	137534
MIZ	•	2346	3007	730
	693			
SIKKI	0	53	30	45
TRIP	578	784	53	79
ARUN	80	87	51	63
MEGH	3018	2929	640	651
NAGA	130	122	77	57
ASSA	9241	9716	1948	2041
MANI	8434	9980	734	765
NER	23827	26678	4263	4394

The social class-wise distribution of entrepreneurship reveals that in Assam, Tripura, Manipur and Sikkim the majority of entrepreneurs are from the'general' category; denoted by'others' who do not belong to scheduled caste, schedule tribe and other backward classes. Similar is the class-wise distribution at the national level also. This pattern is more pronounced in the urban areas. Especially in Manipur, scheduled tribes vie with the'others' in the rural areas while the latter class is much more dominant in the urban areas. In Assam and Tripura, like at the national level, the'other backward classes' secure the second position to the'general' or'others' class. In Manipur and Sikkim they secure the third position. Entrepreneurs from the schedule caste category have a significant presence in Tripura, Assam and Sikkim.

EMPLOYMENT AND OUTPUT

A perusal of available data reveals that while the SSI sector in the North-Eastern Region employed 3.12 percent of the total number of persons engaged in the SSI sector in the country, it turned out goods and services that valued only 1.77 percent of the national SSI sector output (Table-9(A)). At the employment front, the registered SSI enterprises in the NER score a meager 2 percent of the nation; in output the share is even more slender, merely 0.86 percent.

The small-scale enterprises in the NER are more labour intensive. This is indicated by the share of the NER in the market value of fixed asset (as well as the original value of plant and machinery) in the nation vis-à-vis employment of labour. (Table-10). It appears that in the NER capacity utlization of plants also is in the lower side.

Table-9(A): Status of Small Scale Industries in the NE Region

State	No. of Units	Fixed Investment*	Production*	Employment
SIKKIM	415	12.60	44	1580
ARUNACHAL	1411	34.17	69	4330
NAGALAND	15623	378.55	540	66466
MANIPUR	54101	403.67	703	153715
MIZORAM	12529	139.89	207	28622
TRIPURA	27448	329.27	461	62861
MEGHALAYA	25383	164.45	481	75607
ASSAM	219092	1287.39	4907	487871
NER	356002	2749.99	7412	881052
[% to India]	3.02	1.54	1.77	3.12
India	11859000	178699.00	418263	28257000

* in Rs crores. Source: Govt. of India, Ministry of SSI, Annual Report 2005-06

Distribution of employment in the SSI sector by different criteria (gender, social class, etc) are presented in Table-9(B).

Table-9(B): Estimated Percentage Distribution of Persons Employed in Small-Scale Enterprises

State	Male		Female		SC		ST		OBC		Others		Children		Total
	R	U	R	U	R	U	R	U	R	U	R	U	R	U	
SIK	22.40	55.42	8.65	13.44	4.79	8.02	5.83	13.02	7.81	21.67	12.71	26.04	0.00	0.00	100
ARU	39.43	37.47	3.51	19.58	3.92	4.73	12.56	20.86	3.31	3.44	23.16	28.02	0.00	0.00	100
NAG	19.95	67.22	2.38	10.45	2.84	19.11	15.56	38.68	1.19	7.89	2.74	12.00	0.00	0.00	100
MAN	39.85	40.53	14.36	5.27	0.55	0.03	19.65	0.92	2.67	3.37	31.34	41.48	0.01	0.08	100
MIZ	7.45	68.41	1.27	22.88	0.10	2.62	6.83	80.34	1.17	1.11	0.61	7.21	0.00	0.02	100
TRI	49.81	13.39	34.18	2.62	17.25	3.32	15.29	0.21	26.34	3.75	25.10	8.73	0.44	0.01	100
MEG	41.81	28.94	18.51	10.73	1.41	1.68	52.85	33.05	0.78	0.39	5.28	4.56	0.01	0.02	100
ASS	38.32	47.64	8.24	5.81	5.44	7.11	4.95	4.61	10.90	9.64	25.27	32.09	0.13	0.18	100
IND	30.12	54.06	7.35	8.47	6.17	7.87	2.78	4.06	14.95	21.17	13.57	29.43	0.10	0.12	100

In Tripura, Meghalaya and Manipur the small-scale industries have an inclination to generation of employment in the rural areas whereas Mizoram, Nagaland and Sikkim have the urban bias. Assam and Arunachal Pradesh have more or less balanced division between rural and urban employment. The small-scale enterprises in Tripura, Meghalaya, Mizoram and Arunachal Pradesh have exhibited an inclination to employment generation for women. This is partly so due to generally higher involvement of women in the economic and productive activities, characteristic of the NE Region. However, Nagaland and Assam have a clear bias to the male employment generation.

Table-10 : Percentage Distribution Of Principal Characteristics (Regtd Units)

State	No. of Working Units	Market Value of Fixed Assets	Original Value of Plant & Machinery	Employ-ment	Gross Output	Export
SIKKIM	0.01	0.01	0.01	0.02	0.01	0.00
ARUNACHAL	0.02	0.02	0.01	0.02	0.02	0.00
NAGALAND	0.04	0.06	0.07	0.08	0.05	0.01
MANIPUR	0.33	0.09	0.07	0.32	0.05	0.00
MIZORAM	0.20	0.07	0.09	0.15	0.03	0.00
TRIPURA	0.07	0.26	0.08	0.19	0.08	0.00
MEGHALAYA	0.14	0.04	0.07	0.17	0.05	0.00
ASSAM	1.05	0.52	0.73	1.05	0.57	0.04
NORTH-EAST	1.86	1.07	1.13	2.00	0.86	0.05
REST OF INDIA	98.14	98.93	98.87	98.00	99.14	99.95

Distribution of Small-Scale Enterprises in Secondary and Tertiary Sectors

In the rural areas of Arunachal Pradesh, Meghalaya, Tripura, and Manipur, the secondary sector activities are more prominent (Table-11). The secondary sector comprises manufacturing, assembling, processing, repair and maintenance activities. On the other hand, the secondary sector is more prominent in the urban areas of in Nagaland, Mizoram and Sikkim. In other states urban and rural areas balance in matters of the secondary sector activities in the Small-Scale enterprises. Tertiary sector activities (services) are more prominent in the urban areas than in the rural areas. However, in Meghalaya, Assam and Manipur, the service sector also has a significant presence in the rural areas. In Arunachal Pradesh, Mizoram, Sikkim and Nagaland, the tertiary sector activities of the small-scale enterprises are rather subdued.

Table-11: Percentage Distribution of Number of Units by Nature of Activity

State/ India	Rural			Urban			Total
	Mfg/ Assembly/ Processing	Repairing/ Maintenance	Services	Mfg/ Assembly/ Processing	Repairing/ Maintenance	Services	
SIKKIM	37.57	0.00	2.31	41.62	1.16	17.34	100
ARUNACHAL	52.16	0.39	3.92	35.69	1.96	5.88	100
NAGALAND	19.58	0.71	0.35	72.13	4.41	2.82	100
MANIPUR	42.18	0.50	10.31	30.46	1.09	15.46	100
MIZORAM	7.43	0.11	2.27	65.08	1.28	23.83	100
TRIPURA	45.30	1.36	8.66	28.71	0.63	15.34	100
MEGHALAYA	51.60	0.36	15.79	18.73	0.57	12.95	100
ASSAM	35.99	0.70	11.61	38.97	1.13	11.60	100
All India	27.07	0.82	16.44	36.38	1.28	18.01	100

THE OUTPUT PROFILE OF SMALL-SCALE ENTERPRISES IN THE NER

Most of the SSI enterprises in the North-Eastern Region are based on traditional or agriculture/forestry inputs. Among the forest-based units sawn timber, wooden furniture, sleepers and poles, and cane furniture are important. Among the agro-based enterprises, production of molasses, rice processing and milling are important. Poultry and chicken rearing is another activity. Enterprises producing cotton, woolen, silk and nylon clothes with or without embroidery work also are numerous. Beyond these, concrete works and iron grills, gates, and wire nets also are produced by many enterprises. Detailed list of various major enterprises concentrated in different states, their number, fixed assets, gross output and employment are given in Table-12(A) and Table-12(B). Enterprises do not always produce a single output. Particularly in Nagaland more than 3/4th of the total number of small-scale enterprises produce more than one output. On the other hand, in Sikkim, Tripura and Assam more than 70 percent of the SSI units produce a single output, much like in the nation. In Meghalaya and Mizoram more than 50 percent of SSI units produce a single output. While specialization in producing a single output has many advantages, multi-output units have much more resilience and adaptability to dynamic market conditions. The distribution of SSI units according to multiplicity or otherwise of produce is given in Table12(C). Many enterprises specialize in ancillary and SSSBE products. Their state-wise distribution is given in Table-12(D).

Table-12(a): States Having 500 Or More Units Producing The Same Prod/Service (Unregd. Ssi Sector)

State	Product	No. of Units	Fixed Asset (Rs)	Gross Output (Rs)	Employment (no)
Assam	Molasses	4008	52253262	358386775	15022
Assam	Embroidery clothes	1286	18639750	17568500	1286
Assam	Nylon Shirts & Pants	501	10015000	47884219	2003
Assam	Concrete Products	501	4006000	35052500	1002
Manipur	Chicken Live	1255	70294946	124658107	2556
Manipur	Wooden Sleepers & Poles	1130	97185734	10961647	1130
Manipur	Sculpture	514	4623000	34415667	1541
Nagaland	Sawn Timber	910	68775200	206752000	5460
Meghalaya +Assam jointly	Cane Furniture	4052	36504250	188060750	8731

In addition to this, there are more than 500 units each of rice milling, grill gate, fabrication, tailoring, and gold ornaments & jewellery in Assam; rice milling, wooden furniture & fixture, and embroidery work in Manipur; and wooden furniture and fixture in Nagaland as well as Meghalaya, for which details are not available.

Table-12(b): Districts Having 100 Or More Units Producing The Same Prod/Service (Regd. Ssi)

State	District	Product	No. of Units	Fixed Asset (Rs)	Gross Output (Rs)	Employ-ment (no)
Assam	Kamrup	Grill Gate	229	37013235	85764007	1127
Assam	Kamrup	Cotton Garments Knitted	158	9591669	41697916	760
Assam	Kamrup	Iron/Steel Wire-Nets	185	31591478	62673310	954
Assam	Nagaon	Rice & Other Preparations	193	47018415	29768854	501
Assam	Nagaon	Rice milling	126	21223233	16809173	303
Assam	Sonitpur	Rice Raw Excel. Basmati	167	30421560	85880376	528
Assam	Lakhimpur	Wooden Furniture & Fixture	103	5553609	12662423	392
Manipur	Imphal West	Wooden Furniture & Fixture	168	9291148	38484529	641
Manipur	Imphal West	Wooden Almirah Cabinet, Cupboard	164	11563196	33107274	736
Manipur	Imphal West	Rice Raw Excel. Basmati	121	9467272	17813726	402
Manipur	Ukhrul	Woolen Cardigans, Sweaters, etc	101	4176000	7239643	401
Mizoram	Aizawl	Wooden Furniture & Fixture	135	23129543	35647918	559

Table-12(c): Profile Of Regd Units Having Multiple Products/Services.

State			Percentage number of regd. units producing			Total	
	1_Product/ Service	2_Products/ Services	3_Products/ Services	4_Products/ Services	5_Products/ Services	Not Recorded	
SIKKIM	85.63	10.92	2.87	0.00	0.00	0.57	100.00
ARUNACHAL	42.35	21.57	11.76	8.24	15.29	0.78	100.00
NAGALAND	22.54	22.01	23.94	15.49	14.96	1.06	100.00
MANIPUR	48.99	22.31	20.20	5.74	1.22	1.54	100.00
MIZORAM	66.19	16.90	11.56	2.96	1.43	0.95	100.00
TRIPURA	72.68	14.70	9.28	1.88	0.42	1.04	100.00
MEGHALAYA	57.81	14.65	15.52	9.49	1.96	0.57	100.00
ASSAM	71.37	17.25	5.99	1.41	0.44	3.03	100.00
All INDIA	84.76	9.48	2.74	0.73	0.25	2.05	100.00

Table-12(d): State-wise Dist. Of No. Of Regd. Units By Type Of Unit

State	SSI	Ancillary among SSI	SSSBE
ALL INDIA	901291	45826	473683
MIZORAM	2020	67	713
SIKKIM	139	2	35
TRIPURA	730	18	229
ARUNACHAL	230	4	25
MEGHALAYA	1382	7	557
NAGALAND	550	105	18
ASSAM	11098	89	3355
MANIPUR	3414	42	1185
North-East	19563	334	6117

SSSBE = Small Scale Service and Business (Industry-related) Enterprises

THE INPUT PROFILE OF SMALL ENTERPRISES IN THE NER

It has been mentioned before that most of the small enterprises in the North-Eastern Region are based on processing the raw materials obtained from agriculture, animal husbandry and forestry or traditional inputs such as cotton, wool, silk and nylon fabrics, iron and steel, cement, etc., in which the production technology is well-known. Therefore, they do not need much of technological collaboration. Except in Sikkim and Manipur where traces of foreign contacts for technology is found, the SSI enterprises in other states have nothing to do with such contacts (Table-13(A) and Table-13(B)).

Particularly in Mizoram, Arunachal Pradesh, and Meghalaya about 80 percent or more SSI enterprises do not have any contacts with others for the technical know-how. On the other side, enterprises in Nagaland, Manipur and Sikkim have significant contacts with other units, institutions, research and development agencies and organizations in matters of technical know-how. Unregistered enterprises in these states have shown more interest than the registered enterprises in this matter. In the states where little contacts are made for technical know-how, the unregistered units have kept themselves more isolated. In Fig.-12 we present this picture. Note that interaction with other organizations, agencies, research & development institutions regarding technical know-how is an important determinant of efficiency and profitability.

Table-13(A): Utility of Technical Know-how in Unregistered SSI Sector (percentage)

State/India	Abroad	Domestic Collab. Co/Units	DRD/IS	None	Total
All-India	0.67	5.58	4.84	88.91	100
MIZORAM	0.64	0.00	0.67	98.69	100
SIKKIM	0.00	0.00	45.88	54.12	100
TRIPURA	0.12	0.29	22.44	77.15	100
ARUNAL	0.00	0.00	7.32	92.68	100
MEGHA	0.00	1.84	5.72	92.44	100
NAGA	0.00	65.64	9.03	25.32	100
ASSAM	0.10	12.00	6.62	81.27	100
MANI	1.33	17.57	47.02	34.07	100

DRD/ISO=Domestic R&D Institutions/Special Agency/Organization

Table-13(B): Utility of Technical Know-how in Registered SSI Sector (percentage)

State/India	Abroad	Domestic Collab. Co/Units	DRD/IS	None	Total
All-India	0.97	7.54	6.11	85.38	100
MIZORAM	0.51	2.23	2.93	94.33	100
SIKKIM	1.15	3.45	31.03	64.37	100
TRIPURA	0.83	2.19	17.31	79.67	100
ARUNAL	0.39	7.84	18.04	73.73	100
MEGHA	0.88	9.85	8.15	81.12	100
NAGA	0.00	25.18	15.14	59.68	100
ASSAM	0.44	10.87	11.33	77.35	100
MANI	0.80	25.59	27.70	45.90	100

DRD/ISO=Domestic R&D Institutions/Special Agency/Organization

Table –13(c): State-wise Percentage Distribution Of No.of Units By Main Source Of Energy

State	Percentage No. of Units having Main Source of Energy							Total
	No Power Needed	Coal	Oil	LPG	Electricity	Non Conventional Energy	Traditional Energy/ Firewood	
SIKKIM	13.79	1.72	0.57	0.00	82.18	0.00	1.72	100.00
ARUNACHAL	24.22	1.56	30.47	0.78	33.98	0.00	8.98	100.00
NAGALAND	6.70	2.82	3.53	0.00	82.36	0.53	4.06	100.00
MANIPUR	38.92	2.39	4.98	0.33	45.71	0.11	7.57	100.00
MIZORAM	32.53	0.48	1.76	0.66	54.08	0.73	9.77	100.00
TRIPURA	19.94	4.28	1.57	0.84	65.66	0.00	7.72	100.00
MEGHALAYA	56.29	3.35	1.55	1.13	28.87	0.10	8.71	100.00
ASSAM	34.61	1.44	1.12	0.50	57.12	0.76	4.46	100.00
ALL INDIA	26.23	2.10	2.94	0.53	65.43	0.52	2.26	100.00

The source of energy used by a production unit is another determinant of productivity and profitability. It is closely connected to the production technology as well. However, constraints on availability of a particular source of energy often determine technology, productivity and profitability.

In Meghalaya more than 50 percent of SSI units do not need any power. The percentage is well above 30 for Manipur, Mizoram and Assam. On the other hand, in Nagaland only 7 percent enterprises do not need any source of non-human energy. More than 80 percent of SSI units in Sikkim and Nagaland use electricity for energy (Table-13(C)). Interestingly, Meghalaya (a power surplus state) presents a case where electricity as a source of energy for running the SSI plants is the least in use. Coal as a source of energy is not so popular; the same is the case of oil (except in case of Arunachal Pradesh) and LPG. Use of the traditional sources (firewood) for energy is generally more prevalent than the use of coal, oil or LPG. Except in Sikkim, the traditional source (firewood) of energy is quite much in use. This is so due to easy availability of the firewood. The use of non-conventional sources of energy is only rare.

The extent of rural electrification (percentage of village electrified) is a good measure of availability of electrical power for home consumption as well as industrial purposes. If villages are electrified, towns must be electrifies since electrification of urban areas has always been a priority.

However, electrification of villages does not mean availability of regular or assured supply of power. In many cases village electrification is in name only - at the most of a perfunctory relevance, for recording in the annual reports. Nor it means that the residents of an electrified village really consume electricity or use it as input for productive purposes. In Meghalaya, for instance, only 30 percent of the rural inhabitants use electricity for home lighting, etc. Yet, Meghalaya is renowned as an electricity surplus state.

The details of rural electrification in North-Eastern Region are given in Table-13(D). There is some positive relationship between the extent of rural electrification and the use of electricity as a source of energy to run SSI activities/plants. Meghalaya and

Arunachal Pradesh have lower extent of rural electrification and less percentage of SSI units that use electricity as a source of energy. On the other hand, Nagaland and Sikkim have cent per cent village electrification associated with larger percentage of SSI units using electricity for energy. With an increase in the extent of rural electrification the percentage of SSI units depending on firewood (traditional sources) for energy shows a decline. In this way, village electrification conserves the forest resources.

Table-13(d): Rural Electrification In The North-east India

STATE	Percent Villages Electrified	By the Date
SIKKIM	100.0	31.03.2005
TRIPURA	96.0	31.03.2005
ARUNACHAL	71.0	31.03.2005
MEGHALAYA	69.0	31.03.2005
NAGALAND	100.0	31.08.2005
ASSAM	78.0	31.03.2005
MANIPUR	92.4	31.03.2005
INDIA	74.0	30.05.2006
MIZORAM	99.5	31.03.2005

Source: Rural Electrification Corporation Ltd. Govt. of India

IX. Khadi, Handloom and Handicrafts in the North-Eastern Region: Khadi industries encompass cotton, woolen and silken yarns and textiles. These industries also produce honey, soaps, etc. The status of this industry in the NER may be summarized in the Table-14(A) given below.

The NER has the highest concentration of household units in the Handloom sector in the country and more than 50% of weavers belong to the NER states. It is a heavily labour intensive industry. A substantial part of the handloom industry falls in the unorganized sector and the data available on the profile of this sector are somewhat soft.

The Annual Report 2002-03 Ministry of Textiles, Govt. of India observed that handicrafts have a special significance in the country's economy. They generate a sizeable employment and bring in foreign exchange through exports.

Table-14(A): Production and Employment in Khadi Sector in the NE Region

State	Production (Rs. Lakh)					Employment (Lakh workers)				
	1989	1998	1999	2002	2003	1989	1998	1999	2002	2003
SIKKIM	NA	NA	NA	NA	NA	NA	NA	NA	NA	NA
ARUNACHAL	0.13	86.24	35.91	217.13	317.88	NA	0.01	NA	0.01	0.01
NAGALAND	163.90	1946.13	1816.92	4229.41	4583.94	0.04	0.19	0.19	0.28	0.30
MANIPUR	1290.59	2978.57	4457.27	5512.45	5997.52	0.32	0.42	0.42	0.58	0.62
MIZORAM	80.53	2085.46	2412.76	NA	NA	NA	0.12	0.15	NA	NA
TRIPURA	1324.20	1245.46	1186.89	1825.47	2235.29	0.44	0.27	0.23	0.28	0.23
MEGHALAYA	380.03	1411.87	1202.98	3330.60	3100.46	0.06	0.13	0.11	0.23	0.25
ASSAM	1411.90	4066.55	4379.30	8179.00	7476.00	1.10	1.11	1.25	0.11	0.11
NER	4651.28	13820.28	15492.03	23977.07	26452.78	1.96	2.24	2.35	2.85	2.97
INDIA	16872.20	451930.93	511237.46	NA	NA	42.87	56.27	58.29	NA	NA

Estimates based on the population Census, National Sample Survey, NCAER survey and other studies and information available for the unorganized cottage industry sector reveal that the annual growth rate of employment (both direct and indirect) in the handicrafts sector could be around 2.5%.

Based on this, it is estimated that during the 9th Five Year Plan, employment in the handicrafts sector increased from 52.92 lakhs in the year 1997-98 to 56.99 lakhs in 2000-2001 and was estimated to reach 58.41 lakhs by the end of 9th Plan i.e. 2001-2002.

Out of the total work force in this sector, women constitute 46.8 percent, SC/ST 37.11 and minority 23.89 percent.

Table-14(B): Profile of Handloom and Handicrafts in the NE RE Region

State	No. of Handlooms 1998			No. of Handicraft Artisans (Lakh)	Production (Rs. Lakh)
	Domestic *Units (No.)	Commercial *Units (No.)	Cloth Produced (1n 1000 meters)	Year: 1999	Year: 1999
SIKKIM	NA	NA	NA	NA	NA
ARUNACHAL	44937	653	279.6	0.02	85.30
NAGALAND	1750	2170	1852.8	0.80	9464
MANIPUR	265302	283808	582874.6	3.92	889170
MIZORAM	41041	5944	3689.0	0.08	593
TRIPURA	95592	23480	35250.0	2.57	6080
MEGHALAYA	11030	575	3430.9	1.02	2581
ASSAM	1251930	201803	74875.0	1.46	782094
NER	1711582	518433	702251.9	889170	2094108

Total (NER) may not tally due to inconsistencies of compilation from different sources;

* Source: NEC (2000)

Table-14(C): Handicraft Units and Artisans in the NE Region 1995-96

	Handicraft Units			Handicraft Artisans		
	HH	Non-HH	Total	HH	Non-HH	Total
Sikkim	2169	29	2198	9605	163	9768
Arunachal	4011	33	4044	15539	196	15735
Nagaland	17484	119	17603	79285	593	79878
Manipur	97606	445	98051	378123	1865	739988
Mizoram	2185	28	2213	5127	133	5260
Tripura	77266	109	77375	243726	769	244495
Meghalaya	11360	152	11512	52774	790	53564
Assam	29816	544	30360	97363	3119	100482
NE Region	241897	1459	243356	881542	7628	1249170
India	1425414	29642	1455056	4583562	177624	4761186

http://www.india-seminar.com/2003/523/523%20census.htm : Ameta, H.R. (2003) "Census: Handicraft Artisans – 1995-96" : HH = Household

Handicrafts make a special part of micro and small enterprises. They are different than the enterprises that use machine, specially skilled manpower for operating and maintaining them, and the brute labour force. Handicraft-based enterprises need specially skilled artisans. A number of artisan clusters have been identified in the different states of the North-Eastern region. Those clusters have been described in Table-14(D) and Table-14(E). Those clusters specialize in the different handicraft products.

Performance of Micro & Small Enterprises in India

Collection of data by institutions as well as individual researchers often follows the prevailing conceptual schema. The categorization of enterprises into small or large scale entities and looking at them merely as a part of the macro-level concept of'industry' in India generated information in the last 6 decades that may give us only a blurred vision of the problems and prospects of small enterprises in the country. India has had a long tradition of classifying manufacturing and service activities under the generic name of'industries.' In this scheme of classification, we have large-scale industries, heavy industries, capital goods industries, consumer goods industries, small-scale industries, Khadi industries, cottage industries, agro-based industries and so on. Of late, some paradigm change has occurred.

Micro, Small and Medium Enterprises Development Act (MSMED), 2006 introduced the concept of'enterprises' against the earlier concept of'industries'. These'enterprises' have been classified under two major heads that relate to manufacturing and services. In each of these categories, enterprises have further been classified on the criterion of investment as micro, small and medium, described in Table-15(A). It may be noted the Act defined a'medium' enterprise for the first time in India. Earlier,'industries' were under the'small-scale' or the'large-scale' category. This new classification provides a scope to formulate specific policies for the promotion, development and control of enterprises of different sizes in the two sectors (manufacturing and service). Industry-wise classification scheme has also been problematic if an enterprise turned out multiple products, which is very frequent in the small enterprises sector.

Table-15: Classification of Enterprises According to MSMED Act, 2006

Investment	LimitsManufacturing Enterprises			Service Enterprises		
	Micr	Small	Medium	Micr	Small	Medium
Upper limit (Rs. million)	2.5	50.0	100.0	1.0	20.0	50.0
Lower limit (Rs. million)	0.0	2.5	50.0	0.0	1.0	20.0
Nature of Capital	BuiltInvestment in Plant & Machinery			Investment in Equipment		

Traditionally, the small enterprises sector included service enterprises in the form of Small Scale Service and Business (industry-related) Enterprises or the SSSBEs, with investment in fixes assets (excluding land and building) of Rs. 1.0 million or less. A list of activities was also there to define and illustrate the nature of SSSBEs. The MSMED Act, 2006 not only enhanced the upper limit of investment in service enterprises, it also significantly enlarged the scope of activities of the micro/small/medium enterprises (MSMEs).

Table-15(B): Growth Performance of MSE Sector in India

Year	No. of MSEs (lakh)			Employment (lakh persons)	Production (Rs. crore)	
	Registered	Unregistered	Total		Constant Prices	Current Prices
2001-02	14.89	90.32	105.21	294.33	195613	282270
2002-03	15.91	93.58	109.49	260.21	210636	311993
2003-04	16.97	96.98	113.95	271.42	228730	357733
2004-05	17.53	101.06	118.59	282.57	251511	418263
2005-06	18.71	104.71	123.42	294.91	277668	476201

Source: Personal Communication with Shri KK Sarkar, Secretary General, Indian Council of Small Industries Kolkata. dated 25.6.2007

Table-15(C): Growth Performance and Share of MSE Sector in GDP & Industrial Production

Performance Indicator (%)	2000-01	2001-02	2002-03	2003-04	2004-05	2005-06
Share of MSE in the National GDP	6.04	5.77	5.91	5.82	5.81	NA
do in Overall Industrial Production	39.71	39.12	38.89	38.80	38.55	NA
do in Exports	34.47	34.29	34.03	33.49	34.38	NA
Growth rate of MSE Sector	8.23	6.06	7.68	8.59	9.96	10.4
do Overall Industrial Sector	5.0	2.7	5.7	7.0	8.4	8.1

Source: Personal Communication with Shri KK Sarkar, Secretary General, Indian Council of Small Industries Kolkata. on 25.6.2007

Based on the data collected through various Census and Surveys on small scale industries before, it has been estimated that in the year 2005-06 Micro & Small Enterprises (MSEs) sector has some 1.87 million registered and 10.47 million unregistered enterprises that employ about 2.9 million persons and produce about Rs. 2776.68 thousand millions (at constant prices, 1994, or Rs. 4762.01 thousand millions at current prices) worth of goods and services. It contributes about 39 percent of the national manufacturing sector output and roughly 34 percent of exports. The MSE sector is growing much faster and consistently in comparison to the overall industrial sector of the country. A synoptic view of the performance of MSE sector may be obtained from Table-15(B) and Table-15(C).

Prospects and Constraints of Village and Small Enterprises in the NE Region

What constitutes the constraints and prospects of the village and small enterprise sector in its evolution into the engine of economic development (Harper, 2003) in the NE Region? Perhaps, the most important factors to consider in this regard may be classified under three heads:

(i) social-cum-psychological,
(ii) infrastructural and
(iii) technical-cum-technological. In what follows, we will discuss these factors at some length.

Social and Psychological Factors: Enterprises to come up require first of all that enough number of entrepreneurs should be there. What makes an entrepreneur? It is well known that in every living being there are, among many others, two basic instincts: the first to exploit and the second to explore. To copy, imitate, follow and such behaviours are fundamentally exploitative, while to innovate, deviate, etc. are fundamentally explorative.

To exploit is to choose the path of least resistance and to explore is to willingly take the bull by the horns. In particular a man from his very moment of birth begins imitating. His body too is an imitation in part. He receives language, manners, codes of conduct, learning, etc by imitation. It is not surprising, therefore, that the exploitative activities make the major part of his behaviour.

Adam and Eve were punished for explorative activities. In schools, now, children are punished if they are explorative and deviants from the beaten track. These regularities prevailing in the society go against enterprise. As McClelland (1961) tells us, the child has a chance to achieve higher if in his early life he learned the lesson of exploration from his'important others' and a need for achievement could be instilled in him. Entrepreneurship comes from risk disposition, a sense of self-worth and the need to self-determine (Brockhaus-1982). However, the societies where traditionalism is a virtue and heresy is shunned, entrepreneurs are less likely to come up.

Voiculescu (2005) in answering the question "What makes an entrepreneur?" puts forth his observations that may be paraphrased as follows. People do not typically switch on being an entrepreneur. Some come from nature, some from nurture. It is hard for people to be taught to be entrepreneurial: they either have it in their genes or in their upbringing or not at all. People cannot be taught to relish risk taking. Imagination is not taught in the classroom. However, some academics believe that education can help to provide those with a spark with at least some of the skills they will need to turn that spark into something more substantive. They hold that it is possible to give aspiring entrepreneurs some insight and help to build their confidence. Although it may not be possible to teach people to have a good idea but one can always be helped to develop inter-personal skills, sales and marketing and general management skills.

By training one may be made better prepared to reduce the odds against success. Those academics believe that it is crude to say that people are born entrepreneurs; that early experiences and role models shape them is more of a reality. Being an entrepreneur also has negative aspects to it. Many of them tend to be unable to have and miss out on close relationships and the family life that their fellow beings in the society have. Their focus on the business becomes an obsession, which can be likened to drug addiction. Only a few entrepreneurs actually set out to build big businesses and to attain wealth and, interestingly, money is not a prime motivator. Driessen and Zwart provide a list of characteristics and psychological dispositions of entrepreneurs.

Returning back to the NE Region, it may be noted that traditional culture, handicrafts, and artisans are the main planks on which the possibilities and prospects of entrepreneurial breakthrough for economic development in the region are squarely based. It is believed that a little of (short) training, a write up on the features of different types of enterprises and readiness of financial institutions to liberally support the manufacturing and service ventures would bring about a boom of micro and small enterprises in the region. However, there is a need to distinguish between'craftsmanship'/'artisanship' and'entrepreneurship'. Craftsmanship is rooted in the'instinct of workmanship' to use the phrase of Veblen (1898-99; 1914 and others). On the other hand, entrepreneurship and the success of enterprise depend on the'predatory prowess'.

To quote Veblen (1898-99): " *As the predatory culture reaches a fuller development, there comes a distinction between employments. The tradition of prowess, as the virtue par excellence, gains in scope and consistency until prowess comes near being recognized as the sole virtue. Those employments alone are then worthy and reputable which involve the exercise of this virtue. Other employments, in which men are occupied with tamely shaping inert materials to human use, become unworthy and end with becoming debasing.*" SAAP Annual Conference (2007) describes how the predatory prowess uses sabotage as a means to power or control on the creative instincts of craftsmen. Srinath (2002) observes: for the craftsman, it is a struggle to grow up.

His aversion to structure, his preference for personalized relationships and his reluctance to accept constructive criticism makes growth, with its implicit need for a more sophisticated infra- and supra-structure and greater decentralization, increasingly difficult to handle. Hoarding of information, inconsistencies in day-to-day interpretation of company policies, playing favourites and refusal or reluctance to let people really know where they stand do not contribute to an efficient and effective organization. Mediocrity thus becomes an established norm. While the craftsman tends to create a rigid enterprise, the opportunistic entrepreneur creates an adaptive organization. A more drastic type of change is thus needed for `craftsmen' for continued growth and success of the enterprise.

To those who are akin to the socio-economic conditions in the NE region it is a commonplace that in spite of great talents in art and craftsmanship, the region lacks in the prowess that is germane to development of entrepreneurship. Entrepreneurs, whether of local origin or the migrants to the region, live under the fear of extortion, disruption, and bandhs or closure of all activities, including movements, often called on by the unions and associations of a handful of persons - often the politicians in making, and readily observed by the mass either for fear or for the bonus of a pleasant no-work day.

A successful entrepreneur is soon subjected to the envious forces. "A house may be large or small; as long as the surrounding houses are equally small it satisfies all social demands for a dwelling. But if a palace rises beside the little house, the little house shrinks into a hut." writes Lipset (1960, p. 63) quoting Marx. The'house' is soon put to the conditions that lead to its turning into a'hut'. Therefore, the region has experienced a capital flight and exodus, material as well as human, now for decades. Education given to the students prepares them, at its most, to some'unproductive' service sector; jobs in the Government, or the academia. A treasure of funds is poured in by the Government of India every year plus every now and then to help the people in the region to develop. There are other sources of money too.

Easy money, especially in the hands of the youth and a section of the privileged people has turned them to consumerism. Thriftiness is no longer a virtue. The psychological facts are that rejoicing on other' labour is more appealing and the present is more real than the future; consumption relates to rejoicing on others' labour in the present while investment is a step to produce by oneself in the future. Another trait of the Indian populace that has emerged vivid now is in the practice of their identifying themselves by the social groups based on caste, tribe, religion, etc.

It is in fact a symptom of identity crisis; people cannot identify themselves by the groups based on other criteria such as material or intellectual development. The prevalent criteria are grossly opportunistic. On this front at least, the NE Region is not lagging behind the nation. However, all these things go against entrepreneurship. Unless this scenario is altered, entrepreneurial development in the region is a far cry. These observations may appear to be pessimistic, but the ostrich cannot evade adversities by closing his eyes to them.

Infrastructural Factors: Means of transportation and communication, availability of power, market, financial institutions, training institutes, etc. together make the infrastructure that facilitate the feasibility of productive activities and therefore, entrepreneurial activities too. Unfortunately, the North Eastern Region has a less developed transportation system, largely due to its topographical features. In the dawn of freedom in 1947 the erstwhile India was divided into India (present) and Pakistan. East Pakistan (now Bangladesh) was carved out from the North East. As a result, the transportation system was most severely affected and the present North East India was reduced to an almost'unconnected' part of the nation.

Over the years, the transport system in the NER and its connectedness to other parts of the country have improved significantly, but even today the condition is not very satisfactory. Transportation bottlenecks increase the time and pecuniary cost of production, leading to cost disadvantages in the competitive market. The local markets for material, labour and produce are less developed, less connected and less competitive. Villages have been largely electrified, but in want of productive activities, low income, weak product markets and availability of traditional sources of energy almost freely, electrification has not been much effective. There are training institutions, Industrial Training Institutes for instance, but the preference of the people - the students and their parents - is for the general academic courses in colleges and universities. The observation of Veblen, that *employments, in which men are occupied with tamely shaping inert materials to human use, become unworthy and end with becoming debasing*, is well supported in the preference of people against training in the industrial training institutes. These facts are important in planning for the promotion of MSEs in the region.

Technical-cum-Technological Factors: While discussing the involvement of research and development institutions, agencies, etc. it has been mentioned earlier that about 80 percent or more among the small scale industrial units in Mizoram, Arunachal

Pradesh, and Meghalaya do not have any contacts with others for the technical know-how. On the other side, enterprises in Nagaland, Manipur and Sikkim have significant contacts with other units, institutions, research and development agencies and organizations in matters of technical know-how. This is likely to be true of micro and small enterprises also since these enterprises were earlier included under the head of small-scale industries, whether registered or unregistered. Contacts for technical know-how are necessary for process and product development, which has direct bearing on marketability, cost and profit. The reasons for a lack of adoption of new technical know-how are numerous.

Lack of awareness, need to review the possibilities of cost reduction and product development, non-traditional attitude to one's own trade, financial soundness needed for adoption of new techniques, willingness to learn new skill, etc are some major ones among them (Galbraith, 1980). The lack of adoption of new techniques of production has lead to lower productivity in the MSE sector. It has been mentioned earlier that these enterprises employ about 3.12 percent of workers, but produce barely 1.77 percent of output in the nation. Thus the labour productivity of this sector in the region is only 57 percent of that in the nation. Capital investment in the NER small enterprises is only 1.54 percent of that in the nation. Adoption of improved methods will necessarily be more capital intensive, but would increase labour productivity and profitability of enterprises. It has been observed that the rate of closure of rural enterprises is more frequent in the NE region than that in India. In many NE states this is true of the urban enterprises also. The largest number of artisan clusters together with the highest frequency of closure of SSI units in Tripura is intriguing. Sickness and closure can greatly be reduced by technical-cum-technological improvements. The Government has recently formulated a programme to address the problems of technology, marketing and skill upgradation in the MSE sector.

Besides the factors elaborated above, financial and institutional factors (Veblen, 1904) also have a bearing on the success of micro and small enterprises. The MSMED Act, 2006 has provided for a statutory National Board with wide and balanced representation of all stakeholders in MSMEs to advise and recommend policies.

The Act also provides for administration of special funds for the MSMEs, statutory assurance of progressive credit policies, preference to micro and small enterprises in Govt. procurement, policies to counter the problems of delayed payments to the MSEs , etc. Khadi and village Industries Commission Act has been comprehensively amended to facilitate professionalism in Khadi and village enterprises sector.

The Govt. has also formulated a promotional package, which includes measures to address most of the problems relating to infrastructure, technology, marketing, capacity building and support to women entrepreneurs. The Govt. has announced a policy package for stepping up credit to SMEs. In this package the public sector banks have been advised to fix their own targets of credit delivery to SMEs in order to achieve a minimum 20 percent year-on-year growth. The Small Industries Development Bank of India (SIDBI) has been set to work on performance and credit rating of small enterprises and to take necessary steps to help MSEs by cluster development. Micro and small enterprises should take advantage of these opportunities for making the NE Region a hub of productive activities.

IMPORTANT ANTIPOVERTY EMPLOYMENT GENERATION PROGRAMS

Swaranjayanti Gram Swarozgar Yojana (SGRY)Started on April 1, 1999. It has replaced the following programs:Integrated Rural Development Program (IRDP) : Started in 1978 - 79). Training Rural Youth for Self -Employment (TRYSEM): Started in 1978-79. Development of Women and Children in Rural Areas (DWCRA): Started in 1978 -79. Ganga Kalyan Yojana (GKY): Started in 1997. Million Wells Scheme (MWS): Started in 1989. Supply of Improved Tool-kits to Rural Artisans (SITRA). The yojana takes into account all the strengths and weaknesses of the earlier self-employment programs. Every assisted family will be brought above the poverty line. It is proposed to cover 30% of the rural poor in each block.

To Target at atleast 50% Scheduled Castes and Scheduled Tribes, 40% women and 3% disabled.Pradhan Mantri Gramodaya Yojana (PMGY)It was introduced in 2000-01 with the objective of focusing on village level development in five critical areas I.e., primary health, primary education, housing, rural roads and drinking water and nutrition with the overall objective of improving the quality of life of people in rural areas. Rural electrification was added as an additional component from 2001-02. It has the following components: Pradhan Mantri Gram Sadak Yojana (PMGSY) Pradhan Mantri Gramodaya Yojana (Gramin Awas). Pradhan Mantri Gramodaya Yojana (Rural Drinking Water Project).Sampoorna Gramin Rozgar Yojana (SGRY)It was started on Sept. 25,2001, with the mergence of the Employment Assurance Scheme (EAS) and the Jawahar Gram Samriddhi Yojana (JGSY). Earlier Jawahar Rozgar Yojana, which started in 1989, was merged with Jawahar Gram Samriddhi Yojana.

The objective of the program is to provide additional wage employment in rural areas and also to provide food security.Swarna Jayanti Shahari Rozgar Yojana (SJSRY)The SJSRY came into operation in Dec, 1997, through a restructuring and streamlining of the earlier urban poverty alleviation programs, the Nehru Rozgar Yojana (NRY), the Urban Basic Services for the Poor (UBSP) and the Prime Minister's Integrated Urban Poverty alleviation Program (PMIUPEP). It seeks to provide employment to the urban employed or underemployed living below poverty line and educated up to IX standard through encouraging the setting up of self-employment ventures or provision of wage employment.Antyodaya Anna YojanaLaunched on Dec. 25,2000. The scheme aims at providing food security to poor families. The scheme contemplates identification of 10 million'poorest of the poor' families and providing the \m with 25kg of food grains per family per month at a low price of Rs.2 per Kg for wheat and Rs.3 per Kg for rice.Annapurna YojanaInaugurated on March 19, 1999. Initially the scheme provided 10 kg food grains to senior citizens who were eligible fore old age pension but could not get it due to one reason or the other. Later on, it was extended to cover those people who get old age pensions. Food grains are provided to the beneficiaries at subsidized rates of Rs.2 per kg of wheat and Rs.3 per kg of rice.

5

NREGA: A Historic Legislation

A key element that unexpectedly propelled the United Progressive Alliance (UPA) to power in May 2004 was the deep distress in India's countryside. The passage of the National Rural Employment Guarantee Act (NREGA) in 2005 is an important action of the UPA fulfilling mandatc-2004. The Act initially came into force in 200 economically backward districts of the country from February 2, 2006. The formulation and implementation of NREGA constitute a significant step towards poverty alleviation by providing an institutional framework for guaranting supplementary livelihood opportunity to the rural households.

NREGA is the first ever law internationally, that guarantees wage employment at an unprecedented scale. NREGA aims at enhancing livelihood security of households in rural areas of the entire country by providing at least one hundred days of guaranteed wage employment in a financial year to every household whose adult members volunteer to do unskilled manual work. The primary objective of the Act is augmenting wage employment. But its auxiliary objective is strengthening natural resource management through works that address causes of chronic poverty like drought, deforestation and soil erosion and so encourage sustainable development. The process outcomes include strengthening grassroots processes of democracy and infusing transparency and accountability in governance.

Unique features of NREGA include : time bound employment guarantee and wage payment within 15 days, incentive-disincentive structure to the State governments for providing employment as 90 per cent of the cost for employment provided is borne by the Centre or payment of unemployment allowance at their own cost and emphasis on labour intensive work prohibiting the use of contractors and machinery. The Act also mandates 33 per cent participation for women.

During the first year of implementation in 200 districts (financial year 2006-07), 2.10 crore households were employed. In 2007-08. 3.39 crore households were provided employment in 330 districts of the country. In 2008-09, up to mid-September, 2008, 2.9 crore households have been provided employment across the country. Comparing data on employment provided for phase-I and Phase-II districts from April to September, from financial year 2007-08 to financial year 2008-09, there is an increase of 17 per cent. Similarly, there has been an increase of 47 per cent in men generation in Phase-I and Phase-ll districts from financial year 2007-08 to financial year 2008-09 in the period from April to mid-September 2008. Moreover, the average wage paid under NREGA has increased from Rs. 75 to Rs. 80 in the financial year 2008-09 at the national level. The enhanced wage earning has led to a strengthening of the livelihood resource base of the rural poor. In 2007-08, more than 68 per cent of the funds utilized were in the form of wages paid to the labourers. In 2008-09, 71 per cent of the funds have been utilized in the form of wages (up to September 2008).

Significantly, the NREGA Programme had a high workforce participation of marginalised groups, namely, Scheduled Castes and Scheduled Tribes (57 per cent in financial year 2007-08). In financial year 2008-09, up to mid-September 2008, the participation of Scheduled Castes and Scheduled Tribes has been 55 per cent. Women workforce participation has also surpassed the statutory minimum requirement of one-third participation. In the financial year 2007-08, women participation was 43 per cent, which has increased to 49 per cent up to mid-September, 2008.

To avoid irregularities in wage payment, the Government of India has been encouraging the State governments to make wage payment through bank and post office accounts of wage seekers. Up to mid-September 2008, 4.2 crore NREGA bank and post office accounts have been opened to disburse wages. Workers are also being covered under Janshri Bima Yojana and Rastriya Swasthya Bima Yojana for accidental and health insurance.

Salutary effects have also been noted on natural resources through water conservation, land development, and afforestation projects taken up in large measures under NREGA. Enhancement of agricultural productivity has also been made possible through water harvesting, check dams, ground water recharging (particularly in Dungarpur district in Rajasthan and Villupuram district of Tamil Nadu), improve moisture content, check soil erosion and micro-irrigation works. The information from the field in the first year for which details are available shows that 75 per cent of the 8.3 lakh works have been water-harvesting structures, minor irrigation tanks, community wells, land development, flood control, plantations and so on. Benefits include the creation of over 12 crore cubic metres of water .storage capacity, three lakh km of drainage and embankments in water logged areas, 3.5 lakh hectares each of plantations and 1and development. These contribute also to drought proofing in low rainfall and semi-desert regions.

ln the financial year 2007-08, 17.88 lakh works were undertaken, of which 49 per cent constituted water conservation, 17 per cent rural connectivity, 16 per cent land development and provision of irrigation facility to individual beneficiaries constituted around 15 per cent and remaining 3 per cent works related to other activities. In the financial year 2008-09, up to mid- September 2008, 19.14 lakh works have been undertaken, of which 44 per cent relate to water conservation, 15 per cent rural connectivity, 23 per cent land development and provision of irrigation facility to individual beneficiaries constituted around 18 per cent and remaining 1 per cent works related to other activities.

Unlike many other programmes, programme implementation under NREGA has been entrusted to Panchyati Raj institutions which are the main planning and implementation authorities. Gram Sabhas have been assigned a pivotal role in planning. monitoring and social audit of projects under the Act.

A Central Employment Guarantee Council (CEGC) at the national level has been set up with the statutory mandate of monitoring and reviewing the Act. The CEGC and the Executive

Council have been meeting regularly and the EC members visited Jharkhand. Tamil Nadu, Orissa in 2007 and Uttar Pradesh and Maharashtra in 2008. For effective monitoring of the projects 100 per cent verification of the works at the block level. 10 per cent at the district level and 2 per cent at the State level inspections need to be ensured.

STRATEGIES AND PROGRAMMES

The rural economy, as much as urban economy, is an integrated part of the overall Indian economy. Any talk of overall development without rural development, particularly in a country where three-quarters of people below the poverty line reside in rural areas, is flawed. Poverty is indeed a global issue. Its eradication is considered integral to humanity's quest for sustainable development. Reduction of poverty in India, is, therefore, vital for the attainment of international goals.

Poverty alleviation has been one of the guiding principles of the planning process in India. This can be substantiated by the fact that anti-poverty programs have been internalized in the (particularly the ninth) five year plan. This article sheds light on the various "strategies and programs" that form the instruments of the plan.

Integrated Rural Development Program (IRBD)

First introduced in 1978-79, IRBD has provided assistance to rural poor in the form of subsidy and bank credit for productive employment opportunities through successive plan periods. Subsequently, Training of Rural Youth for Self Employment (TRYSEM), Development of Women and Children in Rural Areas (DWCRA), Supply of Improved Tool Kits to Rural Artisans (SITRA) and Ganga Kalyan Yojana (GKY) were introduced as sub-programs of IRDP to take care of the specific needs of the rural population.

Wage Employment Programs

Important components of the anti-poverty strategy, Wage Employment Programs have sought to achieve multiple objectives. They not only provide employment opportunities during lean agricultural seasons but also in times of floods, droughts and other natural calamities. They create rural infrastructure which supports further economic activity. These programs also put an upward pressure on market wage rates by attracting people to public works programs, thereby reducing labour supply and pushing up demand for labour. It encompasses National Rural Employment Program (NREP) and Rural Landless Employment Guarantee Program (RLEGP) which were initially part of the Sixth and Seventh five year Plans.

Employment Assurance Scheme (EAS)

EAS was launched in October 1993 covering 1,778 drought-prone, desert, tribal and hill area blocks. It was later extended to all the blocks in 1997-98. The EAS was designed to provide employment in the form of manual work in the lean agricultural season. The works taken up under the program were expected to lead to the creation of durable economic and social infrastructure and address the felt-needs of the people.

Food for Work Program

The Food for Work program was started in 2000-01 as a component of the EAS in eight notified drought-affected states of Chattisgarh, Gujarat, Himachal Pradesh, Madhya Pradesh, Orissa, Rajasthan, Maharastra and Uttaranchal. The program aims at food provision through wage employment. Food grains are supplied to states free of cost. However, lifting of food grains for the scheme from Food Corporation of India (FCI) godowns has been slow.

Rural Housing

Initiated in 1985-86, the IAY is the core program for providing free housing to families in rural areas, targets scheduled castes (SCs)/scheduled tribes (STs), households and freed bonded laborers. The rural housing program has certainly enabled many BPL families to acquire pucca houses, the coverage of the beneficiaries is limited given the resource constraints. The Samagra Awas Yojana (SAY) was taken up in 25 blocks to ensure convergence of housing, provision of safe drinking water, sanitation and common drainage facilities. The Housing and Urban Development Corporation (HUDCO) has extended its activities to the rural areas, providing loans at a concessional rate of interest to economically weaker sections and low-income group households for construction of houses.

Social Security Programs

Democratic decentralization and centrally supported Social Assistance Programs were two major initiatives of the government in the 1990s. The National Social Assistance Program (NSAP), launched in August 1995 marks a significant step towards fulfillment of the Directive Principles of State Policy. The NSAP has three components: a) National Old Age Pension Scheme (NOAPS); b) National Family Benefit Scheme (NFBS); c) National Maternity Benefit Scheme (NMBS). The NSAP is a centrally-sponsored program that aims at ensuring a minimum national standard of social assistance over and above the assistance that states provide from their own resources. The NOAPS provides a monthly pension of Rs. 75 to destitute BPL persons above the age of 65. The NFBS is a scheme for BPL families who are given Rs. 10,000 in the event of the death of the breadwinner. The NMBS provides Rs. 500 to support nutritional intake for pregnant women. In addition to NSAP, the Annapurna scheme was launched from I April 2000 to provide food security to senior citizens who were eligible for pension under NOAPS but could not receive it due to budget constraints.

Land Reforms

In an agro-based economy of, the structure of land ownership is central to the wellbeing of the people. The government has strived to change the ownership pattern of cultivable land, the abolition of intermediaries, the abolition of zamindari, ceiling laws, security of tenure to tenants, consolidation of land holdings and banning of tenancy are a few measures undertaken. Furthermore, a land record management system is a pre-condition for an effective land reform program. In 1987-88, a centrally-sponsored scheme for Strengthening of Revenue Administration and Updating of Land Records (SRA & ULR) was introduced in Orissa and Bihar.

Although these measures have been successful (to some extent) in curbing poverty , this model has a very basic flaw. Under this model resources are transferred from urban economy to rural economy just for short term political motives. This is affecting both areas, not letting rural economy develop on its own and hampering growth and investments in urban economy. An ideal approach should include the government, panchayats and key village personals, NGOs and private companies. This will not only help reduce this imbalance but will have a multiplier effect on the overall economy. By aligning the goals of the two parts we can convert this seemingly zero sum game into a win-win situation. It would be a very long drawn and difficult battle with conventions but the reward is worth the effort.

BANGLADESH

Bangladesh is without doubt notorious for its poverty. However it deserves the appreciation of being the country where micro-credit policies to eliminate poverty have been most successful. This article tries to explore the reasons for this peculiarity that Bangladesh enjoys.

Despite its short history, the word Bangladesh has become synonymous to poverty. Even nature seems to be against the poverty stricken people of Bangladesh. Whatever life sustaining rural economies they have are served a deathblow by frequent flooding. Ironically, the worst part has not come as yet. In keeping tradition with its huge neighbors (India and Pakistan) the worst characteristic of poverty in Bangladesh is that it is heavily skewed towards women.

Micro-credit plays the crucial role of being the glimmer of hope at the end of this unforgiving tunnel of darkness. It would not be an exaggeration to claim that micro-credit policies have become Bangladesh's very own. This might have come as a surprise to many but micro-credit can in fact work! The problems of repayment, hijacking of programs by elite, corruption and asymmetry of information have in the case of many countries thwarted the success of these micro-credit schemes. Then what is special about Bangladesh that makes micro-crediting work?

A simple but effective answer to this question would be that the whole process of micro-crediting is transparent and focused. Many a times such projects are not continuous and a family once given a loan is left unattended in subsequent years. It is vital to realize that a sudden burst of loans is not what people need. In Bangladesh, NGO's have ensured that people get loans regularly which can help them to achieve a sustainable level of stability in their respective ventures. Also it is made sure that the amount of subsequent loans is linked to the performance in repayments. In this way the credibility of the participants is maintained. Besides this there is a unique requirement for participants to save in groups. The funds accumulated could be used to loan out to any member to fulfill his/her need. The beauty of this process lies in the fact that the participants act as checks and balances on to one another. Since every transaction is carried forward in the presence of other participants who have a direct stake in the success of this process, the chances of default are minimized. Statistics too prove this point and astonishingly the repayment rate of loans given out as micro-credit is substantially higher than those given by the commercial banks. In addition to this, women are given the priority in loan allocation. This is where the focused dimension comes into this whole process. These loans act as lifelines to the deprived Bangladeshi women and empirical studies prove that they make more durable investment choices than men. Also help from the World Bank and Government doesn't hurt either.

So where is the loophole? Although this program is the best in the world but there is always room for improvements. The very bottom stratum of Bangladesh's population does not enjoy the safety net woven by this policy. Bangladesh would do well to include these desperate people into these schemes of micro-financing.

BOSTWANA

Botswana is a situated in Central Africa and can be regarded as one of the rapidly progressing countries in the region. When the country gained independence in 1966, the economy of the state was in shambles. However, soon after the discovery of the diamond mines in the country, the country has registered rapid progress. Though the economy is driven mainly by the diamond mines, Botswana is primarily an agricultural region. And despite having one of the best credit ratings in the area, the country still faces a great deal of poverty. Other major problems being faced by the Botswana government are the rural urban migration and the Aids problem which has seriously afflicted the whole region.

One of the issues which the government is facing regarding the poverty problem is the creation of the slum areas near the outskirts of its cities. This is a serious problem because the land board of the government has all ready assigned lands to the people and so there should not be too many issues. Given the fact that population of Botswana is not really bloated, it makes the situation even more complex. It is a problem for the government because the creation of slum areas leads to the devaluation of the property. The main reason that can be attributed to these slums is the rural urban migration and the fact that people to whom these land have been allotted are selling it for higher prices on account of them being nearer to the city. The Land Reform Board is looking into this problem. Poverty reduction has been very slow and has actually decreased from about 59% to 47% between the years 1985 and 1994.'It further reported that 55 percent of the rural population was found to be below the poverty datum line compared to 46 percent in urban villages and 29 percent in urban areas.' Given this, the urban population has registered an increase of about 90% i.e. it has almost doubled over a period of about 10 years. This is all very disturbing news for the agricultural sector since people are leaving this line and going for the urban lifestyle and to make matters worse, even the poverty levels there are higher.

A problem which plagues most developing nations these days is the curse of HIV/AIDS. This is also true of Botswana,'especially amongst the sexually and economically active portion of the society.' Though the problem is a growing one, Botswana also has one of the most progressive organized plans for dealing with the situation in the whole region. Hopefully then, the situation will not get out of hand.

Basically Botswana is a developing nation which has a great deal of potential to do well economically. Its situation is helped by the fact that it has a lead over its neighboring countries which would give it an upper hand in dealing with them. Its poverty problems can be solved through better land reforms and attracting greater investment from abroad.

BOLIVIA

One word that people associate with Bolivia is high. This Latin American country boasts the highest navigable lake in the world. La Paz is the highest capital city in the world, at over two miles high in elevation. It has the highest gold- oil, gas and mineral reserves.

Yet at the same time it has experienced the highest inflation and highest rates of poverty.Although rich in natural resources it is the poorest country in Latin America. Landlocked and sparsely populated it continues to struggle against repercussions of foreign plundering. In the early 1980s, Bolivia emerged from many years of military rule in an economically impossible position. It had been looted by the generals. Its foreign debt was overwhelming. In 1985, inflation reached a surreal annual rate of 24,000 percent. During the twelve month period from august 1984 to 1985 prices rose alarmingly and during the final months of the hyperinflation the inflation surged to an annualized rate of 60,000 percent. The country was in a fix with people 62% of the people living on incomes of less than $1 in a day. If it continued this way the country would have plunged into an inflationary death swoop. It was then that the country consented to radical treatment.

The young American economist Jeffery Sachs stepped in and designed a blueprint to solve Bolivia's problem The other key player was the Bolivian minister of planning (later president), Gonzalo Sánchez de Lozada. These two men along with other Bolivian reformers led the country to undergo'shock therapy'. To bring about an immediate halt to the hyperinflation, they drastically devalued the currency, abolished the minimum wage, and cut state spending to the minimum. Within ten days the 60000 percent inflation suddenly ended. This seems almost miraculous except that it plunged the economy into severe recession. Wages fell and unemployment skyrocketed. Tin miners, teachers, nurses, and factory workers were especially hard hit. Yet on the whole the'shock treatment' worked, in the sense that prices eventually stabilized and the Bolivian government's good relations with its foreign creditors-and, most importantly, with their de facto enforcement arm, the International Monetary Fund-were restored. There were conditions, of course. The IMF and the World Bank (the Bank's development loans helped keep the country afloat) took effective control of large areas of public policy. Like many poor countries, Bolivia was subjected to what is blandly known as structural adjustment—a set of standardized, far-reaching austerity and "openness" measures that typically include the removal of restrictions on foreign investment, the abolition of public subsidies and labor rights, reduced state spending, deregulation, lower tariffs, tighter credit, the encouragement of export-oriented industries, lower marginal tax rates, currency devaluation, and the sale of major public enterprises. For Bolivia it was the railways and the phone company.

After seventeen years of structural adjustment, Bolivia remains the poorest country in South America. The predicted foreign investment has arrived, largely in the form of multinational corporations taking control of privatized entities. But prosperity has not followed. Inflation is under control, and there has been modest economic growth, but its benefits have been concentrated among the wealthy, exacerbating a centuries-old problem of extreme inequality.

The predicament of Bolivia is that like other underdeveloped countries, its rapidly changing governments realize that obviously their poverty is thc pre condition for the flow of aid and, for the less scrupulous among them; this can turn the poor themselves into a valuable commodity, their pitiful ness a resource not to be squandered through improvement. So Bolivia, like many other countries, spends more on debt servicing than it spends on health care and continues to be entrapped in poverty. The outlook is bleak, as even Jeffrey Sachs, who continues to advise the Bolivian government, concedes. Regarding Bolivia he says that "I always told the Bolivians, from the very beginning, that what you have here is a miserable, poor economy with hyperinflation; if you are brave, if you are gutsy, if you do everything right, you will end up with a miserable, poor economy with stable prices." It has stable prices, so in that sense it can be referred to as a success story!

SRILANKA

The Sri Lankan government aims to raise the socio-economic status of the rural poor by integrating sound economic management with plans to improve the social indicators of the poor. However, it also needs to resolve ethno-national tensions on a fast-track basis, so as to provide sustainable support and direct funds towards productive spending".

Sri Lanka, with a population of about twenty million, is a poor South Asian country where social indicators like high literacy rates and democratic governance coincide with a relatively high incidence of poverty and ethno-nationalist unrest. According to a Country Assistance Plan made by the Asian Development Bank, about a third of the population lives below the poverty line and almost 85 percent of these reside in the country's rural areas mainly in the Central and Southern provinces and in the rural North-East, which is wracked by the decades old Tamil-Sinhalese conflict. Thus, the overall efforts aimed at poverty reduction in Sri Lanka can't be divorced from the government's attempts at facilitating rural development and bringing about peace. The government's Framework for Poverty Reduction plans to reduce poverty through a combination of steps incorporating economic and social initiatives. In addition, the government is actively pursuing a peace process with Tamils to bring stability and relief to the general populace as well as to the North-Eastern poor who are susceptible to recruitment by the rebels.

First, the Sri Lankan government hopes to reduce the incidence of dire poverty through a three-pronged strategy of promoting economic and social opportunities for the poor by broad-basing the benefits of growth, shielding marginalized and non-competitive groups which can't participate in mainstream economic activities and by incorporating people into the processes of governance and ensuring their fundamental rights. Through its aim to identify new and broader roles for local governments and civil society in poverty reduction, the government is holding out an especially attractive promise to the rural poor who stand to gain greater autonomy in devising and practicing ways of combating widespread poverty. To this effect, the government's Samurdhi (Prosperity) Program, functional since 1994, shores up local authorities by providing social support to very poor households. Also, the Framework acknowledges that a stable, overarching macroeconomic situation would contribute greatly to endeavors against poverty. Thus, a plan aimed at privatizing state-owned units and ensuring fiscal stability is working as a part of the overall Framework. Other social initiatives directed at improving the lot of the rural poor include establishing a Child Protection Authority (1997) to protect against exploitation and to impart education to all.

However, economic initiatives alone cannot work in a country like Sri Lanka where civil strife poses a serious threat particularly to the rural poor. The conflict has caused much damage to physical and social infrastructure facilities. In addition, it has led to the displacement of hundreds of thousands of people from their homes and source of livelihood. The only way the government can follow sustainable development policies here is by giving priority to establishing peace through political methods, so as not to further tax the already distressed population. This not only increases welfare access to the poor but it also frees up funds to the tune of 5 percent of the GDP, which are currently being used to finance the conflict. Hence, there is reason to invest hope in a fragile cease fire which has held since February 2002.

Thus, economic development in Sri Lanka hinges on multiple factors that cover economic, social and political areas.

SOUTH AFRICA

To be poor is to be hungry, lack shelter and clothing, to be sick and not be cared for, to be illiterate and not be schooled. But for poor people, poverty is more than this. They are particularly vulnerable to adverse events outside their control. They are often treated badly by the institutions of state and society and excluded from voice and power in those institutions (World Bank 2000)".

Poverty is a defining characteristic of South Africa and has a clearly racial, geographic and gender element. It has been argued that this is a direct result of segregationist policies employed by the colonial regimes. Therefore, the main thrust of post-apartheid ANC government was to eradicate the massive poverty amongst the Black population and make the distribution of income more equitable. However, the problem proved to be far more tenacious than the government assumed and in 2003 the issue of poverty regained importance. The opposition rallied behind the slogan "Life is no better now than in 1994", the government was faced with a stark reality; poverty indicators remained alarming. In South Africa, one is ten Africans is malnourished, one is four children is stunted, 45% of the population lives on less than $2 a day. In 1999, it was estimated that around 45-55% of all South Africans live in conditions of poverty. It was tragic to note that 22% of households reported that members were going hungry because they could not afford to buy food and to make matters worse, 32% of households contained no employed people.

The spatial and gender dimension of poverty reveals that while less than half of the South African population lives in rural areas, they house 72% of the country's poor. The rate of poverty amongst the female-headed households is double (60%) that of male-headed households as unemployment rates are highest amongst the females. The most vulnerable population is children and the old age persons. HIV/AIDS is another phenomenon that has plagued South Africa in recent times. In 1994, some 2.4 million people were infected by HIV.'The illness increases the risk of a household or individual becoming impoverished, and lowers the general level of health in communities because of its close relationship with other communicable and poverty-related diseases such as tuberculosis' . Consequently, national life expectancy has declined dramatically from 60.8 in 1996 to 53.5 in 2001.

Income distribution in South Africa is one the most unequal in the world. The Gini-coefficient is currently 0.58, second highest in the world. There has been an emergence of a new Black elite class but the overwhelming population remains poor.

Poverty reduction strategies employed by the ANC have been seen as a betrayal by most. While the government deserves credit for securing human rights and political freedoms for the Blacks, it has failed to alleviate the problem of poverty. In 1996, ANC adopted the Growth and Redistribution Program (GEAR) that was in line with neo-liberal policy reforms. It focused on economic growth with free market reforms at the expense on social development and redistribution. In conclusion, any solution to poverty in South Africa must consider the following:

- asset redistribution;
- market reforms
- linking growth to development

- spatial development; and
- institutional reform.

INDONESIA

Rural development has been effectively delineated as one of the important solutions towards combating poverty. This article focuses on developing the rural sector through strengthening institutional ties. As a case in point, Indonesia has benefited from increased cooperation and engagement of the communities at the local level

Developing countries are in a perpetual struggle against the elimination of poverty which amongst the many reasons is attributed towards the dualistic nature of development; benefiting a handful at the cost of many living in the rural sectors of the countries. An urban-centered approach and being completely apathetic towards rural development has also been blamed as potentially exacerbating poverty. It is in the wake of these perspectives that focus has been given to the upliftment of the poor through building stronger institutional ties. Formation of local community groups and decentralization is held to be the key for effective service delivery and termed as the means through which poverty can be successfully fought. But the question here arises how important is the need for institutional development and to what degree has it been carried out successfully in Indonesia?

Institutions have been defined as established ways or thoughts of a group of people (Burkett, 1962). Institutions however not only comprise formal institutions such as that of a church, school or hospital but also an abstract set of rules, incentives and values that determine and address the equitable distribution of resources in low-income households in the rural sectors, thus helping them to combat poverty.

Political transition in 1999 after a 44 year rule by President Suharto did not prove an effective solution to the country's aggravating economic problems. The poor remained trapped in a quagmire of problems and did not benefit from the economic growth. New decentralization laws were passed in 2000 to strengthen institutional capacity and boost greater authority and decision making power in the hands of the local populace. A specific attempt in this regard has been the Kemacatan Development Program (KDP) instituted in 1998. The program aims to establish participatory governance, demand-responsiveness, administrative autonomy, greater downward accountability, and enhanced local capacity (World Bank, 2005). Experience has shown that effective partnerships with support of the local governments pave a long way for the implementation of communal goals which act as catalyzing agents for the betterment of all.

Another interesting example substantiating the above fact has that been of the Riung Nature Reserve in Indonesia. A hub of natural diversity comprising both upland forests and a coastal marine zone, it has been the centre of conflict between local farmers and the governmental authorities; the former expanding gardening reserves in the reserve thus defying the latter. Recently a consensus has emerged between the governmental authorities and the local community through increased participation amongst the two has had dual benefits. The reserve has been saved from environmental degradation and locals tap economic advantages helping them to emerge from the poverty trap which engulfed them earlier.

Institutions as effective service deliverers have had a phenomenal impact on pulling people from the abyss of poverty. Acting as agents for rural development they have significant spillover benefits since a contented rural workforce also halts the onset of migration to urban areas and thus in turn over urbanization. Institutional development has not only infused a spirit of cooperation at the local level but has also resulted in the effective reduction of poverty.

Summary

Rural development has been effectively delineated as one of the important solutions towards combating poverty. This article focuses on developing the rural sector through strengthening institutional ties. As a case in point, Indonesia has benefited from increased cooperation and engagement of the communities at the local level.

6

Government Antipoverty Programs

The government has initiated, sustained, and refined many programs since independence to help the poor attain self sufficiency in food production. Probably the most important initiative has been the supply of basic commodities, particularly food at controlled prices, available throughout the country. The poor spend about 80 percent of their income on food while the rest of the population spends more than 60 percent. The price of food is a major determinant of wage scales. Often when food prices rise sharply, rioting and looting follow. Until the late 1970s, the government frequently had difficulty obtaining adequate grain supplies in years of poor harvests. During those times, states with surpluses of grain were cordoned off to force partial sales to public agencies and to keep private traders from shipping grain to deficit areas to secure very high prices; state governments in surplus-grain areas were often less than cooperative. After the late 1970s, the central government, by holding reserve stocks and importing grain adequately and early, maintained sufficient supplies to meet the increased demand during drought years. It also provided more remunerative prices to farmers.

In rural areas, the government has undertaken programs to mitigate the worst effects of adverse monsoon rainfall, which affects not only farmers but village artisans and traders when the price of grain rises. The government has supplied water by financing well digging and, since the early 1980s, by power-assisted well drilling; rescinded land taxes for drought areas; tried to maintain stable food prices; and provided food through a food-for-work program. The actual work accomplished through food-for-work programs is often a secondary consideration, but useful projects sometimes result. Employment is offered at a low daily wage, usually paid in grain, the rationale being that only the truly needy will take jobs at such low pay.

In the 1980s and early 1990s, Indian government programs attempted to provide basic needs at stable, low prices; to increase income through pricing and regulations, such as supplying water from irrigation works, fertilizer, and other inputs; to foster location of industry in backward areas; to increase access to basic social services, such as education, health, and potable water supply; and to help needy groups and deprived areas. The total money spent on such programs for the poor was not discernible from the budget data, but probably exceeded 10 percent of planned budget outlays.

India has had a number of antipoverty programs since the early 1960s. These include, among others, the National Rural Employment Programme and the Rural Landless Employment Guarantee Programme. The National Rural Employment Programme evolved in FY 1980 from the earlier Food for Work Programme to use unemployed and underemployed workers to build productive community assets. The Rural Landless Employment Guarantee Programme was instituted in FY 1983 to address the plight of the hard-core rural poor by expanding employment opportunities and building the rural infrastructure as a means of encouraging rapid economic growth. There were many problems with the implementation of these and otherschemes, but observers credit them with helping reduce poverty. To improve the effectiveness of the National Rural Employment Programme, in 1989 it was combined with the Rural Landless Employment Guarantee Programme and renamed Jawahar Rozgar Yojana, or Jawahar Employment Plan (see Development Programs, ch. 7).

State governments are important participants in antipoverty programs. The constitution assigns responsibility to the states in a number of matters, including ownership, redistribution, improvement, and taxation of land (see The Constitutional

Framework, ch. 8). State governments implement most central government programs concerned with land reform and the situation of small landless farmers. The central government tries to establish programs and norms among the states and union territories, but implementation has often remained at the lower bureaucratic levels. In some matters concerning subsoil rights and irrigation projects, the central government exerts political and financial leverage to obtain its objectives, but the states sometimes modify or retard the impact of central government policies and programs.

DEVELOPMENT PLANNING

Planning in India dates back to the 1930s. Even before independence, the colonial government had established a planning board that lasted from 1944 to 1946. Private industrialists and economists published three development plans in 1944. India's leaders adopted the principle of formal economic planning soon after independence as an effective way to intervene in the economy to foster growth and social justice.

The Planning Commission was established in 1950. Responsible only to the prime minister, the commission is independent of the cabinet. The prime minister is chairperson of the commission, and the minister of state with independent charge for planning and program implementation serves as deputy chairperson. A staff drafts national plans under the guidance of the commission; draft plans are presented for approval to the National Development Council, which consists of the Planning Commission and the chief ministers of the states. The council can make changes in the draft plan. After council approval, the draft is presented to the cabinet and subsequently to Parliament, whose approval makes the plan an operating document for central and state governments (see The Legislature; Local Government, ch. 8).

The First Five-Year Plan (FY 1951-55) attempted to stimulate balanced economic development while correcting imbalances caused by World War II and partition. Agriculture, including projects that combined irrigation and power generation, received priority. By contrast, the Second Five-Year Plan (FY 1956-60) emphasized industrialization, particularly basic, heavy industries in the public sector, and improvement of the economic infrastructure. The plan also stressed social goals, such as more equal distribution of income and extension of the benefits of economic development to the large number of disadvantaged people. The Third Five-Year Plan (FY 1961-65) aimed at a substantial rise in national and per capita income while expanding the industrial base and rectifying the neglect of agriculture in the previous plan. The third plan called for national income to grow at a rate of more than 5 percent a year; self-sufficiency in food grains was anticipated in the mid-1960s.

Economic difficulties disrupted the planning process in the mid-1960s. In 1962, when a brief war was fought with China on the Himalayan frontier, agricultural output was stagnating, industrial production was considerably below expectations, and the economy was growing at about half of the planned rate. Defense expenditures increased sharply, and the increased foreign aid needed to maintain development expenditures eventually provided 28 percent of public development spending. Midway through the third plan, it was clear that its goals could not be achieved. Food prices rose in 1963, causing rioting and looting of grain warehouses in 1964. War with Pakistan in 1965 sharply reduced the foreign aid available. Successive severe droughts in 1965 and 1966 further disrupted the economy and planning.

Three annual plans guided development between FY 1966 and FY 1968 while plan policies and strategies were reevaluated. Immediate attention centered on increasing agricultural growth, stimulating exports, and searching for efficient uses of industrial assets. Agriculture was to be expanded, largely through the supply of inputs to take advantage of new high-yield seeds becoming available for food grains. The rupee was substantially devalued in 1966, and export incentives were adjusted to promote exports. Controls affecting industry were simplified, and greater reliance was placed on the price mechanism to achieve industrial efficiency.

The Fourth Five-Year Plan (FY 1969-73) called for a 24 percent increase over the third plan in real terms of public development expenditures. The public sector accounted for 60 percent of plan expenditures, and foreign aid contributed 13 percent of plan financing. Agriculture, including irrigation, received 23 percent of public outlays; the rest was mostly spent on electric power, industry, and transportation. Although the plan projected national income growth at 5.7 percent a year, the realized rate was only 3.3 percent.

The Fifth Five-Year Plan (FY 1974-78) was drafted in late 1973 when crude oil prices were rising rapidly; the rising prices quickly forced a series of revisions. The plan was subsequently approved in late 1976 but was terminated at the end of FY 1977 because a new government wanted different priorities and programs. The fifth plan was in effect only one year, although it provided some guidance to investments throughout the five-year period. The economy operated under annual plans in FY 1978 and FY 1979.

The Sixth Five-Year Plan (FY 1980-84) was intended to be flexible and was based on the principle of annual "rolling" plans. It called for development expenditures of nearly Rs1.9 trillion (in FY 1979 prices), of which 90 percent would be financed from domestic sources, 57 percent of which would come from the public sector. Public-sector development spending would be concentrated in energy (29 percent); agriculture and irrigation (24 percent); industry including mining (16 percent); transportation (16 percent); and social services (14 percent). In practice, slightly more was spent on social services at the expense of transportation and energy. The plan called for GDP growth to increase by 5.1 percent a year, a target that was surpassed by 0.3 percent. A major objective of the plan was to increase employment, especially in rural areas, in order to reduce the level of poverty. Poor people were given cows, bullock carts, and handlooms; however, subsequent studies indicated that the income of only about 10 percent of the poor rose above the poverty level.

The Seventh Five-Year Plan (FY 1985-89) envisioned a greater emphasis on the allocation of resources to energy and social spending at the expense of industry and agriculture. In practice, the main increase was in transportation and communications, which took up 17 percent of public-sector expenditure during this period. Total spending was targeted at nearly Rs3.9 trillion, of which 94 percent would be financed from domestic resources, including 48 percent from the public sector. The planners assumed that public savings would increase and help finance government spending. In practice that increase did not occur; instead, the government relied on foreign borrowing for a greater share of resources than expected.

The schedule for the Eighth Five-Year Plan (FY 1992-96) was affected by changes of government and by growing uncertainty over what role planning could usefully perform in a more liberal economy. Two annual plans were in effect in FY 1990 and FY 1991. The eighth plan was finally launched in April 1992 and emphasized market-based policy reform rather than quantitative targets. Total spending was planned at Rs8.7 trillion, of which 94 percent would be financed from domestic resources, 45 percent of which would come from the public sector. The eighth plan included three general goals. First, it sought to cut back the public sector by selling off failing and inessential industries while encouraging private investment in such sectors as power, steel, and transport. Second, it proposed that agriculture and rural development have priority. Third, it sought to renew the assault on illiteracy and improve other aspects of social infrastructure, such as the provision of fresh drinking water. Government documents issued in 1992 indicated that GDP growth was expected to increase from around 5 percent a year during the seventh plan to 5.6 percent a year during the eighth plan. However, in 1994 economists expected annual growth to be around 4 percent during the period of the eighth plan.

Four decades of planning show that India's economy, a mix of public and private enterprise, is too large and diverse to be wholly predictable or responsive to directions of the planning authorities. Actual results usually differ in important respects from plan targets. Major shortcomings include insufficient improvement in income distribution and alleviation of poverty, delayed completions and cost overruns on many public-sector projects, and far too small a return on many public-sector investments. Even though the plans have turned out to be less effective than expected, they help guide investment priorities, policy recommendations, and financial mobilization.

THE ROLE OF GOVERNMENT

Early Policy Developments

Many early postindependence leaders, such as Nehru, were

influenced by socialist ideas and advocated government intervention to guide the economy, including state ownership of key industries. The objective was to achieve high and balanced economic development in the general interest while particular programs and measures helped the poor. India's leaders also believed that industrialization was the key to economic development. This belief was all the more convincing in India because of the country's large size, substantial natural resources, and desire to develop its own defense industries.

The Industrial Policy Resolution of 1948 gave government a monopoly in armaments, atomic energy, and railroads, and exclusive rights to develop minerals, the iron and steel industries, aircraft manufacturing, shipbuilding, and manufacturing of telephone and telegraph equipment. Private companies operating in those fields were guaranteed at least ten years more of ownership before the government could take them over. Some still operate as private companies.

The Industrial Policy Resolution of 1956 greatly extended the preserve of government. There were seventeen industries exclusively in the public sector. The government took the lead in another twelve industries, but private companies could also engage in production. This resolution covered industries producing capital and intermediate goods. As a result, the private sector was relegated primarily to production of consumer goods. The public sector also expanded into more services. In 1956 the life insurance business was nationalized, and in 1973 the general insurance business was also acquired by the public sector. Most large commercial banks were nationalized in 1969. Over the years, the central and state governments formed agencies, and companies engaged in finance, trading, mineral exploitation, manufacturing, utilities, and transportation. The public sector was extensive and influential throughout the economy, although the value of its assets was small relative to the private sector.

Controls over prices, production, and the use of foreign exchange, which were imposed by the British during World War II, were reinstated soon after independence. The Industries (Development and Regulation) Act of 1951 and the Essential Commodities Act of 1955 (with subsequent additions) provided the legal framework for the government to extend price controls that eventually included steel, cement, drugs, nonferrous metals, chemicals, fertilizer, coal, automobiles, tires and tubes, cotton textiles, food grains, bread, butter, vegetable oils, and other commodities. By the late 1950s, controls were pervasive, regulating investment in industry, prices of many commodities, imports and exports, and the flow of foreign exchange.

Export growth was long ignored. The government's extensive controls and pervasive licensing requirements created imbalances and structural problems in many parts of the economy. Controls were usually imposed to correct specific problems but often without adequate consideration of their effect on other parts of the economy. For example, the government set low prices for basic foods, transportation, and other commodities and services, a policy designed to protect the living standards of the poor. However, the policy proved counterproductive when the government also limited the output of needed goods and services. Price ceilings were implemented during shortages, but the ceiling frequently contributed to black markets in those commodities and to tax evasion by black-market participants. Import controls and tariff policy stimulated local manufacturers toward production of import-substitution goods, but under conditions devoid of sufficient competition or pressure to be efficient.

Private trading and industrial conglomerates (the so-called large houses) existed under the British and continued after independence. The government viewed the conglomerates with suspicion, believing that they often manipulated markets and prices for their own profit. After independence the government instituted licensing controls on new businesses, especially in manufacturing, and on expanding capacity in existing businesses. In the 1960s, when shortages of goods were extensive, considerable criticism was leveled at traders for manipulating markets and prices. The result was the 1970 Monopolies and Restrictive Practices Act, which was designed to provide the government with additional information on the structure and investments of all firms that had assets of more than Rs200 million, to strengthen the licensing system in order to decrease the concentration of private economic power, and to place restraints on certain business practices considered contrary to the public interest. The act emphasized the government's aversion to large companies in the private sector, but critics contended that the act resulted from political motives and not from a strong case against big firms. The act and subsequent enforcement restrained private investment.

The extensive controls, the large public sector, and the many government programs contributed to a substantial growth in the administrative structure of government. The government also sought to take on many of the unemployed. The result was a swollen, inefficient bureaucracy that took inordinate amounts of time to process applications and forms. Business leaders complained that they spent more time getting government approval than running their companies. Many observers also reported extensive corruption in the huge bureaucracy. One consequence was the development of a large underground economy in small-scale enterprises and the services sector.

India's current economic reforms began in 1985 when the government abolished some of its licensing regulations and other competition-inhibiting controls. Since 1991 more "new economic policies" or reforms have been introduced. Reforms include currency devaluations and making currency partially convertible, reduced quantitative restrictions on imports, reduced import duties on capital goods, decreases in subsidies, liberalized interest rates, abolition of licenses for most industries, the sale of shares in selected public enterprises, and tax reforms. Although many observers welcomed these changes and attributed the faster growth rate of the economy in the late 1980s to them, others feared that these changes would create more problems than they solved. The growing dependence of the economy on imports, greater vulnerability of its balance of payments, reliance on debt, and the consequent susceptibility to outside pressures on economic policy directions caused concern. The increase in consumerism and the display of conspicuous wealth by the elite exacerbated these fears.

The pace of liberalization increased after 1991. By the mid-1990s, the number of sectors reserved for public ownership was slashed, and private-sector investment was encouraged in areas such as energy, steel, oil refining and exploration, road building, air transportation, and telecommunications. An area still closed to the private sector in the mid-1990s was defense industry. Foreign-exchange regulations were liberalized, foreign investment was encouraged, and import regulations were simplified. The average import-weighted tariff was reduced from 87 percent in FY 1991 to 33 percent in FY 1994. Despite these changes, the economy remained highly regulated by international standards. The import of many consumer goods was banned, and the production of 838 items, mostly consumer goods, was reserved for companies with total investment of less than Rs6 million. Although the government had sold off minority stakes in public-sector companies, it had not in 1995 given up control of any enterprises, nor had any of the loss-making public companies been closed down. Moreover, although import duties had been lowered substantially, they were still high compared to most other countries.

Political successes in the mid-1990s by nationalist-oriented political parties led to some backlash against foreign investment in some parts of India. In early 1995, official charges of serving adulterated products were made against a KFC outlet in Bangalore, and Pepsi-Cola products were smashed and advertisements defaced in New Delhi. The most serious backlash occurred in Maharashtra in August 1995 when the Bharatiya Janata Party (BJP—Indian People's Party)-led state government halted construction of a US$2.8 million 2,015-megawatt gas-fired electric-power plant being built near Bombay (Mumbai in the Marathi language) by another United States company, Enron Corporation.

AGRICULTURE

Agriculture has always been India's most important economic sector. In the mid-1990s, it provides approximately one-third of the gross domestic product (GDP—see Glossary) and employs roughly two-thirds of the population. Since independence in 1947, the share of agriculture in the GDP has declined in comparison to the growth of the industrial and services sectors. However, agriculture still provides the bulk of wage goods required by the nonagricultural sector as well as numerous raw materials for industry. Moreover, the direct share of agricultural and allied sectors in total exports is around 18 percent. When the indirect share of agricultural products in total exports, such as cotton textiles and jute goods, is taken into account, the percentage is much higher.

Dependence on agricultural imports in the early 1960s convinced planners that India's growing population, as well as concerns about national independence, security, and political stability, required self-sufficiency in food production. This perception led to a program of agricultural improvement called the Green Revolution, to a public distribution system, and to price supports for farmers (see The Green Revolution, this ch.). In the 1980s, despite three years of meager rainfall and a drought in the middle of the decade, India managed to get along with very few food imports because of the growth in food-grain production and the development of a large buffer stock against potential agricultural shortfalls. By the early 1990s, India was self-sufficient in food-grain production. Agricultural production has kept pace with the food needs of the growing population as the result of increased yields in almost all crops, but especially in cereals. Food grains and pulses account for two-thirds of agricultural production in the mid-1990s. The growth in food-grain production is a result of concentrated efforts to increase all the Green Revolution inputs needed for higher yields: better seed, more fertilizer, improved irrigation, and education of farmers. Although increased irrigation has helped to lessen year-to-year fluctuations in farm production resulting from the vagaries of the monsoons, it has not eliminated those fluctuations.

Food-grain production increased from 50.8 million tons in fiscal year 1950 to 176.3 million tons in FY 1990. The compound growth rate from FY 1949 to FY 1987 was 2.7 percent per annum. Overall, wheat was the best performer, with production increasing more than eightfold in forty years. Wheat was followed by rice, which had a production increase of more than 350 percent. Coarse grains had a poorer rate of increase but still doubled in output during those years; production of pulses went up by less than 70 percent.

The increase in oilseed production, however, was not enough to fill consumer demands, and India went from being an exporter of oilseeds in the 1950s to a major importer in the 1970s and the early 1980s. The agricultural sector attempted to increase oilseed production in the 1980s and early 1990s. These efforts were successful: oilseed production doubled and the need for imports was reduced.

In the early 1990s, India was on the verge of self-sufficiency in oilseed production.After independence in 1947, the cropping pattern became more diversified, and cultivation of commercial crops received a new impetus in line with domestic demands and export requirements. Nontraditional crops, such as summer mung (a variety of lentil, part of the pulse family), soybeans, peanuts, and sunflowers, were gradually gaining importance.

The per capita availability of a number of food items increased significantly in the postindependence period despite a population increase from 361 million in 1951 to 846 million in 1991. Per capita availability of cereals went up from 334 grams per day in 1951 to 470 grams per day in 1990.

Availability of edible oils increased significantly, from 3.2 kilograms per year per capita in FY 1960 to 5.4 kilograms in FY 1990. Similarly, the availability of sugar per capita increased from 4.7 to 12.5 kilograms per year during the same period. The one area in which availability decreased was pulses, which went from 60.7 grams per day to 39.4 grams per day. This shortfall presents a serious problem in a country where a large part of the population is vegetarian and pulses are the main source of protein.

There are large disparities among India's states and territories in agricultural performance, only some of which can be attributed to differences in climate or initial endowments of infrastructure such as irrigation. Realizing the importance of agricultural production for economic development, the central government has played an active role in all aspects of agricultural development. Planning is centralized, and plan priorities, policies, and resource allocations are decided at the central level.

Food and price policy also are decided by the central government. Thus, although agriculture is constitutionally the responsibility of the states rather than the central government, the latter plays a key role in formulating policy and providing financial resources for agriculture.

Land Use

In FY 1987, field crops were planted on about 45 percent of the total land mass of India. Of this cultivated land, almost 37 million hectares were double-cropped, making the gross sown area equivalent to almost 173 million hectares. About 15 million hectares were permanent pastureland or were planted in various tree crops and groves. Approximately 108 million hectares were either developed for nonagricultural uses, forested, or unsuited for agriculture because of topography. About 29.6 million hectares of the remaining land were classified as cultivable but fallow, and 15.6 million hectares were classified as cultivable wasteland. These 45 million hectares constitute all the land left for expanding the sown area; for various reasons, however, much of it is unsuited for immediate cropping. Expansion in crop production, therefore, has to come almost entirely from increasing yields on lands already in some kind of agricultural use.

Topography, soils, rainfall, and the availability of water for irrigation have been major determinants of the crop and livestock patterns characteristic of the three major geographic regions of India—the Himalayas, the Indo-Gangetic Plain, and the Peninsula—and their agro-ecological subregions. Government policy as regards irrigation, the introduction of new crops, research and education, and incentives has had some impact on changing the traditional crop and livestock patterns in these subregions. The monsoons, however, play a critical role in determining whether the harvest will be bountiful, average, or poor in any given year. One of the objectives of government policy in the early 1990s was to find methods of reducing this dependence on the monsoons.

HIMALAYAN RANGES

The Himalayan region, with some 520,000 square kilometers of land, ranks well behind the other two regions in agricultural importance. Despite generally adequate rainfall, the rugged topography allows less than 10 percent of the land to be used for agriculture. The sandy, loamy soils on the hillsides and the alluvial clays in the region's premier agricultural subregion, the Vale of Kashmir—located in the northwestern part of the state of Jammu and Kashmir—provide fertile land for agricultural use. The main crops are rice, corn, wheat, barley, millet, and potatoes. Most of India's temperate-zone fruits (apples, apricots, cherries, and peaches) and walnuts are grown in the vale. Sericulture and sheepherding also are being undertaken. In the eastern Himalayan subregion, the soils are moderately rich in organic matter and are acidic. Although much of the farming is done on terraced hillsides, there is a significant amount of shifting cultivation, which has resulted in deforestation and soil erosion. Rice, corn, millet, potatoes, and oilseeds were the main crops in the early 1990s. The region also is well known for the tea plantations of the mountainous Darjiling (Darjeeling) area in the northern tip of West Bengal.

Indo-Gangetic Plain

The vast Indo-Gangetic Plain, extending from Punjab to Assam, is the most intensively farmed zone of the country and one of the most intensively farmed in the world. Rainfall, most of which comes with the southwest monsoon, is generally adequate for summer-grown crops, but in some years vast areas are seared by drought. Fortunately, much of the land has access, or potential access, to irrigation waters from wells and rivers, ensuring crops even in years of drought and making possible a winter crop as well as a summer harvest. Wheat is the main crop in the west, rice in the east. Pulses, sorghum, oilseeds, and sugarcane are among other important crops. Mango orchards are common. Other fruits of the subregion include guavas, jackfruit, plums, lemons, oranges, and pomegranates.

In the Great Indian Desert, rainfall is scanty and erratic. About 20 percent of the total area is under cultivation, mostly in Haryana and Gujarat states, and comparatively little in Rajasthan. The Indira Gandhi Canal—begun in 1958 as the Rajasthan Canal—was designed to bring water from the north. Progress was slow, and only the first stage was close to completion by the end of the Seventh Five-Year Plan (FY 1985-89). By then, the canal had substantially increased the area under cultivation in Rajasthan, and a new completion date of 1999 is anticipated. The cultivable area is expected to expand further with the development of the canal's second stage during the 1990s. The leading crops of the subregion are millet, sorghum, wheat, and peanuts. Vast expanses of sparse vegetation provide sustenance for sheep and goats. In the late 1980s, dairy farming became important in locations that had sufficient pastureland.

Peninsular India

The east and west coasts, the coastal plains, and the deltaic tracts that extend inland for some 100 to 200 kilometers in Peninsular India benefit from both the June-to-September southwest monsoon and the October-to-November northeast monsoon. Farther inland, as the topography and climate change, so does the pattern of agriculture. The proportion of land under cultivation ranges from about 50 percent along the coastal plain and in the western part of Andhra Pradesh to about 25 percent in eastern Madhya Pradesh. Except in areas of certain developed river valleys, double-cropping is rare. Rice is the predominant crop in high-rainfall areas and sorghum in low-rainfall areas. Other crops of significance along the east coast and in the Central Highlands in the early 1990s were pigeon peas, mustard, peanuts, millet, linseed, castor beans, cotton, and tobacco.

On the Deccan Plateau, deep, alluvial black soils that retain moisture for a long time are the basis for much of the region's output of farm products. However, the region also has many farming areas that are covered by thin, light-textured soils that suffer quickly from drought. Whether a crop is made or lost is, therefore, often dependent on the availability of supplementary water from ponds and streams. About 60 percent of the land in the state of Maharashtra was under cultivation in the early 1990s, less in Madhya Pradesh. About 75 percent of the cropland of the Deccan during this period was planted in food crops, such as millet, sorghum, rice, wheat, and peanuts; most of the remaining cropland was planted in fodder crops.

In the far south of the Peninsula, the area under cultivation varies from about 10 percent in the Western Ghats, to 25 percent in the western coastal tract, to 55 percent on the Karnataka Plateau. Here is the India—the land of spices—that Vasco da Gama and other European navigators came searching for in the fifteenth century. On the Karnataka Plateau, sorghum, millet, pulses, cotton, and oilseeds are the main crops on the 90 percent of the cultivated land that is dry-farmed; rice, sugarcane, and vegetables predominate on the 10 percent that was irrigated in the late 1980s. Coconuts, areca, coffee, pepper, rubber, cashew nuts, tapioca, and cardamom are widely grown on plantations in the Nilgiri Hills and on the western slopes of the Western Ghats.

Land Tenure

Matters concerning the ownership, acquisition, distribution, and taxation of land are, by provision of the constitution, under the jurisdiction of the states (see Local Government, ch. 8). Because of the diverse attitudes and approaches that would result from such freedom if there were no general guidelines, the central government has at times laid down directives dealing with the main problems affecting the ownership and use of land. But it remains for the state governments to implement the central government guidelines. Such implementation has varied widely among the states.

Landholding Categories

India is a land of small farms, of peasants cultivating their ancestral lands mainly by family labor and, despite the spread of tractors in the 1980s, by pairs of bullocks. About 50 percent of all operational holdings in 1980 were less than one hectare in size. About 19 percent fell in the one-to-two hectare range, 16 percent in the two-to-four hectare range, and 11 percent in the four-to-ten hectare range. Only 4 percent of the working farms encompassed ten or more hectares.

Although farms are typically small throughout the country, the average size holding by state ranges from about 0.5 hectare in Kerala and 0.75 hectare in Tamil Nadu to three hectares in Maharashtra and five hectares in Rajasthan. Factors influencing this range include soils, topography, rainfall, rural population density, and thoroughness of land redistribution programs.

Many factors—historical, political, economic, and demographic—have affected the development of the prevailing land-tenure status. The operators of most agricultural holdings possess vested rights in the land they till, whether as full owners or as protected tenants. By the early 1990s, there were tenancy laws in all the states and union territories except Nagaland,

Meghalaya, and Mizoram. The laws provide for states to confer ownership on tenants, who can buy the land they farm in return for fair payment; states also oversee provision of security of tenure and the establishing of fair rents. The implementation of these laws has varied among the states. West Bengal, Karnataka, and Kerala, for example, have achieved more success than other states. The land tenure situation is complicated, and it has varied widely from state to state. There is, however, much less variation in the mid-1990s than in the postindependence period.

Independent India inherited a structure of landholding that was characterized by heavy concentration of cultivable areas in the hands of relatively large absentee landowners, the excessive fragmentation of small landholdings, an already growing class of landless agricultural workers, and the lack of any generalized system of documentary evidence of landownership or tenancy. Land was important as a status symbol; from one generation to the next, there was a tendency for an original family holding to be progressively subdivided, a situation that continued in the early 1990s. This phenomenon resulted in many landholdings that were too small to provide a livelihood for a family. Borrowing money against land was almost inevitable and frequently resulted in the loss of land to a local moneylender or large landowner, further widening the gap between large and small landholders. Moreover, inasmuch as landowners and moneylenders tended to belong to higher castes and petty owners and tenants to lower castes, land tenure had strong social as well as economic impact.

By the early 1970s, after extensive legislation, large absentee landowners had, for all practical purposes, been eliminated; their rights had been acquired by the state in exchange for compensation in cash and government bonds.

More than 20 million former zamindar-system tenants had acquired occupancy rights to the land they tilled. Whereas previously the landlord collected rent from his tenants and passed on a portion of it as land revenue to the government, starting in the early 1970s, the state collected the rent directly from cultivators who, in effect, had become renters from the state. Most former tenants acquired the right to purchase the land they tilled, and payments to the state were spread out over ten to twenty years.

Large landowners were divested not only of their cultivated land but also of ownership of forests, lakes, and barren lands. They were also stripped of various other economic rights, such as collection of taxes on sales of immovable property within their jurisdiction and collection of money for grazing privileges on uncultivated lands and use of river water. These rights also were taken over by state governments in return for compensation. By 1980 more than 6 million hectares of waste, fallow, and other categories of unused land had been vested in state governments and, in turn, distributed to landless agricultural workers.

Land Reform

A major concern in rural India is the huge number of landless or near-landless families, many of whom are wholly dependent on a few weeks of work at the peak planting and harvesting seasons. The number of landless rural families has grown steadily since independence, both in absolute terms and as a proportion of the population. In 1981 there were 195.1 million rural workers: 55.4 million were agricultural laborers who depended primarily on casual farm work for a livelihood. In the early 1990s, the rural work force had grown to 242 million, of whom 73.7 million were classified as agricultural laborers. Approximately 33 percent of the employed rural workers were classified as casual wage laborers.

Because of the large number of landless farmers and the frequent neglect of land by absentee landlords in the early years of independence, the principle that there should be a ceiling on the size of landholdings, depending on the crop planted and the quality of the land, was embodied in the First Five-Year Plan (FY 1951-55). An agricultural census was conducted to provide guidance in setting such ceilings. During the Second Five-Year Plan (FY 1956-60), most states legislated fixed ceilings, but there was little uniformity among the states; ceilings ranged from six to 132 hectares. Certain specialized branches of agriculture, such as horticulture, cattle breeding, and dairy farming, were usually exempted from ceilings.

All the states instituted programs to force landowners to sell their over-the-ceiling holdings to the government at fixed prices; the states, in turn, were to redistribute the land to the landless.

But adamant resistance, high costs, sloppy record keeping, and poor administration in general combined to weaken and delay this aspect of land reform. The delays in legislation allowed large landowners to circumvent the intent of the laws by spurious partitioning, sales, gifts to family members, and other methods of evading ceilings. Many exemptions were granted so that there was little surplus land.

To ensure more uniformity in income, to combat evasion of the intent of the laws, and to secure more land for distribution to the landless, the central government in the 1970s pushed for greatly reduced ceilings. For a family of five, the central government guidelines called for not more than 10.9 hectares of good, irrigated land suitable for double-cropping, not more than 10.9 hectares of land suited for one crop annually, and not more than 21.9 hectares for orchards. Exemptions were continued for land used as cocoa, coffee, tea, and rubber plantations; land held by official banks and other government units; and land held by agricultural schools and research organizations. At the option of the states, land held by religious, educational, and charitable trusts also could be exempted. To protect the states from legal challenges to their land reform laws, the constitution was amended in 1974 to include in its Ninth Schedule the state laws that had been enacted in conformance with national guidelines. Land reform laws enacted after 1974 also were included in the amendment.

By the beginning of the 1990s, all states and union territories, except Goa, Arunachal Pradesh, Nagaland, Manipur, Mizoram, and Tripura, had passed ceiling laws to conform to central government guidelines. In Maharashtra, for example, the revised ceiling law that became effective in 1975 set upper limits at perennially irrigated land, 7.2 hectares; seasonally irrigated land, 10.8 hectares; paddy land in an assured rainfall area, 14.6 hectares; and other dry land, 21.9 hectares.

By the early 1980s, about 150,000 hectares had been declared surplus under this act, about 100,000 of which had been distributed to 6,500 landless persons. A 1973 land reform amendment in Bihar set a range of ceilings on holdings for a family of five, from six to eighteen hectares depending on land quality, and offered an allowance for each additional family member, subject to a maximum of one-and-one-half times the holding. Within five years, the Bihar government had acquired 94,000 hectares of surplus land and had distributed 53,000 hectares to 138,000 landless families. Success nationwide was limited. Of the 2.9 million hectares of land declared surplus, nearly 1.9 million hectares had been distributed by the end of the seventh plan, leaving 1 million hectares still to be distributed as of early 1993.

By the early 1990s, nearly all the states had enacted legislation aimed at the consolidation of each tiller's landholdings into one contiguous plot. Implementation was patchy and sporadic, however. By the early 1980s, the work had been completed only in Punjab, Haryana, and western Uttar Pradesh and had begun in Orissa and Bihar. In most of the other states, nothing had been accomplished by the early 1990s. The Sixth Five-Year Plan (FY 1980-84) set a goal for the completion of the consolidation of holdings within ten years, which was not achieved.

In order to protect tenants from exorbitant rents (often up to 50 percent of their produce), the states passed legislation to regulate rents. The maximum rate was fixed at levels not exceeding 20 to 25 percent of the gross produce in all states except Andhra Pradesh, Haryana, and Punjab. The states also adopted various other measures for the protection of tenants, including moratoriums on evictions, minimum periods of tenure, and security of tenure subject to eviction on prescribed grounds only.

By the early 1980s, most of the cultivated area had been surveyed and records of rights prepared. In most states, revenue assessment—the tax on land—against farmland had been revised upward in keeping with a rise in farm prices. In several states, steps were taken to associate village assemblies, or *panchayat*, with the maintenance of land records, the collection of land revenue, and the management of lands belonging to government; the results of these efforts have frequently been unsatisfactory.

ECONOMIC DEVELOPMENT

Evolution of Policy

The British colonial government of India did not pursue an active policy of agricultural development despite modest efforts to formulate a policy. One such effort was the appointment in

1926 of the Royal Commission on Agriculture, which made some recommendations for improving agriculture and promoting the welfare of the rural population. Most of the commission's recommendations were deferred because of the Great Depression of the 1930s. One outcome, however, was the establishment of the Imperial (later Indian) Council of Agricultural Research in 1929. During World War II, disruptions in international trade also led the government to initiate the Grow More Food Campaign. The government adopted its first agricultural policy statement in the wake of famine in Bengal in 1943. The policy objectives included increased production of food grains, use of better methods of production, improved marketing, better prices for the producers, fair wages for agricultural labor, fair distribution of food, increased production of raw materials, and improvements in research and education. This statement was the basis of many of the policies adopted soon after independence, especially in the First Five-Year Plan, when the central government was committed to giving priority to agricultural production to increase the food supply in the country.

The prolonged neglect of agriculture meant that there was almost no growth in the agricultural sector. From 1891 to 1946, output of all crops grew at 0.4 percent a year; the rate for food grains was only 0.1 percent per year. The land tenure system led to exploitative agrarian relations and stagnation. Farmers had little incentive to invest, and despite great strides in foreign agricultural technology, Indian agricultural technology stagnated. Specifically, there were few improvements in seeds, agricultural implements, machines, or chemical fertilizers.

At the time of independence in 1947, agriculture and allied sectors provided well over 70 percent of the country's employment and more than 50 percent of the gross national product. Agricultural development was a key to a number of national goals, such as reducing rural poverty, providing an adequate diet for all citizens, supplying agricultural raw materials for the textile industry and other industries, and expanding exports. In the mid-1960s, the goal of self-reliance was added to this list. The central government has played a progressively more important role on the agricultural front by providing overall leadership and coordination, as well as by providing a significant part of the financing for agricultural programs. However, the primary responsibility for the design and implementation of agricultural programs, in accordance with the constitution, remained with the states in the late twentieth century.

India's agricultural growth strategy after independence evolved over three distinct phases. In the first phase, roughly covering the period through the Second Five-Year Plan, agricultural growth rested on removing basic socioeconomic constraints through land reform, change in the village power structure, reorganization of the rural poor into cooperatives, and better citizen participation in planning. The initial assumption was that changing the land tenure system by abolishing the zamindar system—a method of revenue collecting and landholding developed during the Mughal and British colonial periods—would stimulate agricultural output.

The second phase occurred during the Third Five-Year Plan (FY 1961-65). The continuing shortages of food in the 1960s and the consequent crises convinced planners that raising agricultural output, especially food grains, was essential for political stability and independence from foreign food aid. Self-sufficiency in food-grain production and development of an adequate buffer stock through procurement became clearly defined goals in the mid-1960s. Keeping in mind the variety of socioeconomic and agroclimatic differences, the government adopted an area-specific approach, and emphasized programs such as the Intensive Area Agricultural Programme and the Intensive Agricultural District Programme.

The third phase is identified predominantly as the Green Revolution. This phase relied on better seeds, more water via irrigation, and improved quantity and quality of fertilizer during the Fourth Five-Year Plan (FY 1969-73), the Fifth Five-Year Plan (FY 1974-78), and the Sixth Five-Year Plan (FY 1980-84). The Green Revolution was successful in meeting the goals of self-sufficiency in food-grain production and adequate buffer stocks by the end of the 1970s. Production was more than 100 million tons in 1978 and 1979. Imports were negligible, and the year-end buffer stocks from 1976-79 averaged more than 17 million tons. After 1980 buffer stocks fell below 10 millions tons only once, in 1988.

In the mid-1990s, the major goals of agricultural policy continued to be self-sufficiency in food staples and adequate food supplies at affordable prices for consumers. Expanding cereal production continued to be a major objective because of the population growth rate of almost 2 percent per year. The budgetary share of agriculture, together with irrigation and flood control projects, remained almost constant in the first six plans, varying between 21 percent and 24 percent.

The Eighth Five-Year Plan (FY 1992-96), as conceived in the early 1990s, not only aimed at continued self-sufficiency in food production, but also included plans to generate surpluses of some agricultural commodities for export. It also aimed at spreading the Green Revolution to more regions of the country with an emphasis on dryland farming.

Development Programs

Within the broad framework of policy, the government has undertaken a wide variety of programs in agriculture to build up the physical and information infrastructures necessary for sustained development. There are programs for the betterment of the rural population; research, education, and extension programs; irrigation development schemes; plans to increase the supply of agricultural inputs, such as seeds, fertilizers, and pesticides; plans to change the institutional framework of land ownership; plans to improve agricultural financing; better marketing techniques; and plans to improve technology. These programs are administered, financed, and run by the central government and by the state governments, and both levels encourage private-sector development through direct or indirect programs.

Some of the specialized programs in place in the 1990s were introduced during the Fifth Plan. Among them were the Small Farmers Development Agency, Minimum Needs Programme, Hill Area Development Programme, and Drought-Prone Areas Programme. In 1989 two other programs, the National Rural Employment Programme and the Rural Landless Employment Guarantee Programme, were merged into a single program called the Jawahar Employment Plan (Jawahar Rozgar Yojana; Jawahar in memory of Jawaharlal Nehru [1889-1964], India's first prime minister; *rozgar* means daily employment in Hindi; and *yojana* means project or plan).

The Integrated Rural Development Programme, launched in FY 1978 and extended throughout India by FY 1980, is a self-employment program intended to raise the income-generation capacity of target groups among the poor. The aim is to raise recipients above the poverty line by providing substantial opportunities for self-employment. During the seventh plan, the total expenditure under the program was Rs33.2 million, and Rs53.7 million of term credit was mobilized. Some 13 million new families participated, bringing total coverage under the program to more than 18 million families. These development programs have played an important role in increased agricultural production by educating farmers and providing them with financial and other inputs to increase yields. They have also alleviated some problems of the rural poor. However, further success has been limited by the lack of efficient administrative mechanisms, the limitation of resources, the magnitude of the task, and the lack of willingness to change the status quo. Many of the program results appear better on paper than the actual results in the field because of lack of implementation and poor monitoring.

Research, Education, and Extension

The central government's Department of Agricultural Research and Education was established in 1973 in the Ministry of Agriculture and Rural Development (later, the Ministry of Agriculture). The department is responsible for coordinating research and educational facilities in agriculture, animal husbandry, and fisheries. The department also provides support services to the Indian Council of Agricultural Research.

Higher education has also seen advances. India has twenty-eight agricultural universities, which include 164 colleges specializing in agriculture, veterinary science, agricultural engineering, home science, fisheries, dairy technology, forestry, horticulture, sericulture, food science, and food-handling technology. They are located through most of the states in India. One of them is a central university that has specialized extension colleges in the seven northeastern states. The undergraduate student enrollment in the early 1990s was around 9,600 and there was a capacity for some 4,500 graduate students.

Agricultural, animal husbandry, and forestry research is conducted under the auspices of the Indian Council of Agricultural Research, central research institutes, and various commodity committees. The council had forty-six institutes in operation in 1992. India's largest such institute is the Indian Agricultural Research Institute, established in 1905 at Pusa, Bihar. Because of an earthquake at Pusa, the research institute moved to New Delhi in 1936. The institute was later accorded university status.

In addition to these agricultural research and education institutions, the Indian Council of Agricultural Research also has a large network of organizations to disseminate agricultural technology information. In the mid-1990s, there were national centers used to demonstrate new crop varieties and production technologies in forty-eight districts throughout the country. There also were seventy nationwide coordinated research projects operating at 120 centers to test specific production technologies.

Agricultural Extension

After independence in 1947, the government's first step toward building an agricultural extension system was expansion of the World War II Grow More Food Campaign. Administrators and extension workers were exhorted to convince cultivators of the gains in yields that could be obtained through the use of improved seeds, compost, farmyard manure, and better cultivation practices. Rural agents, often inundated with other assignments, had little or no training for extension work, however. Gains in yields were minimal, and India's leaders came to realize that converting millions of poor farmers to the use of new technologies was a colossal task.

The Community Development Programme was inaugurated in 1952 to implement a systematic, integrated approach to rural development. The nation was divided into development blocks, each consisting of about 100 villages having populations of 60,000 to 70,000 people. By 1962 the entire country was covered by more than 5,000 such blocks. The key person in the program was the village-level worker, who was responsible for transmitting to about ten villages not only farming technology, but also village uplift programs such as cooperation, adult literacy, health, and sanitation. Although each block was staffed with extension workers, the villagers themselves were expected to provide the initiative and much of the needed financial and labor resources, which they were not in a position to do or inclined to do. Although progress had been made by the early 1960s, it was apparent that the program was spread too thin to bring about the hoped-for increase in agricultural production. Criticism of the program led to more specialized development projects, and some of the functions were taken up by local village bodies. There was only a negligible allocation for community development in the sixth plan, however, and the program was phased out in the early 1980s.

The Intensive Agricultural District Programme, launched in five districts in 1960 by the central government in cooperation with the United States-based Ford Foundation, used a distinctly different approach to boosting farm yields. The program operated under the premise that concentrating scarce inputs in the potentially most productive districts would increase farm-crop yield faster than would a wider but less concentrated distribution of resources in less productive districts. Among these inputs were technical staff, fertilizers, improved seeds, and credit. Under the technical guidance of American cooperative specialists, the program placed unusual emphasis on organizational structures and administrative arrangements. For the first time, modern technology was systematically introduced to Indian farmers. Within a decade, the program covered fifteen districts, 28,000 villages, and 1 million inhabitants. The Intensive Agricultural District Programme was thus a significant influence on the forthcoming Green Revolution.

IRRIGATION

Except in southeastern India, which receives most of its rain from the northeast monsoon in October and November, dryland cultivators place their hopes for a harvest on the southwest monsoon, which usually reaches India in early June and by mid-July has extended to the entire country. There are great variations in the average amount of rainfall received by the various regions—from too much for most crops in the eastern Himalayas to never enough in Rajasthan. Season-to-season variations in rainfall are also great. The consequence is bumper harvests in some seasons, crop-searing drought in others. Therefore, the importance of irrigation cannot be overemphasized.

Irrigation has been a high priority in economic development since 1951; more than 50 percent of all public expenditures on agriculture have been spent on irrigation alone. The land area under irrigation expanded from 22.6 million hectares in FY 1950 to 59 million hectares in FY 1990, an increase of 161 percent in four decades. This increase was about 33 percent of the estimated potential. The overall strategy has been to concentrate public investments in surface systems, such as large dams, long canals, and other large-scale works requiring huge outlays of capital over a period of years, and in deep-well projects that also involve large capital outlays. Shallow-well schemes and small surface-water projects, mainly ponds (called tanks in India), have been supported by government credit but were otherwise installed and operated by private entrepreneurs. Roughly 42 percent of the net irrigated area in FY 1990 was from surface water sources. Tanks, step wells, and tube wells provided another 51 percent; the rest came from other sources.

Between 1951 and 1990, nearly 1,350 large- and medium-sized irrigation works were started, and about 850 were completed. The most ambitious of these projects was the Indira Gandhi Canal, with an anticipated completion date of close to 1999. When completed, the Indira Gandhi Canal will be the world's longest irrigation canal. Beginning at the Hairke Barrage, a few kilometers below the confluence of the Sutlej and Beas rivers in western Punjab, it will run south-southwest for 650 kilometers, terminating deep in Rajasthan near Jaisalmer, close to the border with Pakistan. A dramatic change already had taken place in this hot and inhospitable wasteland by the late 1980s. As a result, desert dwellers switched from raising goats and sheep to raising wheat, and outsiders flocked in to purchase six-hectare plots for the equivalent of US$3,000.

Progress in irrigation has not been without problems. Large dams and long canals are costly and also highly visible indicators of progress; the political pressure to launch such projects was frequently irresistible. But because funds and technical expertise were in short supply, many projects moved forward at a slow pace. The Indira Gandhi Canal project is a leading example. And the central government's transfer of huge amounts of water from Punjab to Haryana and Rajasthan, frequently cited as a source of grievance by Sikhs in Punjab, contributed to the civil unrest in Punjab during the 1980s and early 1990s.

Problems also have arisen as ground water supplies used for irrigation face depletion. Drawing water off from one area to irrigate another often leads to increased salinity in the supply area with resultant effects on crop production there. Some areas receiving water through irrigation are poorly managed or inadequately designed; the result often is too much water and water-logged fields incapable of production. To alleviate this problem, more emphasis is being placed on using irrigation water to spray fields rather than allowing it to flow through ditches. Furthermore, charges of corruption and mismanagement have been levied against government-operated facilities. Cases of bribery, maldistribution of water, and carelessness are frequently raised in the media.

Another major problem has been the displacement of thousands of people, usually poor people, by large hydroelectric projects. Critics also claim that the projects are damaging to the ecology. Smaller projects and such traditional methods for irrigation as tanks and wells are seen as having less serious impact. In the late 1980s and early 1990s, the debate between large-scale versus small-scale projects came to the fore because of the US$3 billion Sardar Sarovar project on the Narmada River. Sardar Sarovar, as conceived, was one of the world's largest hydroelectric and irrigation projects. Some 37,000 hectares of land in Madhya Pradesh, Gujarat, and Maharashtra were slated to be submerged following the construction of some 3,000 dams, 75,000 kilometers of canals, and an electric power generating capacity of 1,450 megawatts of power per year.

Included among the 3,000 dams was the proposed 160-meter-high Sardar Sarovar Dam. In 1985 the World Bank agreed to loan US$450 million for the project. Environmentalists in India and abroad, however, argued that the project was ecologically undesirable. In the face of this strong protest, the World Bank appointed a two-member team in 1991 to review the project. Despite a negative review of the environmental impact by the team, World Bank funding and the project continued. By 1993, however, in the face of continued international protest as well as opposition and a call for a satyagraha by villages in the affected areas, the central government cancelled the dam project loan. Work on the Sardar Sarovar project continues, however, with funds provided by the central government and the governments of the three states involved.

Although India had the second largest irrigated area in the world, the area under assured irrigation or with at least minimal drainage is inadequate. The irrigation potential estimated to have been created by the early 1990s was about 82.8 million hectares. This amount includes the gross irrigated area plus the potential for double cropping provided by irrigation. There was a cumulative gap in irrigated land use of about 8.6 million hectares until FY 1990, by which time the gap had decreased through improved land management.

Seeds

The central government established the National Seeds Corporation in 1963 and the State Farm Corporations of India in 1969 to encourage production and distribution of certified seeds of various crops. Thirteen state seed corporations were established to arrange production and distribution of certified seeds. Production of breeder seed was organized by the Indian Council of Agricultural Research through interested breeders and scientists. The National Seeds Corporation and State Farm Corporations of India also produced breeder seeds. The availability of breeder seeds increased eightfold during the 1980s, from 391.4 tons in FY 1981 to 3,213 tons in FY 1988.

The production and availability of seeds has increased enormously since the late 1970s. The distribution of certified and quality seeds showed an increase from 140,000 tons in FY 1979 to 568,000 tons in FY 1988. A buffer stock of seeds is maintained by the National Seeds Corporation for the northeastern states and by the State Farm Corporations of India for the other states against such unforeseen contingencies as floods, droughts, and diseases.

Fertilizer

The rate of fertilizer consumption increased dramatically after independence, although it was still lower than in most other countries worldwide. India used only sixty-nine kilograms per hectare in 1989, ranking it fifty-sixth worldwide and below all its South Asian neighbors except Nepal. Fertilizer consumption increased from approximately 69,000 tons of nutrients in FY 1950 to 12.6 million tons in FY 1990, and was expected to be about 13.8 million tons in FY 1993. Punjab used the highest amount of fertilizer per hectare followed by Tamil Nadu. The use of fertilizers was high in Punjab and Harayana in the north because of adequate irrigation. In the south, other than in Tamil Nadu, consumption, especially in Andhra Pradesh and Kerala, was higher than the national average. The disparity in the use of fertilizers across states was decreasing, however. Cow dung is an important source of fertilizer—and fuel—in India. Statistics on its usage, however, are not available.

The fertilizer subsidy has been growing since FY 1976. The initial subsidy was a response to the increase in the price of crude oil by the Organization of the Petroleum Exporting Countries. The price increase led to a rise in the cost of naphtha, which in turn increased fertilizer prices. The fertilizer subsidy increased from Rs600 million in FY 1976 to Rs32 billion in FY 1988, to nearly Rs44 billion in FY 1990. Further increases are expected as the decade progresses. Plans in 1992 to cut the subsidy by 40 percent were curtailed following heavy political opposition from the major farming states.

Plant Protection and Pesticides

The government has introduced integrated pest management at the central and state levels for purposes of plant protection. Twenty-five central, integrated pest-management centers have been established in twenty-two states and one union territory for pest surveillance and monitoring, promotion of biocontrol methods of conservation, promotion of nonchemical methods of pest control, training of extension workers and farmers, and demonstration farms. The use of synthetic pesticides has increased steadily because of the spreading use of new high-yielding varieties of seeds and their greater vulnerability to plant pests and diseases. The sale of synthetic pesticides jumped from 8,620 tons in crop year 1960-61 to 65,000 tons in 1982-83 and 85,660 tons in 1989-90. In 1960 only about 6 million hectares received chemical pesticides, but by the early 1980s some 100 million hectares were being treated, and the growth in coverage continues in the 1990s. The rapid rise in the use of plant protection led to the enactment of the Insecticides Act of 1968 to regulate the import, sale, transport, distribution, and use of insecticides.

Technology and Mechanization

Despite the pervasive, large-scale use of draft animals throughout India, agricultural machinery and implements, tractors, in particular, have had an important place in increasing agricultural productivity. The stock of tractors increased from 8,600 in FY 1950 to 518,500 in FY 1982 and continued to grow rapidly throughout the 1980s. The number and sale of power tillers and combine harvesters produced and sold was small, with 4,678 tillers and 110 harvesters sold in FY 1988. There was a significant increase in the number of electric pumps and oil pump sets for irrigation during the 1980s.

The production and use of machinery are hampered by the small size of many operational holdings. However, a number of improved agricultural implements are available for tilling, seeding and fertilizer application, weeding, harvesting, and threshing. The implements include moldboard plows, disc harrows, cultivators, seed drills (more than 110,000 were sold annually in the early 1990s), and mechanical power threshers. These tools have the potential of increasing yields for all crops, but the adoption rate of improved machinery is low. The Central Institute of Agricultural Engineering at Bhopal, Madhya Pradesh, under the aegis of the Indian Council for Agricultural Research, is responsible for coordinating the manufacture and promotion of technology for small and marginal farmers. The government introduced an incentive scheme in 1990 to subsidize the cost of machinery by up to 50 percent to small and marginal farms. Additionally, farmers' agroservice centers are being established to provide custom service for improved implements and machinery. The eighth plan includes a major thrust for upgrading and adopting proven technology.

In a country with a large and growing labor force, too much mechanization in the short run could create fossil fuel shortages as well as social and economic problems. There is, nevertheless, room for improvements in technology. Since FY 1983, there have been attempts to popularize improved animal-drawn agricultural implements and hand tools through demonstrations and subsidies to small and marginal farmers.

Despite these advances in mechanization, most crops are still sown, transplanted, weeded, and harvested through labor-intensive human work. Most grains are harvested by teams of laborers wielding hand-forged iron sickles, binding up sheaves of grain, and carrying loads of sheaves on their heads to bullock carts to be transported to threshing floors. Teams of bullocks are then driven over the sheaves to separate the grains from the stalks, and workers toss basketloads of grain into the air to separate the grain from the chaff. Lentils, a crucial part of the Indian diet, also are harvested through labor-intensive means. Groups of laborers squat down in fields for hours at a time, ripping out lentil plants at the root by hand. Machinery available to lentil farmers has proven difficult to use, and traditional methods are preferred.

Price Policy and Terms of Trade

After independence, India's initial price policy could be characterized as serving the interests of the consumers, particularly where food grains were concerned, and most of all in regard to wheat. Food prices were kept low to provide cheap food for urban consumers under the theory that a cheap and easy supply of wage goods—of which food grains formed the main component—would inhibit inflationary pressures on the economy. This policy, buttressed with imports under the United States Public Law 480 Food for Peace Program, kept prices at a low level during the late 1950s and early 1960s but did not provide incentives for Indian farmers to invest or increase production. The terms of trade vis-à-vis manufacturing were favorable to agriculture in FY 1959 and then on a par with other sectors for three years. Thereafter, when manufacturing prices went up faster than agricultural prices as a result of government policy, terms of trade favored manufacturing and turned against the agricultural sector. This change led to a food crisis in the mid-1960s when agricultural production fell. From about 1965, the need to guarantee remunerative prices to farmers was stressed to ensure self-sufficiency in food-grain production as soon as possible. The Agricultural Prices Commission—in 1993 called the Commission for Agricultural Costs and Prices—was set up to advise the government on agricultural prices, keeping in view the interests of both the consumer and the producer. Of particular concern were prices for wheat, rice, coarse grains, pulses, sugarcane, oilseeds, cotton, and jute. In the late 1980s and early 1990s, the commission was supplied with cost of production data, compiled through sample surveys, to improve its effectiveness in setting prices. The commission was reasonably successful in providing remunerative prices for farmers. It used the price mechanism to increase the production of commodities in demand, such as oilseeds at the end of the 1980s, and to keep prices at a reasonable level for consumers.

Crop Output

The average rate of output growth since the 1950s has been more than 2.5 percent per year and was greater than 3 percent during the 1980s, compared with less than 1 percent per annum during the period from 1900 to 1950. Most of the growth in aggregate crop output was the result of an increase in yields, rather than an increase in the area under crops. The yield performance of crops has varied widely.

The national growth rates mask variability in the performance of different states, but in the regions with the greatest increases three categories are discernible. The first category includes states or areas that have an exceptionally high agricultural growth rate—Punjab, Haryana, and western Uttar Pradesh. The second is states or areas that have high growth rates, but not as high as the first category—Andhra Pradesh, Maharashtra, and Jammu and Kashmir. A third category has a lesser growth rate and includes Bihar, Gujarat, Karnataka, Orissa, Rajasthan, Tamil Nadu, eastern Uttar Pradesh, and West Bengal. These eight states, however, comprise 55 percent of the total food-grains area.

Some observers believe that the increase in productivity has been an important factor explaining the satisfactory growth of food-grain production since the mid-1960s. However, the gains in productivity remain confined to select areas. Between FY 1960 and FY 1980, yields increased by 125.6 percent in North India (Punjab, Haryana, and western Uttar Pradesh). The increase in the other regions was much less: central India, 36 percent; eastern, 22.7 percent; southern, 58.3 percent; and western India, 31.6 percent. The national average was nearly 40.9 percent. Part of this disparity can be explained by the fact that during this period Punjab and Haryana were way ahead of other states in terms of irrigated area, intensity of irrigation, and intensity of cropping. Availability of irrigation is one of the crucial factors governing regional variations.

As a result of a good monsoon during FY 1990, food grain production reached 176 million tons, 3 percent more than in FY 1989. The production of rice and wheat was 74.6 million and 54.5 million tons, respectively. Among the commercial crops, sugarcane and oilseeds reached production levels of 240.3 million tons and 21.8 million tons, respectively. The increased production in FY 1990 was mainly the result of continuing increases in yields for all the main crops—rice, wheat, pulses, and oilseeds. In the case of oilseeds and sugarcane, higher production was also the result of the increased number of hectares planted.

The growth in food-grain production did not occur in a linear trend, but as a series of spurts depending mostly on the weather, input availability, and price policy. Aggregate growth was composed of an even split between area expansion and yield growth before FY 1964. Since FY 1967, the contribution of growth in yields has become dominant and attests to the vigor with which agriculture has responded to the opportunities opened up by new seed, water, and fertilizer technology.

Food-Grain Production

Food grains include rice, wheat, corn (maize), coarse grains (sorghum and millet), and pulses (beans, dried peas, and lentils). In FY 1990, approximately 127.5 million hectares were sown with food grains, about 75 percent of the total planted area. The total number of hectares increased by 31 percent over the forty-year period from FY 1950 to FY 1990. Most of this increase occurred in the 1950s; there was almost no change in the sown number of hectares through the 1980s. Around 33 percent of cropland was given over to rice, about 29 percent to coarse grains, and the rest evenly divided between wheat and pulses.

Rice, India's preeminent crop, is the staple food of the people of the eastern and southern parts of the country. Production increased from 53.6 million tons in FY 1980 to 74.6 million tons in FY 1990, a 39 percent increase over the decade. By FY 1992, rice production had reached 111 million tons, second in the world only to China with its 182 million tons. Since 1950 the increase has been more than 350 percent. Most of this increase was the result of an increase in yields; the number of hectares increased only 40 percent during this period. Yields increased from 1,336 kilograms per hectare in FY 1980 to 1,751 kilograms per hectare in FY 1990. The per-hectare yield increased more than 262 percent between 1950 and 1992.

Wheat production showed an 843 percent increase, from nearly 6.5 million tons in FY 1950 to 54.5 million tons in FY 1990 to 56.7 million tons in FY 1992. Most of this greater production was the result of an increase in yields that went from 663 kilograms per hectare in FY 1950 to 2,274 kilograms in FY 1990. Along with the excellent performance in yields, improved wheat production resulted from an increase in the area planted from nearly 9.8 million hectares in FY 1950 to 24.0 million hectares in FY 1990.

Sorghum and millet, the principal coarse grains, are dryland crops most frequently grown as staples in central and western India. Corn and barley are staple foods grown mainly near and in the Himalayan region. As the result of increased yields, the production of coarse grains has doubled since 1950; there was hardly any change in the area sown for these grains. The production of pulses did not fare well, increasing by only 68 percent over the four decades. Land devoted to pulses increased by 28 percent, and yields were up by 30 percent. Pulses are an important source of protein in the vegetarian diet; the small improvement in production along with the increase in population meant a reduced availability of pulses per capita.

Before the Green Revolution, coarse grains showed satisfactory rates of growth but afterward lost cultivated areas to wheat and rice, and their growth declined. The area sown with coarse grains increased from FY 1950 to FY 1970 by roughly 20 percent but declined subsequently up to the early 1990s. In FY 1990 the area sown was 3 percent less than in FY 1950 and 20 percent less than in FY 1970. The area sown with two coarse grains, *jowar* (barley) and *bajra* (millet), increased from FY 1950 to FY 1970 and then declined during the 1970s and the 1980s. The area sown with *jowar* increased from 15.6 million hectares in FY 1950 to 17.4 million hectares in FY 1970 and then decreased to 14.5 million hectares in FY 1990. The area sown with *bajra* increased from 9.0 million hectares in FY 1950 to 12.9 million hectares in FY 1970 and stood at 10.4 million hectares in FY 1990. A similar pattern existed for other coarse grains. Overall, India's coarse-grain production increased from 15.4 million tons in 1950 to 29 million tons in 1980 to 33.1 million tons in 1990 and 33.7 million tons in 1993.

Oilseeds

India in the mid-1990s has almost attained self-sufficiency in the production of oilseeds to extract vegetable oil, essential in the Indian diet. Peanuts, grown mainly as a rain-fed crop on part of the semiarid areas of western and southern India, account for the largest source of the nation's production of vegetable oils. The second-ranking source of vegetable oils in the early 1990s was rapeseed. Cottonseed, an important by-product of cotton fiber and once mostly fed to cattle, was another source of vegetable oils. Soybeans and sunflower seeds were relatively new as significant oilseeds, but their production increased rapidly in the 1980s.

The production of oilseeds increased from 5.2 million tons in FY 1950 to 21.8 million tons in FY 1990. Specific information regarding area planted is not available for all oilseeds, but it increased in the 1980s, as did the yields. The growth of production before the mid-1970s was not adequate to meet the needs of the increasing population, and large quantities had to be imported from the 1970s to the mid-1980s, using scarce foreign exchange.

Commercial Crops

India is the largest producer of sugar in the world, harvesting 12 million tons in 1993, followed by Brazil's 9 million tons and China's 7 million tons. Sugar availability per capita increased from 4.7 kilograms per year in FY 1960 to 12.5 kilograms per year in FY 1990, following the more than fourfold increase in production from 57 million tons in FY 1950 to 240 million tons in FY 1990. This increase in production was a result of the doubling of the yield per hectare and a doubling of the area sown with sugar. Imports of sugar were negligible in FY 1992 and FY 1993. However, in the FY 1995 budget presentation to the Lok Sabha in March 1995, Minister of Finance Manmohan Singh said it was necessary to supplement the public distribution system with "necessary imports of sugar."

Raw cotton is the most important nonfood commodity produced on India's farms. Cotton was an important export crop in the 1950s, but thereafter it provided the raw material for India's textile industry, which grew greatly to meet the needs of an expanding population. Cotton fabrics found an expanding international market in the 1980s and earned valuable foreign exchange. The foreign exchange earned from raw cotton, cotton yarn, and fabrics of all textile materials increased from US$163 million in FY 1960 to US$1.4 billion in FY 1980 to nearly US$3.9 billion in FY 1990 and US$3.8 billion by FY 1992. Cotton production increased from 600,000 tons in FY 1950 to nearly 1.7 million tons in FY 1990. These improvements largely resulted from increased yields, as there was little increase in the sown area devoted to cotton.

Raw jute is second only to cotton as a farm-produced industrial raw material. Before partition in 1947, India was the world's main supplier of jute and jute goods used as packaging material. As a result of the partition of India and Pakistan, the main jute growing area was in East Pakistan (eastern Bengal, after 1971 the independent nation of Bangladesh), and the factories manufacturing jute goods were in West Bengal, which remained part of India after partition. Jute also had been India's main source of export earnings. As a result, there was a concerted effort to increase raw jute production. The area sown with jute increased from 571,000 hectares in FY 1950 to nearly 1.2 million hectares in FY 1985 but then decreased to 692,000 hectares in FY 1988. Yields increased steadily from 1,040 kilograms per hectare in FY 1950 to 1,803 kilograms per hectare in FY 1990. These two factors combined to more than double jute production from 595 million tons in FY

1950 to 1.4 billion tons in FY 1990, with a maximum production of nearly 2 billion tons in FY 1985. Because technological changes in packaging reduced the worldwide demand for jute, production in the early 1990s was mainly for the domestic market. In FY 1990, jute provided less than 1 percent of export earnings.

The Green Revolution

The introduction of high-yielding varieties of seeds after 1965 and the increased use of fertilizers and irrigation are known collectively as the Green Revolution, which provided the increase in production needed to make India self-sufficient in food grains. The program was started with the help of the United States-based Rockefeller Foundation and was based on high-yielding varieties of wheat, rice, and other grains that had been developed in Mexico and in the Philippines. Of the high-yielding seeds, wheat produced the best results. Production of coarse grains—the staple diet of the poor—and pulses—the main source of protein—lagged behind, resulting in reduced per capita availability.

The total area under the high-yielding-varieties program was a negligible 1.9 million hectares in FY 1960. Since then growth has been spectacular, increasing to nearly 15.4 million hectares by FY 1970, 43.1 million hectares by FY 1980, and 63.9 million hectares by FY 1990. The rate of growth decreased significantly in the late 1980s, however, as additional suitable land was not available.

The major benefits of the Green Revolution were experienced mainly in northern and northwestern India between 1965 and the early 1980s; the program resulted in a substantial increase in the production of food grains, mainly wheat and rice. Food-grain yields continued to increase throughout the 1980s, but the dramatic changes in the years between 1965 and 1980 were not duplicated. By FY 1980, almost 75 percent of the total cropped area under wheat was sown with high-yielding varieties. For rice the comparable figure was 45 percent. In the 1980s, the area under high-yielding varieties continued to increase, but the rate of growth overall was slower. The eighth plan aimed at making high-yielding varieties available to the whole country and developing more productive strains of other crops. The Green Revolution created wide regional and interstate disparities. The plan was implemented only in areas with assured supplies of water and the means to control it, large inputs of fertilizers, and adequate farm credit. These inputs were easily available in at least parts of the states of Punjab, Haryana, and western Uttar Pradesh; thus, yields increased most in these states. In other states, such as Andhra Pradesh and Tamil Nadu, in areas where these inputs were not assured, the results were limited or negligible, leading to considerable variation in crop yields within these states. The Green Revolution also increased income disparities: higher income growth and reduced incidence of poverty were found in the states where yields increased the most and lower income growth and little change in the incidence of poverty in other states.

Livestock and Poultry

A large number of farmers depend on livestock for their livelihood. In addition to supplying milk, meat, eggs, and hides, animals, mainly bullocks, are the major source of power for both farmers and drayers. Thus, animal husbandry plays an important role in the rural economy. The gross value of output from this sector was Rs358 billion in FY 1989, an amount that constituted about 25 percent of the total agricultural output of Rs1.4 trillion.

In FY 1992, India had approximately 25 percent of the world's cattle, with a collective herd of 193 million head. India also had 110 million goats, 75 million water buffalo, 44 million sheep, and 10 million pigs. Milk production in FY 1990 was estimated to have reached 53.5 million tons, and egg production had reached a level of 23.3 billion eggs. Dairy farming provided supplementary employment and an additional source of income to many small and marginal farmers. The National Dairy Development Board was established in 1965 under the auspices of Operation Flood at Anand, in Gujarat, to promote, plan, and organize dairy development through cooperatives; to provide consultations; and to set up dairy plants, which were then turned over to the cooperatives. There were more than 63,000 Anand-style dairy cooperative societies with some 7.5 million members in the early 1990s. The milk produced and sold by these farmers brought Rs320 million a day, or more than Rs10 trillion a year. The increase in milk production permitted India to end imports of powdered milk and milk-related products. In addition, 30,000 tons of powdered milk were exported annually to neighboring countries.

Operation Flood, the world's largest integrated dairy development program, attempted to establish linkages between rural milk producers and urban consumers by organizing farmer-owned and -managed dairy cooperative societies. In the early 1990s, the program was in its third phase and was receiving financial assistance from the World Bank and commodity assistance from the European Economic Community. At that time, India had more than 64,000 dairy cooperative societies, with close to 7.7 million members. These cooperatives established a daily processing capacity of 15.5 million liters of whole milk and 727 tons of milk powder.

Forestry

Some 50 million hectares, about 17 percent of India's land area, were regarded as forestland in the early 1990s. In FY 1987, however, actual forest cover was 64 million hectares. However, because more than 50 percent of this land was barren or brushland, the area under productive forest was actually less than 35 million hectares, or approximately 10 percent of the country's land area. The growing population's high demand for forest resources continued the destruction and degradation of forests through the 1980s, taking a heavy toll on the soil. An estimated 6 billion tons of topsoil were lost annually. However, India's 0.6 percent average annual rate of deforestation for agricultural and nonlumbering land uses in the decade beginning in 1981 was one of the lowest in the world and on a par with Brazil.

Many forests in the mid-1990s are found in high-rainfall, high-altitude regions, areas to which access is difficult. About 20 percent of total forestland is in Madhya Pradesh; other states with significant forests are Orissa, Maharashtra, and Andhra Pradesh (each with about 9 percent of the national total); Arunachal Pradesh (7 percent); and Uttar Pradesh (6 percent). The variety of forest vegetation is large: there are 600 species of hardwoods, *sal* (*Shorea robusta*) and teak being the principal economic species.

Conservation has been an avowed goal of government policy since independence. Afforestation increased from a negligible amount in the first plan to nearly 8.9 million hectares in the seventh plan. The cumulative area afforested during the 1951-91 period was nearly 17.9 million hectares. However, despite large-scale tree planting programs, forestry is one arena in which India has actually regressed since independence. Annual fellings at about four times the growth rate are a major cause. Widespread pilfering by villagers for firewood and fodder also represents a major decrement. In addition, the forested area has been shrinking as a result of land cleared for farming, inundations for irrigation and hydroelectric power projects, and construction of new urban areas, industrial plants, roads, power lines, and schools.

India's long-term strategy for forestry development reflects three major objectives: to reduce soil erosion and flooding; to supply the growing needs of the domestic wood products industries; and to supply the needs of the rural population for fuelwood, fodder, small timber, and miscellaneous forest produce. To achieve these objectives, the National Commission on Agriculture in 1976 recommended the reorganization of state forestry departments and advocated the concept of social forestry. The commission itself worked on the first two objectives, emphasizing traditional forestry and wildlife activities; in pursuit of the third objective, the commission recommended the establishment of a new kind of unit to develop community forests. Following the leads of Gujarat and Uttar Pradesh, a number of other states also established community-based forestry agencies that emphasized programs on farm forestry, timber management, extension forestry, reforestation of degraded forests, and use of forests for recreational purposes.

Such socially responsible forestry was encouraged by state community forestry agencies. They emphasized such projects as planting wood lots on denuded communal cattle-grazing grounds to make villages self-sufficient in fuelwood, to supply timber needed for the construction of village houses, and to provide the wood needed for the repair of farm implements. Both individual farmers and tribal communities were also encouraged to grow trees for profit. For example, in Gujarat, one of the more aggressive states in developing programs of socioeconomic importance, the forestry department distributed 200 million tree seedlings in 1983.

The fast-growing eucalyptus is the main species being planted nationwide, followed by pine and poplar.

The role of forests in the national economy and in ecology was further emphasized in the 1988 National Forest Policy, which focused on ensuring environmental stability, restoring the ecological balance, and preserving the remaining forests. Other objectives of the policy were meeting the need for fuelwood, fodder, and small timber for rural and tribal people while recognizing the need to actively involve local people in the management of forest resources. Also in 1988, the Forest Conservation Act of 1980 was amended to facilitate stricter conservation measures. A new target was to increase the forest cover to 33 percent of India's land area from the then-official estimate of 23 percent. In June 1990, the central government adopted resolutions that combined forest science with social forestry, that is, taking the sociocultural traditions of the local people into consideration.

Since the early 1970s, as they realized that deforestation threatened not only the ecology but their livelihood in a variety of ways, people have become more interested and involved in conservation. The best known popular activist movement is the Chipko Movement, in which local women decided to fight the government and the vested interests to save trees. The women of Chamoli District, Uttar Pradesh, declared that they would embrace—literally "to stick to" (*chipkna* in Hindi)—trees if a sporting goods manufacturer attempted to cut down ash trees in their district. Since initial activism in 1973, the movement has spread and become an ecological movement leading to similar actions in other forest areas. The movement has slowed down the process of deforestation, exposed vested interests, increased ecological awareness, and demonstrated the viability of people power.

Fishing

Fish production has increased more than fivefold since independence. It rose from only 800,000 tons in FY 1950 to 4.1 million tons in the early 1990s. Special efforts have been made to promote extensive and intensive inland fish farming, modernize coastal fisheries, and encourage deep-sea fishing through joint ventures. These efforts led to a more than fourfold increase in coastal fish production from 520,000 tons in FY 1950 to 2.4 million tons in FY 1990. The increase in inland fish production was even more dramatic, increasing almost eightfold from 218,000 tons in FY 1950 to 1.7 million tons in FY 1990. The value of fish and processed fish exports increased from less than 1 percent of the total value of exports in FY 1960 to 3.6 percent in FY 1993.

The important marine fish in the mid-1990s are mackerel, sardines, Bombay duck, shark, ray, perch, croaker, carangid, sole, ribbonfish, whitebait, tuna, silverbelly, prawn, and cuttlefish. The main freshwater fish are carp and catfish; the main brackish-water fish are *hilsa* (a variety of shad), and mullet.

Great potential exists for expanding the nation's fishing industry. India's exclusive economic zone, stretching 200 nautical miles into the Indian Ocean, encompasses more than 2 million square kilometers. In the mid-1980s, only about 33 percent of that area was being exploited. The potential annual catch from the area has been estimated at 4.5 million tons. In addition to this marine zone, India has about 1.4 million hectares of brackish water available for aquaculture, of which only 60,000 hectares were being farmed in the early 1990s; about 1.6 million hectares of freshwater lakes, ponds, and swamps; and nearly 64,000 kilometers of rivers and streams.

In 1990 there were 1.7 million full-time fishermen, 1.3 million part-time fishermen, and 2.3 million occasional fishermen, many of whom worked as saltmakers, ferrymen, or seamen, or operated boats for hire. In the early 1990s, the fishing fleet consisted of 180,000 traditional craft powered by sails or oars, 26,000 motorized traditional craft, and some 34,000 mechanized boats.

Fisheries research and training institutions are supported by central and state governments that deserve much of the credit for the expansion and improvements in the Indian fishing industry. The principal fisheries research institutions, all of which operate under the Indian Council of Agricultural Research, are the Central Institute of Marine Fisheries Research at Kochi (formerly Cochin), Kerala; the Central Inland Fisheries Institute at Barrackpore, West Bengal; and the Central Institute of Fisheries Technology at

Willingdon Island near Kochi. Most fishery training is provided by the Central Institute for Fishery Education in Bombay (or Mumbai in Marathi), which has ancillary institutions in Barrackpore, Agra (Uttar Pradesh), and Hyderabad (Andhra Pradesh). The Central Fisheries Corporation in Calcutta is instrumental in bringing about improvements in fishing methods, ice production, processing, storing, marketing, and constructing and repairing fishing vessels. Operating under a 1972 law, the Marine Products Export Authority, headquartered in Kochi, has made several market surveys abroad and has been instrumental in introducing and enforcing hygiene standards that have gained for Indian fishery export products a reputation for cleanliness and quality.

The implementation of two programs for inland fisheries—establishing fish farmers' development agencies and the National Programme of Fish Seed Development—has led to encouragingly increased production, which reached 1.5 million tons during FY 1990, up from 0.9 million tons in FY 1984. A network of 313 fish farmers' development agencies was functioning in 1992. Under the National Programme of Fish Seed Development, forty fish-seed hatcheries were commissioned. Fish-seed production doubled from 5 billion fry in FY 1983 to 10 billion fry in FY 1989. A new program using organic waste for aquaculture was started in FY 1986. Inland fish production as a percent of total fish production increased from 36 percent in FY 1980 to 40 percent by FY 1990.

Apart from four main fishing harbors—Kochi (Kerala), Madras (Tamil Nadu), Vishakhapatnam (Andhra Pradesh), and Roychowk in Calcutta (West Bengal)—twenty-three minor fishing harbors and ninety-five fish-landing centers are designated to provide landing and berthing facilities to fishing craft. The harbors at Vishakhapatnam, Kochi, and Roychowk were completed by 1980; the one at Madras was completed in the 1980s. A major fishing harbor was under construction at Sassoon Dock in Bombay in the early 1990s, as were thirteen additional minor fishing harbors and eighteen small landing centers. By early 1990, there were 225 deep-sea fishing vessels operating in India's exclusive economic zone. Of these, 165 were owned by Indian shipping companies, and the rest were chartered foreign fishing vessels.

The government provides subsidies to poor fishermen so that they can motorize their traditional craft to increase the range and frequency of operation, with a consequent increase in the catch and earnings. A total of about 26,171 traditional craft had been motorized under the program by 1992.

The banning of trawling by chartered foreign vessels and the speedy motorization of traditional fishing craft in the 1980s led to a quantum jump in marine fish production in the late 1980s. The export of marine products rose from 97,179 tons (Rs531 billion) in FY 1987 to 210,800 tons (Rs17.4 trillion) in FY 1992, making India one of the world's leading seafood exporting nations. This achievement was largely a result of significant advancements in India's freezing facilities since the 1960s, advancements that enabled India's seafood products to meet international standards. Frozen shrimp, a high-value item, has become the dominant seafood export. Other significant export items are frozen frog legs, frozen lobster tails, dried fish, and shark fins, much of which is exported to seafood-loving Japan. During the eighth plan, marine products were identified as having major export potential.

There are several specialized institutes that train fishermen. The Central Institute of Fisheries Nautical and Engineering Training in Kochi instructs operators of deep-sea fishing vessels and technicians for shore establishments. It has facilities in Madras and Vishakhapatnam for about 500 trainees a year. The Integrated Fisheries Project, also headquartered in Kochi, was established for the processing, popularizing, and marketing of unusual fish. Another training organization, the Central Institute of Coastal Engineering for Fisheries in Bangalore, has done techno-economic feasibility studies on locations of fishing harbor sites and brackish-water fish farms.

To improve returns to fishermen and provide better products for consumers, several states have organized marketing cooperatives for fishermen. Nevertheless, most traditional fishermen rely on household members or local fish merchants for the disposal of their catches. In some places, marketing is carried on entirely by fisherwomen who carry small quantities in containers on their heads to nearby places. Good wholesale or retail markets are rare.

Agricultural Credit

Credit institutions serving agricultural-sector needs developed in three phases. In the first phase, which lasted from 1947 to 1969, cooperative agencies were the primary vehicle providing credit. In the second phase, after nationalization of banks in 1969, commercial banks were assigned a role in providing agricultural credit but were supplementary to cooperatives. In the last phase starting in 1975, regional rural banks were established to provide credit. In the 1990s, agricultural credit is provided through a multiagency approach in the form of cooperatives, commercial banks, and regional rural banks. These institutions have gradually ensured that credit reaches the most remote agricultural and rural areas.

Since the inception of central economic planning in 1950, the government has favored cooperative societies as a channel for providing credit and as a means of broadening the experience of villagers in such activities as marketing, community farming, and consumer purchasing. Credit societies were the first to be established and continue to be the most extensive and important group of cooperatives. Of the roughly 250,000 cooperatives in India in 1980, about 100,000 were primarily agricultural credit cooperatives. By the late 1980s, because regional rural banks were doing more lending, the number of agricultural credit cooperatives had decreased to 87,300. By 1988 there were 93,000 primary agricultural credit societies operating in rural areas, with a membership of 89.8 million.

The societies aimed for universal membership in order that poorer members of society could join cooperatives and use their services. Total loans advanced by such societies amounted to nearly Rs36.9 billion during FY 1987. These agricultural credit societies had a share capital of about Rs10.1 billion at the end of June 1988.

Cooperatives played a significant role in the production and distribution of agricultural inputs. For example, during FY 1988 nearly 3.5 million tons, representing more than 33 percent of total fertilizer (less cow dung), were distributed through a network of 76,000 cooperative retail outlets. Cooperatives also distributed other inputs, such as seeds, pesticides, and agricultural implements.

The overall control of rural credit for the development of agriculture and the rural sector is under the control of the National Bank for Agriculture and Rural Development, which was established in July 1980. It was chartered to oversee the workings of regional rural banks, and in the mid-1990s was slated to establish a rural infrastructure development fund to provide loans to state governments and state-owned corporations to enable completion of irrigation, soil conservation, watershed management, and other rural infrastructure projects in progress. By June 1991, there were 14,522 regional rural banks in India.

Public-sector banks, including commercial and regional rural banks, increased their activities in the countryside after the nationalization of banks. Many bank branches were opened in rural areas. One indicator of increased availability of credit through public-sector banks was the increase in the number of accounts. The number went from 164,000, with outstanding loans of Rs1.6 billion, to nearly 21.8 million accounts, with an outstanding balance of nearly Rs165.2 billion in March 1990.

In economic terms, the growth in credit supply has been satisfactory, but the growth in deposits has not kept pace with credit supply and there has been a high rate of loan defaults. Field-level rural financial institutions have increased, however, even though there are fewer primary agricultural credit societies. The large increase in the number of branches of commercial banks in the rural areas and the expansion of regional rural banks led to the reduction.

Agricultural Taxation

Agricultural property and some agricultural income were being taxed in the early 1990s, but the revenue from these taxes was negligible. In the early 1950s, however, land revenue agricultural property taxes were a significant form of government income, providing just under 10 percent of the tax revenue of the central, state, and union territory governments. At the end of the 1980s, that proportion was less than 1 percent because land revenue had been fixed. For instance, land revenue was an average of Rs28 per hectare in Kerala and Rs23 per hectare in Uttar Pradesh, the two states with the highest assessment rates. The national average was Rs16.50 per hectare. Agricultural property also was subject to stamp duties and registration fees. (All property transactions have to be made on official, stamped forms, and registration fees have to be paid to register transactions.) No data were available in early 1993 on the proportion of these fees that came from the agricultural sector, but a taxation inquiry committee put it at approximately 20 percent. Between 1950 and 1990, only about 1.5 percent of the total taxes collected by the central, state, and union territory governments came from the agricultural sector. Overall, the impact of tax on agricultural property was negligible but was a likely target for economic reform in the mid-1990s.

Since the 1950s, agricultural income tax has been collected as a federal tax, but it has been levied only on income from plantations. All other agricultural income has been exempt from tax. The total collection from this tax was less than 1 percent of the total taxes collected by the central, state, and union territory governments in FY 1950; in the late 1980s, it had dropped below 0.3 percent.

MARKETING, TRADE, AND AID

Marketing and Marketing Services

The agricultural marketing system operates primarily according to the forces of supply and demand in the private sector. Government intervention is limited to protecting the interests of producers and consumers and promoting organized marketing of agricultural commodities. In 1991 there were 6,640 regulated markets to which the central government provided assistance in the establishment of infrastructure and in setting up rural warehouses. Various central government organizations are involved in agricultural marketing, including the Commission for Agricultural Costs and Prices, the Food Corporation of India, the Cotton Corporation of India, and the Jute Corporation of India. There also are specialized marketing boards for rubber, coffee, tea, tobacco, spices, coconut, oilseeds, vegetable oil, and horticulture.

A network of cooperatives at the local, state, and national levels assist in agricultural marketing. The major commodities handled are food grains, jute, cotton, sugar, milk, and areca nuts. Established in 1958 as the apex of the state marketing federations, the National Agricultural Cooperative Marketing Federation of

India handles much of the domestic and most of the export marketing for its member organizations.

Large enterprises, such as cooperative sugar factories, spinning mills, and solvent-extraction plants mostly handle their own marketing operations independently. Medium- and small-sized enterprises, such as rice mills, oil mills, cotton ginning and pressing units, and jute baling units, mostly are affiliated with cooperative marketing societies.

In the late 1980s, there were some 2,400 agroprocessing units in the cooperative sector. Of all the cooperative agroprocessing industries, cooperative sugar factories achieved the most notable success. The number of licensed or registered units remained at 232, of which 211 had been installed by March 1988. During the October 1987-September 1988 sugar season, 196 cooperative sugar factories were in production. They produced nearly 5.3 million tons of sugar, accounting for about 57.5 percent of the country's total production of 9.2 million tons. The National Federation of Cooperative Sugar Factories rendered advice to member cooperatives on technical improvement, financial management, raw materials development, and inventory control.

In the early 1990s, the cooperative marketing structure comprised 6,777 primary marketing societies: 2,759 general-purpose societies at the *mandi* (wholesale market) level and 4,018 special commodities societies for oilseeds and other such commodities. There were also 161 district or central societies covering nearly all important *mandis* in the country and twenty-nine general-purpose state cooperative marketing federations. The total value of agricultural produce marketed by cooperatives amounted to about Rs54.2 billion in FY 1988, compared with Rs18 billion in FY 1979. The total value of food grains handled by marketing cooperatives increased from Rs5 billion in FY 1979 to about Rs11.3 billion in FY 1986.

The Ministry of Agriculture's Directorate of Marketing and Inspection is responsible for administering federal statutes concerned with the marketing of agricultural produce. Another function is market research. The directorate also works closely with states to provide agricultural marketing services that constitutionally come under state purview.

Under the Agricultural Produce (Grading and Marketing) Act of 1937, more than forty primary commodities are compulsorily graded for export and voluntarily graded for internal consumption. Although the regulation of commodity markets is a function of state government, the Directorate of Marketing and Inspection provides marketing and inspection services and financial aid down to the village level to help set up commodity grading centers in selected markets. By the 1980s, warehouses for storing agricultural produce and farm supplies played an increasing role in government price support and price control programs and in distributing farm commodities and farm supplies. Because the public warehouses issue a receipt to the owners of stored goods on which loans can be raised, warehouses are also becoming important in agricultural finance. The Central Warehousing Corporation, an entity of the central government, operates warehouses at major points within its jurisdictions, and cooperatives operate warehouses in towns and villages. The growth of the warehousing system has resulted in a decline in weather damage to produce and in loss to rodents and other pests.

Most agricultural produce is sold by farmers in the private sector to moneylenders (to whom the farmer may be indebted) or to village traders. Produce is sold in various ways. It might be sold at a weekly village market in the farmer's own village or in a neighboring village. If these outlets are not available, then produce might be sold at irregularly held markets in a nearby village or town, or in the *mandi* . Farmers also can sell to traders who come to the work site. The government has adopted various measures to improve agricultural marketing. These steps include establishing regulated markets, constructing warehouses, grading and standardizing produce, standardizing weights and measures, and providing information on agricultural prices over All India Radio (Akashvani), the national radio network.

The government's objective of providing reasonable prices for basic food commodities is achieved through the Public Distribution System, a network of 350,000 fair-price shops that are monitored by state governments. Channeling basic food commodities through the Public Distribution System serves as a conduit for reaching the truly needy and as a system for keeping general consumer prices in check. More than 80 percent of the supplies of grain to the Public Distribution System is provided by Punjab, Haryana, and western Uttar Pradesh. The Food Corporation of India was established in 1965 as the public-sector marketing agency responsible for implementing government price policy through procurement and public distribution operations. It was intended to secure for the government a commanding position in the food-grain trade. By 1979 the corporation was operating in all states as the sole agent of the central government in food-grain procurement. The corporation uses the services of state government agencies and cooperatives in its operations. The Food Corporation of India is the sole repository of food grains reserved for the Public Distribution System. Food grains, primarily wheat and rice, account for between 60 and 75 percent of the corporation's total annual purchases. Food-grain procurement was 8.9 million tons in FY 1971, 13.0 million tons in FY 1981, and 17.8 million tons in FY 1991. Food grains supplied through the Public Distribution System amounted to 7.8 million tons in FY 1971, 13.0 million tons in FY 1981, and 17.0 million tons in FY 1991. The corporation has functioned effectively in providing price supports to farmers through its procurement scheme and in keeping a check on large price increases by providing food grains through the Public Distribution System.

External Trade

Agricultural exports were 44 percent of total exports in FY 1960; they decreased to 32 percent in FY 1970, to 31 percent in FY 1980, to 18.5 percent in FY 1988, and to 15.3 percent in FY 1993. This drop in agriculture's share was somewhat misleading because agricultural products, such as cotton and jute, that were exported in the raw form in the 1950s, have been exported as cotton yarn, fabrics, ready-made garments, coir yarn, and jute manufactures since the 1960s.

The composition of agricultural and allied products for export changed mainly because of the continuing growth of demand in the domestic market. This demand cut into the surplus available for export despite a continuing desire, on the part of government, to shore up the constant foreign-exchange shortage. In FY 1960, tea was the principal export by value. Oil cakes, tobacco, cashew kernels, spices, and raw cotton were about equal in value but were only one-eighth of the value of tea exports. By FY 1980, tea was still dominant, but coffee, rice, fish, and fish products came close, followed by oil cakes, cashew kernels, and cotton. In 1992-93 fish and fish products became the primary agricultural export, followed by oil meals, then cereals, and then tea. The share of fish products rose steadily from less than 2 percent of all agricultural exports in FY 1960, to 10 percent in FY 1980, to approximately 15 percent for the three-year period ending in FY 1990, and to 23 percent in FY 1992. The share of tea in agricultural exports fell from 40 percent in FY 1960 to roughly 17 percent in the FY 1988-FY 1990 period, and to only 13 percent by FY 1992.

External Aid

Foreign aid—financial and technical—since the 1950s has made a significant contribution to the agricultural progress in rural India. Aid has come from many sources: the United States government, the Ford Foundation, the Rockefeller Foundation, the World Bank, the Food and Agriculture Organization of the United Nations (UN), the European Economic Community, the former Soviet Union, Britain, and Japan, among others. Agricultural aid also has come in many forms. Between 1963 and 1972, for example, under a program of the United States Agency for International Development, some 400 American scientists and scholars served on the faculties of India's agricultural universities, while more than 500 faculty members from Indian institutions received advanced training in the United States and other countries. Several hundred agricultural research projects, financed with funds generated from sales of American farm commodities under the United States Public Law 480 program, fueled technological breakthroughs in Indian agriculture.

Aid to the agricultural sector continued in the late 1980s and the early 1990s; the FAO, the European Union, the World Bank, and the United Nations Development Programme (UNDP) provided the bulk of the assistance. The FAO provided technical assistance in a number of emerging areas; it provided quality control for exports; videos for rural communication and training; and market studies for wool processing, mushroom production, and egg and poultry marketing. Operation Flood—a dairy development program—was jointly sponsored by the European Economic Community, the World Bank, and India's National Dairy Development Board. The UNDP provided technical assistance by sending foreign experts, consultants, and equipment to India. The World Bank and its affiliates supported agricultural extension, social (community-based) forestry, agricultural credit, dairy development, horticulture, seed development, rain-fed fish farms, storage, marketing, and irrigation.

India has not only been a receiver of aid. Increasingly since independence, India has been sharing its agricultural technology with other developing countries. Numerous foreign scientists have received special and advanced training in India; hundreds of foreign students have attended Indian state agricultural universities. Among other international agricultural endeavors, India has contributed scientists, services, and funds to the work of the International Rice Research Institute, headquartered in the Philippines. In the late 1980s and early 1990s, India provided short- and long-term training courses to hundreds of foreign specialists each year under a variety of programs, including the Technical Cooperation Scheme of the Colombo Plan for Cooperative Economic and Social Development in Asia and the Pacific (Colombo Plan—see Glossary) and the Technical Cooperation Scheme of the Commonwealth of Nations Assistance Program.

Impact of Economic Reforms on Agriculture

The serious foreign-exchange crisis in 1990 led to a number of well-publicized economic reforms in the early 1990s dealing with trade, industrial licensing, and privatization. The reforms had an impact on the agricultural sector through the central government's effort to withdraw the fertilizer subsidy and place greater emphasis on agricultural exports. The cut in the fertilizer subsidy was a result of the government's commitment to reduce New Delhi's fiscal deficit by removing grants and subsidies from the budget. The government action led to a reduction in the use of chemical fertilizers and protests by farmers and opposition political parties. The government was forced to continue the subsidies but at a somewhat lower level.

New import and export policies aim at enhancing export capabilities of the agricultural sector by increasing productivity and promoting modernization and competitiveness. The measures to facilitate export growth include allowing the import of capital for the agricultural sector, reducing the list of agricultural products that cannot be exported, and removing the minimum export price from a number of products. Agricultural exports increased by 30 percent in FY 1991 and 14 percent in FY 1992 in terms of rupee value, but declined by 8 percent from FY 1990 to FY 1992 in United States dollar terms because of the devaluation of the rupee in 1991.

In the mid-1990s, it was expected that agriculture would continue to be the most important sector of the economy for the rest of the decade in terms of the proportion of GDP. However, even when it is not the sector providing the largest share of GDP, the importance of agriculture is not likely to diminish because of its critical role in providing food, wage goods, employment, and raw materials to industries. Despite their preoccupation with industrial development, India's planners and policy makers have had to acknowledge the critical role of agriculture in the early 1990s by changing basic policy. The gains in agricultural production should not lead to complacency, however. Continuing increases in productivity, developing allied activities in rural areas, and building infrastructure in rural areas are essential if India is to continue to be self-reliant in food and agricultural products and provide a modest surplus for exports.

There is abundant literature on Indian agriculture, and much of it is highly detailed. A source that brings together a wide variety of useful information is Subhash C. Kashyap's *National Policy Studies*, which provides a good overview of agricultural policy. A critical review of agricultural development and policy is provided by B.M. Bhatia's *Indian Agriculture: A Policy Perspective* . N.S.S. Narayana, K.S. Parikh, and T.N. Srinivasan's *Agriculture, Growth, and Redistribution of Income* is a more rigorous analysis of policy issues that also contains a large amount of descriptive information. The Indian Ministry of Information and Broadcasting's *India: A Reference Annual* is a valuable source. The Ministry of Finance's annual *Economic Survey* gives a detailed account of developments in agriculture. The *Economic and Political*

Weekly is India's premier source of news and analysis regarding all issues connected with agriculture. At present, the enumeration process is on in Orissa, Andhra Pradesh (ap), and Tamil Nadu (tn). Even as these states have so far steamrollered dissent, the activists are planning to approach the Supreme Court (sc) to stall the survey. The'right to food' campaign, which is spearheading the protest, is an informal group of individuals and non-governmental organisations (ngos). Several ngos from each district of Orissa will petition the apex court in the coming weeks. Pressure groups in ap and tn have resolved to follow suit. This decision was taken at a workshop on the right to food during the Asian Social Forum that was held in Hyderabad in January 2003.

To be sure, the states are conducting the bpl census in compliance with an sc directive. It is noteworthy that the apex court order came in response to a petition filed by the People's Union for Civil Liberties (pucl), Rajasthan, which is at the forefront of the'right to food' drive. The human rights organisation sought that the availability of food be made the people's right. It also wanted the government to be asked to utilise the country's huge food stocks for staving off starvation in many states. During the hearing of the case, it came to light that several states had not identified the number of bpl families. Consequently, in September 2002 the sc directed the Union and state governments to carry out a fresh survey. The estimation of bpl households is crucial as this is an eligibility criterion for various poverty eradication programmes. "Initially the governments delayed the process. Now, as the deadline nears, they want to rush through the exercise," alleges Kavita Srivastav, a Rajasthan-based activist. Significantly, states have to complete the survey by March 31 this year. "In two of Orissa's drought-stric-ken districts - Balangir and Nuapada - at least 50,000 families have migrated to other places. So if the survey takes place now, they will be excluded from various poverty alleviation programmes," points out Sanjay Mishra of Vikalpa, an ngo based in Balangir.

Some states see the logic of this argument. Rajasthan, reeling under a drought for the fifth consecutive year, even urged Union rural deve-lopment minister Shanta Kumar to delay the survey. According to chief minister Ashok Gehlot, the bpl census would deprive about 10 lakh families of the benefits of government schemes. But Damodar Rout, Orissa's panchayati raj minister, differs: "The claim of migration is exaggerated. The government pegs the number at 20,000, and some method of assessment will be devised for these people. The survey cannot be postponed as it is crucial for disbursing anti-poverty benefits."

A District Rural Development Agency official based in Kalahandi concedes that "the estimate may not be exact". An ap official says: "Though our survey may run into problems in the drought-affected areas, the numbers will not be as skewed as the ngos are fearing."

The other issue that has raised the pressure groups' hackles is the basis of bpl calculation. In fact, the debate over estimation methods has been raging for a long time. India was projected to have undergone a sharp decline in poverty during 1994-1999, with the percentage of bpl population coming down from 35.97 per cent in 1993-94 to 26.1 per cent in 1999-2000 . But the census figures remain contested to date. The latest estimates provided by the Planning Commission point to a drop in percentage of rural bpl population from 37.27 per cent to 27.09 per cent.

Over a period of 10 years, the estimation of bpl population has undergone changes in parameters. Earlier it was done on the basis of calorie intake, then it became income-based and in 1992 monthly expenditure was considered the yardstick.

The current survey is being conducted on the basis of material status with assets such as land, television, radio and clothes forming the indicators. This method is, however, said to be flawed since these assets are now counted as necessities in rural areas. In the case of land, quantity - not quality - is the benchmark.

"These parameters would bring down the number of bpl households drastically," feels Biren Nayak of global ngo Action Aid. "For instance, poor families may own large tracts that are unproductive. They will be omitted from the survey," he adds. It is also being alleged that despite the apex court's order to involve ngos, governments have not done so. In Orissa, police officials are carrying out the census as teachers have refused to participate.

7

The District Rural Development Agency (DRDA)

The District Rural Development Agency (DRDA) has traditionally been the principal organ at the District level to oversee the implementation of different anti-poverty programmes. Since its inception, the administrative costs of the DRDAs were met by way of setting apart a share of the allocations for each programme.

However, of late, the number of the programmes had increased and while some of the programmes provided for administrative costs of the DRDAs, others did not. There was no uniformity among the different programmes with reference to administrative costs. Keeping in view the need for an effective agency at the district level to coordinate the anti-poverty effort, a new Centrally Sponsored Scheme for strengthening the DRDAs has been introduced with effect from 1st April, 1999. Accordingly, the administrative costs are met by providing a separate budget provisions. This scheme which is funded on a 75:25 basis between Centre and States, aims at strengthening and professionalsing the DRDAs.

ROLE AND FUNCTIONS OF THE DISTRICT RURAL DEVELOPMENT AGENCY

If effective programme design is critical to successful implementation of rural development programmes, so is an effective delivery agency. None of the anti-poverty programmes can have impact unless they are implemented with clarity of purpose and a commitment to the task. It is here that the DRDAs play a critical role. The DRDAs are not the implementation through overseeing the implementation of different programmes and ensuring that necessary linkages are provided. To this extent the DRDA is a supporting and facilitation organization and needs to play a very effective role as a catalyst in development process.

The district Rural Development Agency is visualised as specialized and a professional agency capable of managing the anti-poverty programmes of the Ministry of Rural Development on the one hand and to effectively relate these to the overall effort of poverty eradication in the District. In other words, while the DRDA will continue to watch over and ensure effective utilization of the funds intended for anti-poverty programmes, it will need to develop a far greater understanding of the processes necessary for poverty alleviation/eradication. It will also need to develop the capacity to build synergies among different agencies involved for the most effective results. It will therefore need to develop distinctive capabilities rather than perform tasks that are legitimately in the domain of the PRIs or the line departments. The role of the DRDA will therefore be distinct from all the other agencies, including the Zilla Parishad.

DRDAs must themselves be more professional and should be able to interact effectively with various other agencies. They are expected to coordinate with the line department, the Panchayati Raj Institutions, the banks and other financial institutions, resources required for poverty reduction effort in the district. It shall be their endeavour and objective to secure inter-sectoral and inter-departmental coordination and cooperation for reducing poverty in the district. It is their ability to coordinate and bring about a convergence of approach among different agencies for poverty alleviation and would set them apart.

The DRDAs are expected to coordinate effectively with the Panchayati Raj Instutions. Under no circumstances will they perform functions of PRIs.

The DRDAs will maintain their separate identity but will function under the chairmanship of the Chairman of Zill Parishad. They are expected to be a facilitating and supporting organization to Zill Parishad, providing necessary excutive and technical support in respect of poverty reduction efforts. Wherever the Zilla Parishads are not in existence of are not functional, the DRDAs would function under the Collector/District Magistrate/Deputy Commissioner, as the case may be.

The DRDAs are expected to oversee the implementation of different anti-poverty programmes of the Ministry of Rural Development in the district. This is not be confused with actual implementation, which will be by the Panchayati Raj and other Institutions. The DRDAs will monitor closely the implementation through obtaining of periodic reports as well as frequent field visits. The purpose of the visit should be to facilitate the implementing agencies in improving implementation process, besides ensuring that the quality of implementation of programmes is high. This would include overseeing whether the intended beneficiaries are receiving the benefits under the different programmes.

The DRDAs shall keep the Zella Parishad, the State and Central Government duly informed of the progress of the implementation of the progremmes through periodic reports in the prescribed formats. Special report, as and when called for, shall be provided.

It shall be the duty of the DRDAs to oversee and ensure that the benefits specifically earmarked for certain target groups (SC/ST, women and disabled) reach them. They shall all necessary steps to achieve the prescribed norms.

The DRDAs shall take necessary step to improve the awareness regarding rural development and poverty alleviation particularly among the rural poor. This would involve issues of poverty, the opportunities available to the rural poor and generally infusing a sense of confidence in their ability to overcome poverty. It would also involve sensitizing the different functionaries in the district to the different aspects of poverty and poverty alleviation programmes.

The DRDAs will strive to promote transparency in the implementation of different anti-poverty programmes. Towards this end, they shall publish periodically, the details of the different programmes and their implementation.

Keeping in view, the substantial investment that are being made in poverty alleviation programmes, the DRDAs shall ensure financial discipline in respect of the funds received by them, whether from Central of State Governments. They shall also ensure that the accounts are properly maintained including in respect of the funds allocated to banks or implementing agencies in accordance with the guidelines of different programmes.

Thus the role of the DRDA is in terms of planning for effective implementation of anti-poverty programmes; coordinating with other agencies-Governmental, non-Governmental, technical and financial for successful programme implementation; enabling the community and the rural poor to participate in the decision marking process, overseeing the implementation to ensure adherence to guidelines, quality, equity and efficiency; reporting to the prescribed authorities on the implementation; and promoting transparency in decision making and implementation.

In addition the DRDAs shall coordinate and oversee the conduct of the BPL Census and such other surveys that are required from time to time.

The DRDAs shall also carry out / aid in carring out action research/ or evaluation studies that are initiated by the Central/ State Governments.

The DRDAs should deal only with the anti-poverty programmes of the Ministry of Rural Development. If DRDAs are to be entrusted with programmes of other ministries or those of the State Governments, it should be ensured that these have a definite antipoverty focus. Entrusting of any programme to the DRDAs, other than anti-poverty programmes of the Ministry, be it of any other Ministry of Government of India or the respective State Government will have to be done with the approval of the Secretary, Rural Development of the respective State (s), who should examine such request in consultation with the Ministry of Rural Development, Government of India. In such cases, it must be ensured that adequate provision is made for requisite staffing needed for proper implementation of the programme.

ORGANISATIONAL STRUCTURE OF THE DRDAS

Each district will have its own District Rural Development Agency. Ordinarily it would be a society registered under a Societies Registration Act. In respect of such states where DRDA does not have a separate identity a separate cell should be created in Zill Parishad which maintains a separate identity and separate accounts, so that the accounts are capable of being audited separately. This Cell should be directly under the charge of CEO or alternatively an officer who has the qualifications to be a Project Director. The accounts of DRDAs should under no circumstances be merged or amalgamated with those of the Zilla Parishads.

In order to be effective, the DRDA must have an appropriate staffing structure as well as suitable personnel policy. Keeping in view the rule and functions of the DRDA listed in the previous chapter, the staffing structure of DRDA must include positions for Planning for poverty alleviation, Project formulation, Social Organization and Capacity builing , Gender concerns, Engineering Supervision and Quality control, Project Monitoring, Accountancy and Audit functions as well as Evaluation and impact studies. An indicative staffing structure is given in Annexure and is also detailed below. The State Government may modify the structure suitably, but without altering the basic design, to take care of the needs of individual districts keeping in view their size as well as specificity. However, this will also be subject to the overall ceiling of administrative costs admissible to the DRDAs in the State. By and large the staff appointed should be dedicated to DRDA-related works and should not be frequently transferred.

The Staffing structure will as follows:

Project Director

Each DRDA should be headed by Project Director, who should be the rank of a Additional District Magistrate. The Project Director should preferably be a senior scale officer of All India Services or a senior officer of the State Service, eligible of appointment to the All India Services. He would be in overall charge of the activities of the DRDA and responsible for interaction with the District/ State administration as well as with the Government of India. The PD should be exclusively for DRDA work.

In some State, such as Maharashtra, the CEO of Zilla Parishad is the Chairman of the Zilla Parishad. Government of India have suggested to all the State Government that the chairman, Zilla Parishad should be the chairman of the governing body of the

DRDA. In the light of this, such states, the CEO of Zilla Parishad could also be designated as the Project Director of the DRDA.

Each DRDA should have the following wings:

(a) Self - employment Wing;

(b) Women's wing;

(c) Wage employment wing;

(d) Engineering wing;

(e) Account wing;

(f) Monitoring and Evaluation wing;

(g) General Administration wing;

Self- Employment Wing

(i) The self-employment Wing, shall be headed by a Project Officer and should have APOs in the field of planning, social mobilization, credit and Technology. The Project Officer may be specifically responsible for any of these four functions. The APO (Planning) would look after the activity clusters, district/block. Village group plan, guiding the BDOs and others in plan preparation, planning for infrastructure including marketing infrastructure. He would coordinate with the district officers, the banks as well as other institutions in the district. The APO (Social Mobilisation) would look after group formation, capacity building, monitoring of groups, choice of activities for groups, release of revolving funds and coordination. The APO (Credit), who should be from the commercial banking sector, would coordinate with the banks in all matters relating to credit, including the interface between the bankers and the beneficiaries/ beneficiary groups, loan disbursements as well as loan recovery. The APO (Technology) would look after issues concerning Technology upgradation as well as transfer of technology.

(ii) The DRDAs would be drawing up projects for specific activities under the Self-employment programmes, it would be necessary to have suitable experts to oversee the successful implementation of such projects. As part of the overall programme management, the DRDAs may take outside expert on a consultancy basis. Secretary, Rural Development of each state should develop guidelines for selection of consultants so as to avoid any wrong use of such provisions and to see that only those who have a proven practical expertise are engaged. Such experts to be engaged on project specific basis will function under the overall control and supervision of the Project Officer, self-employment programms.

Women's Wing

In order to ensure that women receive adequate attention in all the anti- poverty programmes, a Women's Cell should be sit up in each DRDA.

This cell would establish necessaty synergy with departments such as Women & Child Development, Education and health Departments to ensure that women not only receive their due share in the anti-poverty programmes but are also able to receive benefits of other programmes. The Women's wing will be headed by an Assistant Project Officer, who will function under the overall co-ordination of the Project Officer of the self employment wing. Assistant

Wage Employment Wing

The central concern of the DRDA in the wage-employment programmes should relate to planning, monitoring and vigilance by a technical wing. The DRDA should not concern itself with the actual implementation and execution of works which can be done by the line department / engineers or the Panchayati Raj Institutions. At the same time, the magnitude of the wage employment wing, with a Project officer assisted by a small complement of staff.

Watershed Wing

A Watershed Wing will be set up in the DRDA in all such districts where IWDP / DPAP /DDP is in operation. This wing should consist of a Project Officer, assisted by a small complement of staff. This staff would be independent of the programme support in the form of PIAs or Watershed committees.

Engineering Wing

Each DRDA should have a technical wing, which should also be responsible for innovations in design or use of materials, as well as training of the engineering personnel of the line departments or the PRIs.

This wing should be manned by an Executive Engineer assisted by one or two Assistant / Junior Engineers.

Account Wing

(i) Wherever it has not been done, the DRDAs should shift over to commercial accounting systems from the existing government account system. They should publish an annual report alongwith the balance sheet. The accounts wing of the DRDA should be headed by a Sr. Accounts Officer, either on deputation or by engaging the services of a chartered accountant. He should be supported by an Accounts Officer each for self-employment programmes and wage employment programmes duly assisted by accountants. Wherever the Watershed programmes (IWDP/DPAP/DDP) are under implementation, an additional post of Accounts Officer may be sanctioned. For Indira Awaas Yojana, one Accountant at the district level should be available to monitor the progress of the programme and the accounts.

(ii) One of the Accounts Officers should perform the role of internal audit.

Monitoring Wing

These should be a separate Monitoring and Evaluation wing headed by a Project Economist and functioning directly under the supervision of the Project Director.

Apart from monitoring the progress of all the programmes., this wing should also carry out evaluation /impact studies regularly by independent by independent institutions /experts including NGOs.

The cost of such studies will be met from the respective programme funds. This wing should also monitor issues relevant to poverty in the district.

ADMINISTRATIVE COSTS

Administrative costs were earlier admissible under different programmes. In order to enable the DRDAs to develop a proper personnel structure and to ensure its proper growth over years, the practive of meeting the administrative costs as percentages of each programme allocation has been given up. It will, on the other hand, be taken up as a new scheme called 'DRDA Administration with effect from 1st April, 1999. This scheme will be funded on a 75.25 by the central and state government.

Till 31.3.1999, administrative costs of the DRDAs were being met by way of a part of the programme fund of IRDP, JRY, EAS, DPAP, etc. With the introduction of the scheme of 'DRDA Administration' the administrative costs earlier available under different programmes stand withdrawn from 1.4.1999 and provision of administrative support to the DRDAs will be only under the scheme of 'DRDA Administration'.

Since the salary structure in different States different, the States may follow their own salary structure. However, the administrative cost ceiling fixed should be met entirely by the State government.

A maximum of 30% of the salary cost may be allocated towards contingencies inclusive of Rents, POL, office expenses, etc.

The administrative cost per district is fixed as follows:

- Category A districts (<6 blocks) Rs. 46 lakh per year
- Category B districts (6-10 blocks) Rs. 57 lakh per year
- Category C districts (11-15 blocks) Rs. 65 lakh per year
- Category D districts (>15 blocks) Rs. 67 lakh per year

The above limits will be applicable from the year 1999-2000. This ceiling will be raised every year, on a compounding basis, upto 5% to set off the increases due to inflation etc. The state governments are allowed a sum upto 10% of the above costs, to be calculated at 10% of the total admissible cost to all the districts in the state.

PERSONNEL POLICY OF THE DRDAS

Currently, there is no uniform policy for engaging and/or recruiting the staff by the DRDA. In many States, there are staff both directly recruited as well as on deputation. It is essential that prudent personnel policies are followed if the DRDA are to be a professional agency or are to perform the tasks expected of them. The following principles are laid down which must necessarily be followed.

As a matter of policy, the DRDA should not have any permanent staff. Taking employees on deputation to the DRDA for specific periods has the advantage of better choice of staff, flexibility in staffing pattern and of motivating the staff. The objective of strengthening of DRDAs is to provide them with certain professional capacity and have a flexible-standing pattern. To start with, DRDAs shall no longer be allowed to make any direct recruitment. In respect of the Staff that is currently borne on the DRDA, the State Rural Development Department should immediately draw up a 3-5 year plan for absorption of the staff into the line departments.

The Project Directors, Project Officers, APOs and all technical posts are to be manned by officer with proven capability and motivation and are selected in an objective manner by specific Selection Committees. The Project Directors should be selected by a Committee headed by the Chief Secretary / Development Commissioner / Addl. Chief Secretary of the State and with the Secretary (RD) being the member convenor, similarly, for officers at the level of APOs and other technical officers, there should be a selection Committee headed by Secretary (RD). For other staff too, other than ministerial and lower rank, the selection should be by an appropriate selection committee.

In the selection of Project Directors and APOs, emphasis should be on selecting officers of young age. Indicatively, the PDs and APO should be more than 40-45 years of age, and in any case not more than 50 years of age.

Lack of sufficient length of tenure to the project personnel has been a worrisome factor in the implementation of the anti-poverty programmes. In order to avoid this risk, it is necessary to insist on a minimum tenure and also ensure its compliance. The Project Directors, APOs and other technical staff must have a minimum tenure of 2-3 years and only under exceptional circumstances can theyh be shifted that too after recording the specific reasons in writing. Any violation should mean suspension of funds to the concerned DRDA.

The Secretary, Rural Development of the state should be in overall charge of the Project Directors of DRDAs. To start with, after selection the posting orders of Project Directors (the project officers, APOs) should be issued by the Secretary, Rural Development and not by any other department. The cadre controlling authority of the Project Directors / other officers may place the services of the concerned officers (after selection) at the disposal of the Rural Development Department for appointment to the concerned posts. The Secretary, Rural Development should also be responsible for making incharge arrangements when Project Directors go on long leave. The Secretary, Rural Development should actively associate himself / herself in the training requirements of Project Directors and other DRDA staff.

In order to make the DRDA a professional body, the officials and staff of DRDAs should be constantly trained in the general field of management of rural areas and poverty. The personnel to be posted to the DRDA should be given a pre-service training to orient them suitably to their tasks.

There should also be a system of an annual in-service training where the officers could be given the updates about the relevant fields and which would also afford them an opportunity of exchanging their experiences.

Suitable training programmes will be designed by the Ministry in consultation with professional institutes of the national importance. The State Government may also identify suitable state-level institutions in consultation with the Ministry of Rural Development.

ADMINISTRATION OF DRDAS

An indicated, the role of the DRDA is to perform tasks which are distinctly different from other institutions / departments. However, the DRDAs are very much a part of the district. They shall function accordingly.

The DRDA shall be a registered society registered under a Societies Registration Act or a district cell in the Zilla Parishad having a separate identity. The chairman of the Zilla Parishad shall be the chairman of governing body of the DRDA. The Executive and financial functions shall however lie with CEO, Zilla Parishad / District Collector who shall be designated as the Chief Executive Officer or Executive Director. It shall be his responsibility to ensure that the administration of DRDA and the programmes are conducted in accordance with the guidelines. Wherever the Zilla Parishads are not in existence or are not functional, the DRDAs would function under the Collector / District Magistrate /Deputy Commissioner of the District, as the case may be. The administration of the DRDA shall be carried out by a governing body. The Governing Body of the DRDA will provide policy directions, approve the annual plan and also review and monitor the implementation of the plan, including the different programmes. They shall give such directions to the DRDA as may be necessary from time to time. The Governing Body of the DRDA will meet once in a quarter.

The composition of the governing body shall be as follows.

1. Chairman of Zilla Parishad Chairman
2. All MPs and MLAs and MLCs of the District
3. 1/3rd of Panchayat Samiti Chairpersons to be nominated by rotation in alphabetical order for a tenure of one year, one of whom must belong to SC/ST and another a woman.
4. CEO of Zilla Parishad / District Collector – Chief Executive Officer / Executive Director
5. Head of the Central Cooperative Bank of the District
6. Chairman Regional Rural Bank
7. District Lead Bank Officer
8. Representative of the Reserve Bank of India at district level
9. NABARD representative at district level
10. General Manager, DIC
11. Representative of KVIB
12. District Officer in charge of Scheduled Caste / Scheduled Tribe Welfare
13. District women & Child welfare officer

14. District officer dealing with welfare of the disabled
15. One representative from technical institutions
16. Two representatives of NGOs
17. Two representatives of the weaker sections, one of whom may be drawn from SCs and STs
18. One representative of rural women
19. Proejct Director, DRDA - Member Secretary

Wherever the Zilla Parishads are not in existence, the State Governments may nominate elected members of the State Legislature from the concerned districts to act as Chairman of the Governing Bodies of the DRDAs.

Executive Committee (EC)

All executive and financial powers of the DRDA shall be exercised by the executive committee as per a scheme of delegation of financial and executive powers to be determined by each State/ UT Government and this Committee will be fully accountable in all matters of DRDA to the governing body as well as to the Government. The Executive Committee of DRDA shall be headed by the Chief Executive Officer / Executive Director and shall consist of all the District level officers and any other officer deemed necessary for planning and implementation of the anti-poverty programmes. The Project Director DRDA will be the Member-Secretary of the EC. The Executive Committee will meet at least once in a month.

FINANCIAL PROCEDURES

The scheme of 'DRDA Administration' shall be a centrally sponsored scheme. The funds required under this progreamme shall be shared between the Centre and the States in the ratio of 75:25 Funds will be released directly to the DRDAs, in accordance with the guidelines under this programme.

The Centre will release funds in two installments.

Release of First Installment

(i) The release of first installment can be made without any formal request if the second installment in the previous year had been released without any condition. If latter installment was not released at all or was released with some conditions, formal requests for release of first installment are required from the DRDAs after the conditions have been fulfilled / reasons for non-release of the second installment have been met. For the first year i.e., 1999-2000 all the DRDAs will be released first installment on an ad-hoc basis.

(ii) The release of the first installment should ordinarily be completed by the end of the second month of the financial year.

Release of Second Installment

(i) The quantum of the second installment shall be subject to actual requirement within the overall ceiling. The second installment of Central funds shall be released on the request of the DRDAs in the prescribed performa on fulfillment of the following conditions.

- Budget provision for the current year may be indicated by the State Governments. The Central release will not exceed it proportionately.
- The State Government should have released its contribution during the previous year. Deficiency in release of its share will be deducted from the second installment. Also the contribution of the State Government for the first current year should have been released.
- Available funds including carry forward funds should have been utilized at least to 60%.
- The opening balance of the DRDAs should not exceed 15% of the allocation of the year in which funds are being released. In case, the opening balance exceeds this limit, the Central share of the amount by which it exceeds this limit will be deducted at the time of release of second installment.
- Audit reports, utilization certificates for the previous year should be furnished. This will not be required in the first year i.e., 1999-2000.

- Any other terms and conditions imposed at the time of the last release should have been met.

(ii) The DRDA shall maintain the fund under the head 'DRDA Administration', in a separate bank account in any o the nationalized bank. Interest earned on the funds will necessarily be used only for admissible items of expenditure under DRDA administration. They shall not be used for any programme funding or non-admissible items of expenditure, such as construction of building and purchase of vehicles.

Maintenance of Accounts

Principles

Separate accounts shall be maintained of this scheme and each other scheme under which the DRDA receives funds. Such maintenance of accounts is governed by the principles that the expenditure incurred is not repugnant to the objective of the scheme and is made, in accordance with the prescribed procedures. DRDA accounts are to be maintained on double entry system. The accounting procedure for DRDAs has been described in detail in the Government of India, Ministry of Rural Development Publication entitled "Revised Accounting Procedure for District Rural Development Agencies / Societies", 1984 and subsequent instruction issued / to be issued from time to time. Internal Audit Cells should be specifically charged with the responsibility of overseeing and the observance of these principles. One of the Accounts Officers should perform the role of internal audit.

Audit of the Accounts

- The Project Director should cause the annual accounts of the DRDA to be prepared by a date not later than 30th June comprising Receipt and Payment Accounts, Income and Expenditure Account and Balance sheet. After approval by the Governing body, he shall have the accounts audited by the Chartered Accountant or any other auditor appointed for the purpose. A copy of such audit report (duly signed by auditor) alongwith the annual statement of accounts certified by the auditor and the Chairman of the DRDA thereon should be furnished simultaneously to Government of India and the State Government not later than 30th September.

- The Comptroller and Auditor General (CAG) has the right to conduct the audit of the accounts of the society and for this purpose shall have the right of access to the books of accounts and other relevant records of the DRDA. For this purpose a copy of the annual accounts alongwith the audit report and the comments of the DRDA thereon shall be sent to the audit office nominated by CAG.
- The accounts of the DRDA shall also be open to inspection by such individual or parties as are nominated to carryout such inspections by the Ministry of Rural Development at the State level or at the level of the Government of India. All Officers of and above the level of Under Secretary in the Ministry of Rural Development, Government of India and such officer as may be authorized by the State Government may also inspect the accounts.
- A Statement showing the schedule of Fixed Assets held by the DRDA / Agency at the end of the financial year should be sent to the State Government and Government of India with the form prescribed alongwith the annual statement of accounts. No depreciation should be charged and value of assets to be shown at the original cost in the accounts.
- All the Agencies should send a utilization certificate to the Government of India (Department of Rural Development) in the prescribed Performa alongwith annual statement of accounts. The utilization certificate must be prepared strictly on the basis of the Receipts and Payment Accounts and opening / closing balances in both Receipts and Payment Accounts Utilisation Certificate must also tally.
- The above provisions are in addition to the statutory requirements under relevant law under which the DRDAs are registered.

8

Rural Development in India

INTRODUCTION

Rural development has always been an important issue in all discussions pertaining to economic development, especially of developing countries, throughout the world. In the developing countries and some formerly communist societies, rural mass comprise a substantial majority of the population. Over 3.5 billion people live in the Asia and Pacific region and some 63% of them in rural areas. Although millions of rural people have escaped poverty as a result of rural development in many Asian countries, a large majority of rural people continue to suffer from persistent poverty. The socio-economic disparities between rural and urban areas are widening and creating tremendous pressure on the social and economic fabric of many developing Asian economies. These factors, among many others, tend to highlight the importance of rural development. The policy makers in most developing economies recognize this importance and have been implementing a host of programs and measures to achieve rural development objectives. While some of these countries have achieved impressive results, others have failed to make a significant dent in the problem of persistent rural underdevelopment.

LITERATURE ON INDIAN RURAL DEVELOPMENT

Therefore, any development plan bringing not the betterment or uplift of rural sector in the developing countries would lose its significance. On account of this fact, an attempt went on being made throughout the world to generate the literature on rural development. Thereby, the literature on rural development has become so wide that to decide from where the deliberation should be started, is a difficult task. As regards to the literature pertaining to Indian rural development, we can see three separately different themes therein.

(1) The literature coming under the first theme is the literature comprised of the conceptual part and importance of rural development in the national economic development. The greatest part of this literature was generated by European economists or the Indian economists educated in Europe.

(2) The literature under the second theme presents a detail of programmes and projects related to the main issues pertaining to rural development which are:

(i) Literacy and Education: - The simple literacy (basic reading, writing and numeracy) and the functional literacy had been presented as panaceas in the 1950s and the 1970s, respectively, with a view that if everybody learned how to read and write or learned this would enhance development. The literacy, also including functional computer literacy, is still being presented as panacea by the governments of developing countries, UNESCO, World Bank, IMF and numerous aid organizations, with a view that this will solve development problems. On the other hand, education plays an important role in the progress of an individual's mind and country. Ignorance and poverty, the two major speed-breakers in the swift developing country, can be overcome easily through education.

(ii) Construction of Link-Roads: - Though unknown, a potentially important share of the benefits to the poor from rural roads cannot be measured in monetary terms. This is extremely important if the benefits of development have to move beyond the limited confines of cities to the vast hinterland so that the millions of toiling farmers can also become partners in progress. Urban-rural road links play a vital role for carrying urban prosperity into the heartland of a developing economy.

(iii) Self-Employment Generation: - Employment generation, especially the self employment generation in rural sector attach great importance to poverty alleviation and mitigation specifically of the wide variations across States and the rural-urban division. A set of prudentially selected programmes of self employment in rural sector plays as the panacea to remove multi-dimensional nature of poverty through helping a lot the anti-poverty strategy's three broad components - promotion of economic growth, promotion of human development and targeted programmes of poverty alleviation.

(iv) Health Awareness: - The goal of health awareness programme of rural development is to create awareness, a stirring of both heart and mind, about health care conditions, challenges, and solutions among the rural people.

(v) Giving awareness of opportunities availability for them:- Awareness of opportunities availability in rural sector means to provide relevant and usable information to the rural youth regarding (both the skilled and the unskilled) labour markets and access to relevant training to help them make decisions about the labour market options available to them.

(vi) Family Planning: - Population growth is though a global problem but in heavily populated developing countries the problem is rather acute. An effective family planning programme is necessary there so as to curb high population growth that erodes the increase in employment opportunities and per capita income begot on account of the therein launched development programmes.

(vii) Land Reforms: - Land reform means deliberate change in the way agricultural land is held or owned, the methods of its cultivation, or the relation of agriculture to the rest of the economy. The most common objective of land reform is to abolish feudal or colonial forms of landownership, often by taking land away from large landowners and redistributing it to landless peasants.

(viii) Extension of rural or agricultural credit: - An Integrated Rural Development Programme (IRDP) needs to identify the poor, give them credit and subsidy to purchase a productive asset to raise their earnings, recover loans, and recycle loans progressively to help poor villagers. There is a need to popularise banking facilities and make villagers account-holders. New type of accounts to suit their requirements should be considered. Moreover, the main problem in rural credit is not mere credit but the way in which it is spent. Therefore, the agencies providing rural credit should aim to promote sustainable and equitable prosperity of the villagers through effective credit support, related services, institution development and other innovative initiatives.

(ix) Extension of canal irrigation: - Irrigation is an essential component of progressive agriculture. In fact, development of irrigation has become synonymous with agricultural development and rural prosperity. Canal irrigation system is much more challenging than the groundwater irrigation systems. It is the dominant water transfer technique in developing countries and is performing well in many parts of the world.

(x) Rural Electrification: - Rural electrification means to facilitate availability of electricity for accelerated growth and for enrichment of quality of life of rural population. It is argued that rural electrification is essential in the longer term perspective of rural development since electricity is considered as a prerequisite for economic development and improvement of overall standard of living of the rural inhabitants. Electricity is also considered as a potent force capable of elevating and providing the much needed dynamism into the rural economy.

In this literature some programmes and projects pertaining to the national economic development (such as extension of mobile telephone service, extension of highway network, heavy industrialization etc.) also have been referred to as rural development programmes.

(3) The literature under the third theme is most critical. This literature comprises of the deliberations of the writers perhaps over enthusiastic to get them-selves enlisted in the line of economists. They have written to prove even some phenomena like the rural-urban migration and the emergence of small and rare urban patches in the form of campus of one or more heavy industries, to be the signs of rural development. I think, rural-urban migration gains impetus when there becomes acute shortage of employment opportunities in rural sector. Similarly, the above mentioned urban patches too have relation not with the process of rural development but with the rural-urban transformation. Some writers put one more step further by using the terms rural development and urbanization as synonymous. I don't understand why they differentiate not between the rural and the urban economies. The basic difference between the rural and the urban economies is that of their dependence and not of the amenities or facilities of life available for the people living there.

A rural economy substantially depends on land and agriculture. On the other hand, an urban economy substantially depends on any one or a combination of industry, trade and commerce. If we want to develop a rural economy we should develop land and agriculture. The land and agriculture development would increase income of the rural people whereby they would tend to raise their living standard by letting urban amenities, facilities and traditions enter in their life. Whatever the high level of living standard is achieved there on the basis of increased income generated on account of land and agriculture development, the economy remains rural, all the same. It becomes developed but is not converted into an urban economy. The rural villages in United States of America look far better than Indian cities but those are still the part of U.S. rural sector because the economy of those villages is still land and agriculture based. This course of strengthening a rural economy is "Rural Development'.

If the urban way of living is made available to the rural mass without raising their income through land and agriculture, their consumption, traditions and living become urban. This is urbanization and not rural development. Urbanization is enjoyed by rural people till it is free of cost for them. As soon as it starts costing to them, either they revert to their pre-urbanization living standard or, if they have become habitual, they indulge in illegal activities to earn more income to maintain the enjoyed living standard. That is why the urban youths in India are day by day advancing towards crime. Therefore, urbanization can pay nothing positive to rural mass in real sense. Nor, urbanization means rural development. Each of the rural development, the rural extension, the urbanization, the urban development, the urban extension and the rural urban transformation has its separate meaning.

Therefore, this third theme of the rural development literature is totally unacceptable. But, all the same, this theme seems to have crept into and exerted its pressing effect in India's development plan formulation. This becomes amply clear if we reflect on net result of India's long journey, worth more than 55 yrs, on the path of planned economic development.

PREINDEPENDENCE RURAL INDIA

Before independence the picture of India could have been seen in the wrinkled faces, flushed cheeks, concavo bellies, folded hands in praying posture and wet eyes of its rural mass residing in the wide spread rural sector and constituting more than 70 % of India's total population. The real India resided in their privation, poverty, starvation, helplessness, wretchedness and mass unemployment. Some sentimental citizens, having realized this situation of their nation, stepped on the way of freedom movement since the foreign rule was taken as the sole causal factor of that pitiable state of India. The movement went on advancing and masses went on being involved in it. Ultimately in 1947 India became independent whereby we became free to decide our future.

PERFORMANCE OF INDIA"S PLANNED ECONOMIC DEVELOPMENT

We started our planned economic development since 1951

having in our hands the experience, a wide literature of well proved strategies and variegated plans pertaining to, used by and created or formulated by the well developed western economies, apart from our available natural resources. We were over enthusiastic and over ambitious on account of having the ready and well proved weapons sought from the western world for combating the problem of development. Therefore, instead of starting from the very beginning and covering the whole path we, being enticed and allured by the surprisingly fascinating fruits of industrialization, started our efforts but having longed for being developed and grabbing fruits thereof in a haste. Thus we lost sequences in our development path. We ignored agriculture that was the spine of our economy. Thereby our agricultural development lagged far behind the level required for feeding our industrialization up to the mark. Agriculture based small and cottage industries became shattered and the villages became ruined. This raised a huge bulk of unemployed people in the widely spread rural sector.

The unemployed persons started migrating to the urban areas in search of job. The urban development and industrialization there had not sufficient level to absorb the whole migrating mass and to provide them proper urban life facilities. As a result thereof a mushroom growth of slums came about fast which eventually turned into big slum spots in cities and towns within a no longer period of 20 or 25 years. This hampered urban growth and urban life. On the other hand, in rural areas there emerged acute shortage of energetic workforce, service centres, infrastructure, intellectuals etc. This hampered the rural development whereby agricultural development and rural life remained slang lower. That is why, even having travelled a long path of planned economic development, the state of affairs of rural India still remains almost the same as it was before planning. There is a big gulf between urban and rural people regarding wealth, wage, education and income. Moreover, the rural-urban migration, due to the pitiable state of affairs in rural areas, resulted to unchecked urban growth.

Thus, instead of overall development, an unbalanced and unfair development of our economy became resulted therein. Consequently a wide spread general unemployment prevailed in both the rural and the urban areas (as per ECONOMIC APPRAISAL 2006-07, the estimated number of unemployed persons rose from 7.98 million in 1983 to 9.02 million in 1993-94, to 10.51 million in 1999-2000 and to 13.10 million in 2004-05.

In addition to this a considerable number of politically, socially and economically sound and effective elites emerged in cities and urban towns. These elites interfered in the formulation and execution of development plans, on one hand, and in the fixation of priorities, on the other. Thereby our development plans became urban oriented and concentrating on rich minority.

Thus the poor majority and the rural economy became ignored. The unemployment situation in both the rural and the urban sectors became almost uncontrollable. The government became politically weak.

Therefore its priority became to please the rich minority so that it may run. To mitigate unemployment and poverty among the general mass it has to play pseudo role to remedy some times the rural and some times the urban mass alternately through various unsuccessful employment programmes and plans. Due to the general unemployment the condition of rural mass became more embarrassing than that of urban mass since the rural people had already been subsisting in privation. The fruits of the development programmes in rural sector were grabbed by the social elites in villages.

Therefore, the general rural mass, instead of observing their economic uplift, rather found them-selves lagging behind in the run of economic development. The village industries had to be liquidated; rural artisans or handicraftsmen either became unemployed or had to migrate to urban cities or towns; the socio-cultural, cheap and some times free entertainment sources (like village dramas, swangs, street magicians, community chorus, community games, rural fairs, community festivals etc.) were snatched by costly media based means.

Modern road and rail transport replaced the traditional transport. Rural weekly markets and village shopkeepers came to their end in the want of adequate demand. This resulted to a rapid increase in the cost of living of the rural people but their income remained far behind.

CAUSES OF THE REGRESSIVE EFFECTS ON THE RURAL LIFE

There have been three causes of this stinging situation. The first was our galloping along the development path instead of travelling along the true locus by creeping walking and running as and when needed. The second cause refers to the distortion in the concept of rural development which made the formulation of development plans and strategies incompatible to rural economy. The third cause was the rapid population growth which added a lot to make the unemployment situation a mammoth. The first cause relates to our over enthusiasm and the second cause relates to the hereinabove discussed third theme of rural development literature. The third cause relates to the increasing difference of birth rate over death rate and the insignificant performance of'Family Planning Programme'.

On account of extended medical facilities, uplift of living standard due to increased national income, control over epidemics, check on famines, alleviation of starvation, extension of maternity services etc. during the development process in the plan period, the death rate considerably went down (from 27.4 per thousand per year during 1941-50 to 7.6 per thousand per year in 2005) but the birth rate remained slang high (it was 39.9 per thousand per year during 1941-50 and came down only to 23.8 per thousand per year in 2005). Therefore population growth attained an increasingly high rate that was however tried unsuccessfully to be lowered through the'Family Planning Programme'.

FACTORS RESPONSIBLE FOR CHILD BIRTH

If we go in full detail of why a child is born, we will come across the various factors making a child take birth. The factors making a child take birth can be grouped under four heads namely (i)Biological Factor, (ii)Socio-cultural Factors, (iii)Religious Factors and (iv)Economic Factors.

BIOLOGICAL FACTOR

The biological factor refers to the child bearing as a byproduct of sexual gratification. This is one of the most effective factors determining birth rate of the population. A person in the state of aggravated sexual agitation can forgo all social, cultural, religious (spiritual) and economic gains for sexual gratification.

SOCIO-CULTURAL AND RELIGIOUS FACTORS

The socio-cultural and the religious factors refer to the social customs, cultural traditions and religious faiths which play dominant role in the life of people especially in poor and backward communities. The social factors induce a person to have more sons as the sons are believed to be the reliable means of social security and social status for a family. Moreover, they are deemed to care their old, physically wasted and worn-out parents, on one hand, and to provide safety to the family in case of conflicts and death of supportive member/s of the family. The religious factors refer mainly to four beliefs. One states that peace is rendered to the soul after death only if the cremation is performed by a real son. The second speaks of higher spiritual gain or place in Elysium of heaven after death for a person having more sons. The third relates the production of more children to religious service and the fourth specifies child bearing as the pious duty of a woman because she is believed to be sent by God only for increasing progeny.

ECONOMIC FACTORS

Apart from the socio-cultural and the religious factors, the economic factors are very much effective like the biological factor. A person in acute economic privation leaves even deeply instilled socio-cultural, religious and some times biological allurements too for economic gains. The need of economic support in old age and the poverty are two main economic factors making people tend to produce more children. In old age, when a person becomes generally sick, pulled, worn-out, and non-earning, he becomes dependant to his heirs for food, clothing, medical treatment and other expenses. More the sons or heirs he has, lesser will be the share of burden of supporting him. As regards to poverty, it generates three causes of inducement to the high rate of child-birth.

(a) The prevailing media based fascinating means of entertainment are not only out of the reach of poor man but these have also snatches the old socio-cultural, cheap and some times free entertainment sources from him. Therefore a poverty stricken person has to search the way of entertainment in sex and that too being circumstantially unprotected whereby childbirth goes on taking place one after one successively.

(b) In poor families a child becomes earning hand at the age of seven or eight yrs. On account of the subsistence level of family's living, the expenditure on child's feeding is considerably lower than the wage he earns. Therefore, the surplus of his earning over his consumption adds to family income and thus contributes to the uplift of family's standard of living. The sentiments and feelings regarding education or future welfare of the child droop before the agony of unsatisfied basic needs due to privation. Therefore, a child in a poor family is proved an asset rather than liability, in its stead.

(c) There are some types of family occupations where a number of faithful workmen are required. The required manpower from own family is most desirable there. If a person is owner of a series of units of small scale industries, cottage industries, small business units etc. the hired managing persons generally prove costlier, unfaithful and non-devoted. If a family member is deployed at each such unit the safety and profitability is increased. Similar is the position in a single cottage industry unit where margin of profit is low and hired labour makes the profit uncertain. If family manpower instead of hired one is used the profitability there becomes increased on account of devotedness, faithfulness and per need flexibility in working hours of the working force. Moreover, wage rate of a family labour is generally lower than that of a hired labour because the cost of living of one member of the family is lower than that of the whole family of hired man. Therefore the requirement of man power is tried to meet out by producing more children in the family.

PERFORMANCE OF FAMILY PLANNING PROGRAMME

As regards to the check on high population growth the prevailing'Family Planning Programme' has been proved insufficient and incomplete.

Census figures reveal that the'Family Planning Programme' in India has fallen short of the goals with which it was implemented. India's family planning program was initiated in 1952 to curb population growth and in due course was given highest priority along with other developmental programs.

All the same, India's population that was below half billion in 1960 crossed the figure of one billion in 2000.

It is well proved that the programme failed to instill among the general mass the spirit of'children by choice and not by chance'.

Introduction of target free approach in 1996-97, reduced thrust on family planning, poor access to family planning services and inadequate attention on need based methods of sterilization have been the causal factors of the inadequacy and insufficiency of family planning programme in controlling population growth especially in rural areas where it should have been proved but successful.

CONCLUSION AND SUGGESTIONS

The whole length of the above discussion makes amply clear that incompatibility of the development process and inadequacy of family planning programme are the two factors responsible for slackness in rural development in India.

Therefore, to accelerate rural development the development process should be made compatible by rectifying the conceptual mistake in the development move and the high population growth should be checked by making the family planning programme strong and effective.

As far as the question of rectification of mistake in development move is concerned, the time of making the mistake good by starting afresh has gone far back.

Therefore, we should better take a drastic turn to re-fix our priorities, reformulate our strategies, re-select our programmes and reconstruct our plans so as to make our development move rural oriented, congenial to micro-level needs of the people, akin to the over all development and compatible to the extenuation of economic disparities.

This will bring about fast agricultural development, uplift of village life and revival of village industries, artistry and handicraft to check the rural-urban migration.

On the other hand, the'Family Planning Programme' should be made strong and effective by reformulating it in a way that all the factors making a child take birth are extenuated as suggested below.

(1) To check unintended child-birth on account of purely the biological factor the contraceptives should be made so affluently available that in every case of coitus for mere gratification the use of a suitable contraceptive is made sure.

(2) The socio-cultural and the religious factors should be weakened by old age house facility, old age pension, dependent minors allowance scheme, unemployment allowance, community insurance, extension of education, literacy and poverty alleviation programmes etc.

(3) The population growth on account of economic factors should be checked by so designing the media based means of entertainment that these become under the easy reach of poor people, making the family occupations joint ventures, launching subsidy schemes and market protection schemes for rural cottage or small scale industries and accelerating agricultural development.

It is finally concluded that for achieving rural development the development plans and the family planning programme both should be reformed on the hereinabove suggested lines so that extra employment opportunities may be generated fast and population growth may be checked in a way that growth of employment opportunities considerably exceeds the population growth in rural sector.

NATIONAL RURAL RODS DEVELOPMENT AGENCY

MEMORANDUM OF ASSOCIATION

1. The name of the Society will be'National Rural Roads Development Agency'.
2. The Registered Office of the Society shall be at Room No. 552-A, Krishi Bhavan, New Delhi-110001.
3. Background

   Government of India have embarked upon a programme of construction of Rural Roads under the Pradhan Mantri Gram Sadak Yojana. The programme envisages the setting up of a National Rural Roads Development Agency (NRRDA) to extend support to the programme through advice on technical specifications, project appraisal, appointment of part-time Quality Control Monitors, Management of Monitoring Systems and submission of Periodic Reports to the Ministry of Rural Development. This Agency is envisaged as a compact, professional and multi-disciplinary body.
4. Objectives
   a. To discuss with different Technical Agencies and arrive at appropriate Designs and Specifications of Rural Roads and, thereafter, to assist the Ministry of Rural Development in prescribing the Designs and Specifications of Rural Roads, including Bridges and Culverts.
   b. To determine the tasks to be performed by the Principal Technical Agencies and State Technical Agencies.
   c. To appoint reputed Technical Institutions as Principal Technical Agencies and State Technical Agencies to perform the tasks to be entrusted to them.
   d. To render assistance to States or Union Territories in preparing District Rural Roads Plans.
   e. To scrutinize or arrange to scrutinize the proposals received from States and Union Territories for consideration by the Ministry of Rural Development.
   f. To oversee and inspect or arrange to inspect through

Independent Monitors, the execution of the road-works cleared by the Ministry and being implemented by States or Union Territories through their Executing Agencies.

g. To appoint serving or retired Engineers, Academicians, Administrators and other Agencies, with experience in Rural Roads, as Independent Monitors to ensure proper execution of road works by the State Agencies.

h. To monitor the progress of the road-works with particular reference to time frame for completion, Technical Specifications, Project Appraisal and Quality Control methods.

i. To set up an "On-line Management and Monitoring System", incorporating both intranet and internet-based system, for obtaining updated information to facilitate a ready viewing and screening of data.

j. To send periodic reports to the Ministry of Rural Development on the progress of implementation of road works by the States or Union Territories.

k. To Monitor the planning for and plantation of fruit bearing and other suitable trees on both sides of the rural roads undertaken by the States or Union Territories, under the Pradhan Mantri Gram Sadak Yojana.

l. To Monitor the expenditure incurred by the States or Union Territories in implementation of the *Pradhan Mantri Gram Sadak Yojana,* with reference to the funds released by Ministry of Rural Development through expenditure reports obtained form the States or Union Territories and through'Online Management and Monitoring System.

m. To take up research activities relating to Rural Roads, including execution of Pilot Projects.

n. To study and evaluate different Technologies in respect of Rural Roads and to take up pilot projects involving different technologies.

o. To enter into collaboration with Institutions, Agencies

or Bodies of repute, both national and international, in respect of Rural Roads.

p. To arrange suitable Training Programmes for *officers* of the Ministry as well as the State Governments or Union Territories concerned with the implementation of the Rural Roads Programme in reputed institutions.

q. To advise on measures to improve the Quality and Cost-norms of the Rural Roads.

r. To publish books, literature, take up or arrange for production of publicity material, print, audio or audio-visual in respect of the *Pradhan Mantri Gram Sadak Yojana.*

s. To organise and sponsor Workshops and Seminars in respect of Rural Roads.

t. To purchase, lease and hire equipment or machinery required in the construction of Rural Roads.

u. To take up such activities as necessary to further the objective of the Programme and assist the Ministry of Rural Development in Planning and Implementation of the *Pradhan Mantri Gram Sadak Yojana* and such other related Programmes as may be taken up.

5. Pursuant to the aforesaid objectives, the Agency -

   i. shall be a compact, professional and multi-disciplinary body and the personnel will be obtained or engaged on deputation or hired on contract basis. There will be no permanent appointment to the NRRDA.

   ii. will draw Monitors from different Disciplines, States, Union Territories and other Organisations (Public Sector or Private Sector), on part-time basis, for some days in a month, to serve as Independent Monitors.

   iii. may do all such other acts and things, either alone or in conjunction with other organizations or persons, as the National Rural Roads Development Agency may consider necessary, incidental or conducive to the attainment of the objectives mentioned above.

The Agency may raise funds by way of the following:-

Grants-in-aid by the Central Government.

a. Contributions from other sources.

The names, occupations and address of the first members of the General Body are as follows:

Name	Occupation & Address	Designation in the NRRDA
Shri M. Venkaiah Naidu	Minister of Rural Development Government of India, Krishi Bhavan, New Delhi	President
Shri Arun Bhatnagar	Secretary, Ministry of Rural Development, Government of India Krishi Bhavan, New Delhi	Vice-President
3. Shri Lalit Mathur	Additional Secretary & Financial Advisor, Ministry of Rural Development, Government of India Krishi Bhavan, New Delhi	Member
Dr. J. S. Sarma	Joint Secretary, Ministry of Rural Development, Government of India Krishi Bhavan, New Delhi	Director-General
Shri Sunil Kumar	Director, Ministry of Rural Development, Government of India Krishi Bhavan, New Delhi	Member
Shri R. P. Nath	Director, Ministry of Rural Development Krishi Bhavan, New Delhi	Member
Shri Shahabuddin Ahmad	Deputy Secretary, Ministry of Rural Development Krishi Bhavan, New Delhi	Member

It is acknowledged and admitted by all concerned that the National Rural Roads Development Agency is established by the Ministry of Rural Development, Government of India in public interest. In case, if necessary, the Agency can be dissolved as per the provisions laid down under Section 13 and 14 of the Societies Registration Act, 1860. We, the several members, whose names and address are given below, having associated ourselves for the purpose described in this Memorandum of Association, do hereby subscribe our names to this Memorandum of Association and set out several and respective hands hereunto and form ourselves into Society under the Societies Registration Act, 1860 on this day, the 10th of January, 2002.

Name, Address & Occupation of Members	Signature of Members
Shri M. Venkaiah Naidu, Minister of Rural Development, Government of India, Krishi Bhavan, New Delhi	
Shri Arun Bhatnagar, Secretary, Ministry of Rural Development, Government of India, Krishi Bhavan, New Delhi	
Shri Lalit Mathur, Additional Secretary & Financial Advisor, Ministry of Rural Development, Government of India, Krishi Bhavan, New Delhi	
Dr. J. S. Sarma, Joint Secretary, Ministry of Rural Development, Government of India, Krishi Bhavan, New Delhi	
Shri Sunil Kumar, Director, Ministry of Rural Development, Government of India, Krishi Bhavan, New Delhi	
Shri R. P. Nath, Director, Ministry of Rural Development, Krishi Bhavan, New Delhi	
Shri Shahabuddin Ahmad, Deputy Secretary, Ministry of Rural Development, Government of India, Krishi Bhavan, New Delhi	

RULES AND REGULATIONS

a.1. The Rules and regulations be called the Rules of National Rural Roads Development Agency. These Rules shall come into force from the date on which the Agency, namely the National Rural Roads Development Agency, is registered under the Societies Registration Act, 1860.

Short title and commencement

a. 2. 'Agency' means the National Rural Roads Development Agency

b. 'General Body' means the General Body of the National Rural Roads Development Agency.

c. 'President' means the President of the General Body of the National Rural Roads Development Agency.

d. 'Vice President' means the Vice President of the National Rural Roads Development Agency.

e. 'Director-General' means the Director General of the National Rural Roads Development Agency.

'Year' means, unless the context otherwise requires, the financial year of the Government of India.

Definitions

3. The registered office of the National Rural Roads Development Agency shall be situated at 552-A, Krishi Bhavan, New Delhi-110001.

Headquarters of the Agency

4. The number of Members of the Agency shall not exceed 21. The Members of the Agency shall be nominated by the Members of President. The membership of the Agency will be from the following:-

i. Representatives of Central, State Governments or any other Government authority as Ex-officio Members.

ii. Registered bodies, Institutions engaged in any activity connected with Rural Roads or any of the objectives of the National Rural Roads Development Agency.

Persons possessing special expertise, ability or experience

relevant to the furtherance of the objectives of the Agency. The representation may be by name or designation, as may be deemed appropriate.

Members of the Agency

5. Where a person becomes a Member of the Agency by virtue of the office or appointment which he/she holds, his/her Membership of the Agency shall stand terminated when he/she ceases to hold that office or appointment.

Termination of ex-officio membership

6. Membership of Members, other than ex-officio Members, Membership of Members, other than ex-officio Members, following events:-

i. on the expiry of the period of Membership for which nominated;
ii. death, resignation, insolvency, lunacy or conviction for a criminal offence involving moral turpitude; when a Member does not attend three-consecutive meetings of the General Body without proper leave of absence.

Termination of membership of others

a. 7. Subject to the other provisions, a Member of the Agency, other than ex-officio Members, shall hold office for a period of two years from the date of his nomination and shall be eligible for re-nomination by the President.

If a casual vacancy exists during the two year period, such vacancy shall be filled in like manner as the original vacancy and the admitted Member shall hold office for the unexpired portion of the term.

Terms of Membership

8. When a Member desires to resign his/her membership of the Agency, he/she shall forward his/her letter of resignation to the President.

Resignation

9. The Agency shall function notwithstanding any vacancy in any of its bodies and no act, direction or proceeding of the Agency

shall be invalid merely by reason of such vacancy or any defect in the appointment of any of its Members.

VALIDATION OF ACTS

Authorities of the Agency

10. The following shall be the authorities of the Agency:-

i. General Body
ii. President
iii. Vice-President
iv. Executive Committee
v. Director General

Such other officers of the Agency as the General Body may from time to time appoint.

GENERAL BODY

11. There shall be a General Body of the Agency and it shall be composed of all the Members of the Agency.

12. The General Body shall meet normally once in 6 months but at least once every year, on such date, time and place as may be determined by the President. It shall also be open to the President to call for an Extraordinary Meeting.

13. All Meetings of the General Body shall be called by Notice in writing by and under the hand of the Director General.

a. Every Notice calling a Meeting of the General Body shall state the date, time and place of the Meeting and shall be delivered or sent by post to every Member of the Agency normally 15 clear days before the day appointed for the Meeting.

Any inadvertent omission to give notice to or the non-receipt or late receipt of notice by any Members shall not invalidate the proceedings of the Meetings and proof that the envelope containing such notices was properly addressed and duly posted will be sufficient proof of such notice.

14. The General Body shall have following powers and functions, namely to:

i. give over- all Policy Guidelines and directions for efficient functioning of the Agency
ii. approve the Annual Plan of Action including the Annual Budget for functioning of the Agency
iii. consider the Balance Sheet and Audited Accounts for the previous financial year
iv. add and amend the Rules of the Agency
v. frame, bye-laws not inconsistent with these Rules, for the regulation of the business of the Agency
vi. monitor the functioning of the Agency
vii. approve of the Annual Report of the Agency
viii. determine the staff strength and the terms and conditions of service of personnel to be appointed by the Agency
ix. appoint the Principal Technical Agencies and determine the tasks to be performed by them delegate such of its powers to other authorities of the Agency as it may consider necessary and proper.

PRESIDENT

a. 15. The Union Minister incharge of the Ministry / Department dealing with the Agency shall be the ex-officio President of the Agency.

b. In case the votes for and against a particular issue are equal the President shall exercise his casting vote.

The President shall be entitled to invite any other person to attend the Meetings of the Agency but such person(s) shall have no power of voting.

a. 16. The President shall preside over the Meetings of the General Body. In his absence the Vice President shall preside over the Meetings.

b. The President shall nominate Members to the General Body.

c. The President shall exercise the powers of the General Body of the Agency in the interregnum between two Meetings of the General Body. All decisions taken by the President, acting in such capacity, shall be placed in the next Meeting of the General Body for ratification.

The President may, in writing, delegate such of the powers, as he may consider necessary, to the Vice-President or the Director-General.

VICE-PRESIDENT

a. 17. The Secretary incharge of the Ministry / Department dealing with the Agency shall be the ex-officio Vice-President of the Agency.

b. In the absence of the President, the Vice-President shall preside over the Meetings of the General Body.

The Vice President shall exercise such powers and perform such duties as President may delegate him.

EXECUTIVE COMMITTEE

18. There shall be an Executive Committee of the Agency and shall comprise of the following Members:

i. Director-General - Ex-officio Chairman.

ii. Five Members to be appointed by the President, of which one shall be Finance Member and the remaining four shall be from among the Principal Technical Agencies,

Such officials of the Agency, not exceeding two, to be nominated by the President.

19. The Executive Committee shall meet as often as is necessary but at least once in two months.

a. 20. All meetings of the Executive Committee shall be called by notice in writing by and under the hand of the Director General.

b. Every notice calling a meeting of the Executive Committee shall state the date, time and place of the meeting of the Executive Committee normally seven clear days before the day appointing for Meeting.

c. The Chairman may, in special circumstances, call a Meeting at a notice shorter than seven days.

Any inadvertent omission to give notice of the nonreceipt or late receipt of notice by any member shall not invalidate the proceedings of the meeting.

21. The powers and functions of the Executive Committee shall be as follows:

a. Subject to the general control and supervision of the General Body, the Executive Committee shall generally pursue and carry out objectives of the Agency as set forth in the Memorandum of Association.

b. The Executive Committee shall exercise all executive and financial powers of the Agency, subject to such directions as may be issued by the Government of India and General Body from time to time.

c. In particular and without prejudice to the generality of the foregoing provisions, the Executive Committee shall have the power to

i. Prepare and execute detailed plans and programmes for the furtherance of the objectives of the Agency.

ii. To consider the annual and supplementary budgets placed before it and pass them with such modifications as may be deemed necessary, for submission to the general body.

iii. Prepare annual report and accounts of the society for the consideration of the General Body.

iv. Appoint staff as per strength sanctioned by the General Body.

v. Appoint the State Technical Agencies and determine the tasks to be performed by them.

vi. To Monitor the progress of road works and expenditure incurred by the States/ Union Territories under Pradhan Mantri Gram Sadak Yojana.

vii. To appoint Independent Monitors to inspect and report on the Quality of road-works.

viii. To take up research activities relating to Rural Roads, including execution of pilot projects by appropriate Technical Institutions.

ix. To engage the services of Technical Experts as and when necessary.

x. To arrange suitable Training Programmes for officers of the Ministry as well as the State Governments and Union Territories concerned with the implementation of the Rural Roads Programme in reputed institutions.

xi. Receive and to have custody of the funds of the Society and manage the property of the Society.

xii. Incur expenditure, subject to the provisions of the approved budget.

xiii. Enter for, and on behalf of the Agency, into Agreements.

xiv. Lay down terms and conditions governing scholarships, deputations, consultancy, grantsin- aid, research schemes and projects.

xv. 14 Enter into arrangements with the Government of India and, through the Government with foreign and international agencies and organisations, the State Government and other Public or Private bodies, or organisations or individuals, provided that nothing shall be inconsistent with the objectives of the Society or the policy of the Government of India.

xvi. Appoint sub-committees, and panels consisting of persons who may or may not be the Members or employees of the Agency to deal with any matter and make recommendations thereon.'

xvii. Impose and recover fee and charges for the services rendered by the Agency.

xviii. Make deposits in Scheduled Commercial Banks.

xix. Consider any other matter deemed fit by the General Body/ President.

The EC may delegate any of its powers to the Director General or any officer of the Agency.

Director-General

a. 22. The Joint Secretary in Government of India dealing with Rural Connectivity and the Agency shall, exofficio be the Director General of the National Rural Roads Development Agency.

He shall Chair all the Meetings of the Executive Committee.

a. The Director General shall see that affairs of the Agency are run efficiently and in accordance with the provisions of the Memorandum of Association, Rules and Regulations and by-laws of the Agency.

b. The Director General shall preside over the Meetings of the Executive Committee.

c. The Director General may call a meeting of the Executive Committee at any time.

d. The Director General shall exercise such financial powers as are delegated by the Executive Committee.

e. The Director General shall be the Appointing Authority for all the posts sanctioned by the General Body, on deputation, contract or part-time basis to the Agency.

f. The Director General shall be entitled to invite any other persons to attend the Meeting of the Executive Committee.

g. The Director General shall exercise the powers of the Executive Committee of the Agency in the interregnum between two Meetings of the Executive Committee. All decisions taken by the Chairman, acting in such capacity shall be placed in the next Meeting of the Executive Committee for ratification.

The Director General may, in writing, delegate such of the powers, as he may consider necessary, to any officer of the Agency.

FUNDS OF THE AGENCY

The funds of the Agency shall consist of the following:

a. Grants made by the Ministry of Rural Development, Government of India;

b. Fees and charges imposed by the Agency for services rendered by it;

c. Income from Deposits;

d. Income and receipts from other sources; and

Such other funds as may be received by the Agency.

The bankers of the Agency shall be any Scheduled Commercial Bank.

AUDIT OF ACCOUNTS

The Agency shall cause regular accounts to be kept of its money. The Accounts shall be maintained in such form as may be applicable to Central Government Accounts. The Accounts of the Agency shall be audited annually by a Chartered Accountant and the Officers of the Comptroller & Auditor General of India.

The Chartered Accountant or the Auditor shall have the right to demand the production of books, accounts, connected vouchers and other necessary documents and papers.

The results of Audit shall be communicated by the Auditor to the General Body of the Agency, who shall submit a copy of the Audit Report along with its observations to the Ministry/ Department of the Government of India, dealing with the Agency. The Auditor shall also forward a copy of the report direct to the Ministry/Department of the Government of India dealing with the Agency.

ANNUAL REPORT

The Annual Report of the working of the Agency and all work undertaken during the year, together with Balance Sheet and Audited Accounts, shall be prepared by the Executive Committee for information of the General Body and the Ministry of Rural Development. A draft of the Annual Report along with the Audited Accounts of the Agency, and the Auditor's Report thereon, shall be placed before the General Body in its Annual Meeting.

AMENDMENTS

With prior approval of the Ministry of Rural Development, Government of India, the Agency may alter, extend or abridge the purpose for which it is established, or to amalgamate the Agency either wholly or partly with any other Agency in accordance with the provisions of the Societies Registration Act, 1860, as applicable to Delhi.

The Rules of the Agency may at any time be altered by a Resolution passed by a majority of the Members of the General Body, present and voting, at a Meeting of the General Body convened for the purpose.

The Agency may with prior approval of the Ministry of Rural Development, Government of India, change its name by a resolution passed by majority of the members of the General Body, present and voting, at a Meeting of the General Body convened for the purpose.

As and when there is any change in the nomenclature of the Ministry/Ministries, Department(s), Institution(s) and designation(s) mentioned in the Rules, such change(s) shall automatically stand incorporated in these Rules and it shall not be treated as an amendment of the Rules under Rule 26 above. If, on the winding up or dissolution of the Agency, there shall remain, after the satisfaction of all its debts and liabilities, any property whatsoever, the same shall not be paid to, or distributed among, the Members of the Agency or any of them, but shall accrue to the Government of India by escheat.

MISCELLANEOUS

Every officer of the Agency shall be indemnified out of the funds of the Agency against all losses and expenses incurred in the discharge of his duties except such as shall happen through his/her own neglect, willful act or default and such one shall be answerable only for his/her own acts, neglect or defaults and not for those of any other person. Once in every year a list of Members of the General Body shall be filed with the Registrar of Societies required under Section 4 of the Societies Registration Act, 1860. The Agency may sue or be sued in the name of the Administrative Officer, NRRDA as per provisions laid down under Section 6 of the Societies Registration Act, 1860. All the provisions of the Societies Registration Act, 1860 (Punjab Amendment Act, 1957) as extended to the Union Territory of Delhi will apply to this Agency. In case, if necessary, the Agency can be dissolved as per the provisions laid down under Section 13 and 14 of the Societies Registration Act, 1860. Certified that this is the correct copy of the Rules and Regulations of the Society.

NEW INITIATIVES

The Rural Road Programme has established several new standards in its endeavour to construct roads of highest possible quality. The new initiatives taken as part of the PMGSY programme include the following.

Formulation of District Rural Roads Plan

For the first time systematic District Rural Roads Plans have been prepared listing out the complete network of all roads in the district i.e., Village Roads, Major District Roads, State Roads and National Highways.

Rural Roads Manual

The original Manual, called Manual on Route Location, Design, Construction and Maintenance of Rural Roads was brought out by the Indian Roads Congress as a publication in 1979 (IRC: SP:20-1979). Following the launch of the PMGSY, the Ministry of Rural Development constituted 3 Committees in January 2001 to go into various aspects of rural road construction and the manuals on these different aspects brought out by the committees were combined into a separate'Rural Roads Manual' and published as an IRC publication (IRC:SP 20-2002) in supercession of earlier manual. This Manual is now the basis of all works under the PMGSY.

Implementation of concept of Core Network

The concept of Core Network has been operationalised for the first time in order to focus on the set of roads which are considered essential to provide connectivity to all habitations of the desired size. The Core Network will be the basic instrumentality for prioritisation of construction and allocation of funds for maintenance. It is proposed to develop GIS-based applications to further enhance the utility of the Core Network.

Standard Bidding Documents

To standardise the PMGSY works tendering process in the States, a Standard Bidding Document is being published.

Book of Specifications and Standard Data Book

In order to streamline the process of estimating and standardise contracts, a separate Book of Specification and Standard Data Book is being prepared for rural roads. This will replace the present publication brought out by the Ministry of Roads and Highways, and will be in consonance with the Rural Roads Manual.

Computerised Online management of construction

For the first time a nation-wide programme is being managed and monitored online. Special application software has been developed by C-DAC which envisages that the DPIUs will upload the data regarding the road proposals and construction progress comprising both physical and financial data on to the PMGSY website. The site data will be used for decision making, and in due course for transactional decisions, monitoring and analysis.

Use of new technology and materials

Rural Roads have been a neglected sector. The focus given to it through the PMGSY is now enabling the channelisation of R&D efforts to this sector. Use of cement concrete, modified bitumen, fly ash as well as soil stabilisation techniques and other new methodologies, is now one of the thrust areas of the Programme.

Quality consciousness

The execution of programme has brought to light that rural road sector required enormous emphasis on quality control and management if the effort is to succeed. A 3-tier quality control system has been put in place including 2 level of independent quality monitoring. For the first time concerted effort is being made to ensure that testing facilities at the contractors level and executing agency level is brought to a high standard that enables measurement of quality at site. Quality Control Handbook has been published for specific application to rural roads construction.

Outsourcing of technical inputs

In order to manage the programme at the national level and yet ensure that adequate technical inputs are locally available for planning and execution of rural roads programme, an elaborate structure consisting of Principal Technical Agencies (national level technical institutions) as well as State Technical Agencies (regional level technical institutions) has been successfully brought into the framework of the programme planning and execution through a Government – academia partnership.

Additional funding

In order to generate additional resources for the programme discussions have been held with the World Bank and ADB both of whom have agreed in principle to fund the Rural Roads Programme. Funding is likely to commence in late 2003-2004.

9

District Rural Development Agency: ANGUL

The India lives in its villages . Govt. therefore accords high priority for Rural development . DRDA is the bed rock for implementation and supervision of anti-poverty, wage employment , rural housing programmes etc. of Ministry of Rural development , Govt. of India. DRDA,Angul started functioning w.e. from 02.07.1993 as a society registered under the Provisions of SRA (Soceities Registration Act,1860). Both district level officials and public representative like M.P. , MLA ,Panchayat Samiti Chairpersons etc are the member of the Society. President, Zilla Parisad is the Ex-Officio Chairman of DRDA. All administrative and financial power are vested on Collector. The Project Director of the Agency looks after day to day administrartion. DRDA releases funds under various anti poverty programmes under Ministry of Rural Development,govt. of India and State Govt. to various banks / executing agencies. It monitors the implementation of schemes, utilization of fund very closely. Following important schemes are implementated through DRDA.

SGSY

Poverty is an obstruction to a dignified life. A life of dignity is the right of every citizen. Self-employment is a significant step to have sustained incomes and remove the shackles of poverty. Earlier programme like IRDP was not adequate to meet all the requirements. Government have introduced a Self-Employment Programme- Swarnajayanti Gram Swarojagar Yojana or SGSY with effect from 1.4.1999.Under SGSY assistance is given to the poor families living below the poverty line in rural areas for taking up self-employment. The persons taking up self employment are called "Swarojagaries". The may take up activities either individually or group, called Self-Help groups.

RURAL HOUSING SCHEME

Every one would like to have a roof that they can call their own . Government has recognized shelter as a basic human requirement, To fulfil this objective under Rural Housing Schemes IAY, PMGY(GA) are being implementated through DRDA. 10310 houses under IAY sanctioned by Gvt. Of India are being implemented in Blocks affected by flood/ heavy rain 2001.

SGRY

The objectives of the SGRY are to provide additional wage employment in all rural areas and thereby provide food security and improve nutritional levels. The second objective is for creation of durable community and social economic assets and infrastructural development in rural areas.

This scheme is opened to all rural poor who are in need of wage employment in and around their village/ habitation. This scheme is being implemented under two streams i.e. Stream-I and Stream-II . Stream I is being implemented at the district and Panchayat Samity level. Funds and food grains available under the first stream are distributed between the Panchayat Samitties and Zilla Parishad . The second stream is being implemented at the village Panchayat level and the funds and food grains are earmarked for the Panchayats .

WATERSHED

Agriculture is the main stay of Indian economy. Land and water therefore, are of critical importance. Vas tracks of the land are degraded but can be brought under plough with some efforts. Such lands are known as wastelands. Productivity of this land is very low and people owning these lands are poor and their source of living is wage employment. Redressing of these lands is regarded as powerful tool of taking the issue of poverty and backwardness.

Government of India have therefore launched Integrated Water Shed Development programme. In our district 2 Watershed projects under IWDP i.e. Angul-I and Angul-II are under progress.

These schemes are mainly meant of poor people, living below poverty line . The poor people are identified through a survey known as BPL survey, at the begning of each five year plan. The last survey was conducted in the year 1997 and 120608 nos of people were identified to be living below the poverty line (BPL) in rural areas. It constitutes 59 % of the rural population.

Presently a survey is underway to identify people living below the poverty line (PL). This survey utilizes 13 parameters such access to drinking water, land holding, education status of the household etc.

TALCHER ANGUL DEVELOPMENT AUTHORITY

With establishment of industries like FCI, NALCO & TTPS and expansion of local mining activities , Govt. of Orissa fell the need for development of Talcher – Angul area in a planned manner. Hence the provision of the Orissa Town Planning & Improved Trust Act,1956 were enforced over 231 revenue villages of Angul , Talcher and Motonga Police stationin Nov'1982. Talcher Angul Meramandali Regional Improvement Trust (TAMRIT) was constituted having the jurisdiction over the area w.e. from 1st July'1983. The area of operation is spred over 451 sq km. Initially the headquater of the Trust was located at Dhenkanal. Subsequently the office was shifted to Angul on 01.01.1986.

The responsibility of the Trust was to prepare a comprehensive Master Plan of the area , prevent unauthorized constructions and take up various developmental activities such as housing scheme TAMRIT developed a housing colony with 238 houses at Angul in the year 1993. TAMRIT was renamed as Talcher Angul Development Authority (TADA) w.e.from 1.9.1995. TADA has plans to develop two sites and services schemes and a new bus stand at Angul.

DISTRICT URBAN DEVELOPMENT AGENCY (D.U.D.A.)

District Urban Development Agency , Angul has been registered vide Registration No. ANL-190/39 of 95-95 dt.12.5.94.

It is the coordinating agency at district level for formulating different developmental schemes in urban areas. The following schemes/programmes are being implemented under the supervision of DUDA.

Swarna Jayanti Sahari Rojgar Yojana, which is currently in operation with effect from 1.12.97 is an substitution of the earlier programmes like Urban Basic Services for the Poor (UBSP), Prime Minister Integrated Urban Poverty Eradication Yojana(NRY), Environmental Improvement of Urban Slums (EIUs). Under the scheme SJSRY, the following programmes are being implemented in all the ULBs of this district.

- Community structure (Information Education and Communication (IEC) Component.
- Urban Self Employment Programme (USEP)(subsidy)
- Development of Women and Children in Urban Areas (DWCUA)
- Thrift and Credit Society
- Urban Wage Employment Programme(UWEP)
- U.S.E.P (Skill upgradation Training)
- Administration and Office expenses (A & O.E.)

POUDI BHUYAN DEVELOPMENT AGENCY (P.B.D.A),PALLAHARA

The micro project named Paudi Bhuyan Development Agency was constituted by State Government vide Notification No.7176/ HTW dated 16.03.1978 it has been registered under Society Registration Act 1860 bearing registration No. 13329 of 1978-79. The project area comprises 5 G.Ps (Nagira, Bandhabhuin, Saida, Seegarh & Pechamundi) covering 27 villages. The project is spread over 188 sq.Kms. The responsibility of this Agency is to take up projects for the socio economic development of Paudi Bhuyan Primitive Tribes, so that they will cross the poverty line.

State of Rural Healthcare in India-NRHM Report

India's rural health centers are critically short of trained medical personnel. The country's 22,669 primary health centers are in sorry state of affairs increasing people's suffering. According to the recent National Rural Health Mission report nearly 8% PHC don't have a doctor while nearly 39% were running without a lab technician and about 17.7% without a pharmacist. The PHCs are supposed to have one medical officer supported by paramedical staff.

To compound the problem PHCs in some states donot have adequate labour rooms and operation theatres.While not a single of UP's 3,660 PHCs have either a labour room or an operation theatre,the number stands at 208 labour rooms (13%) and 218(13%) OTs in Bihar's 1,641 PHCs,105 (20%) Lrs and 50 (10%)O Ts in Chattisgarh's 518 PHCs and 131 (4%) LR s and 108 (12%) O Ts in Kerala's 909 PHCs.

The condition of 3,910 community health centers supposed to provide specialized medical care is equally appalling.Out of the sanctioned posts, about 59.4% of surgeons,45% of obstetricians and gynaecologists,61.1% of physicians and 53.8% of pediatricians were found to be vacant.Moreover there is a shortfall of 70.2% specialists at the CHCs. The report says there is a huge challenge to meet the shortfall for rural health infrastructure specially the manpower.

According to Planning Commission figures India's CHCs require 3,910 surgeons. While only 2,372 are sanctioned, just 972 are in position creating a vacancy of 1,381 posts for surgeons and a shortfall of 2,376 surgeons in CHCs.As for physicians CHCs require 3,910 of them. There are only 832 in position with 1,296 vacant posts and a shortfall of 2,516 physicians. Of the 3,910 pediatricians required only 1,951 posts are sanctioned of which just 837 are in position. There is a vacancy of 953 posts and a shortfall of 2,511 pediatricians.

Chronic Poverty in India

India is the second largest country in the world by population (after China), and one of the largest in area. Many Indian states are larger than most countries in Asia or Africa. The Indian vision of 'development' has been extremely influential. Its struggle for independence that helped precipitate the end of European colonial administration across Asia and Africa; its mixture of planned and market economic strategies steered a course between the Cold

War superpowers' geopolitics; and now its economic boom is felt across the world. Since independence, the country has made great progress in reducing poverty and improving human development indicators, and is now classed as a middle income country with a per capita GDP of $2892 in 2003 (UN figures).

Nevertheless, it is also a country of huge inequalities, and it is estimated that there are from 78 to 130 million people in India living in chronic poverty. The Millennium Development Goals and India's Plan targets (in particular those relating to poverty ratios, education and gender) cannot be met without addressing chronic poverty. Chronic poverty analysis matters for policy-makers because policies designed to assist the transitorily poor may not be effective for those trapped in chronic poverty. Also, the chronically poor are a heterogeneous group, and policies targeted at them will thus also need to be varied.

Who are the chronically poor in India?

There are many processes driving and maintaining chronic poverty in India. However, some broad characteristics, which most chronically poor peoplewill experience some of, can be identified.

Casual labour: a great many of the chronically poor are not excluded from the economy, but included on adverse terms. Insecure employment, low wages and poor working conditions trap people in poverty. Casual labour is on the increase in India: 41% of all households reported casual labour as their main income source in 1999-2000, and there are around 132 million rural casual labourers. Casual labour is strongly associated with household poverty: many casual labourers never emerge sustainably from poverty.

Persistently poor states: Uttar Pradesh (and Uttarakhand), Bihar (and Jharkand), Madhya Pradesh (and Chattisgarh) and Orissa are states having persistent and severe poverty and the majority of India's most deprived districts. Adverse land relations inherited from feudalism and the zamindari system, political instability and upper caste domination of political power, poor green revolution performance and weak infrastructure have all combined to reproduce this pattern.

Remote Rural Areas: Nevertheless, chronic poverty exists in every state in India, with "pockets" in even relatively wealthy or low-poverty-rate states such as Maharashtra, Andhra Pradesh or Tamil Nadu. Rural areas poorly connected to urban centres are associated with particular problems.

Remote forested areas often form such pockets of chronic poverty. Despite rich natural resource bases, a combination of physical isolation and entitlement failures – of access to these resources, to information, to wider markets and public services and to anti-poverty programmes - maintain many tribal people in chronic poverty. Environmental degradation or climate change may emerge as additional factors maintaining those poor households most dependent on natural resources in chronic poverty.

Many dryland areas are sites of livelihood insecurity. Both commercialisation of agriculture and out-migration have helped households cope, and indeed contributed to growth and poverty reduction. But there is a danger that pressure on water tables and recipient-area economies could block these mechanisms and increase chronic poverty.

Social status: Despite progress in some areas, members of Scheduled Tribes (ST) and Scheduled Castes (SC) remain disproportionately poor. Evidence also suggests that ST face particular challenges (linked to remote rural area problems) in escaping poverty. But social status factors affect others too, in particular, women. Evidently not all women are poor, but discrimination expressed in many areas of life, from labour markets to intra-household decision-making, makes many women especially vulnerable to poverty and makes it harder for poor women to escape from poverty. Other social categories that are often linked to poverty and discrimination include "life-cycle" categories – old age or childhood, and certain forms of ill-health, such as physical disability, HIV/AIDS, leprosy or mental illness.

Household composition: Household size by itself does not appear to be statistically associated with greater likelihood of chronic poverty. But chronically poor people do tend to live in households with a greater number of dependents (e.g. children), or lesser access to the labour market (e.g. with more women).

Multi-dimensional deprivation: chronic poverty is related to nutrition and food insecurity, ill-health (including environmental health) and lack of social well-being as well as income. There is a higher incidence of chronic illnesses among the poor, who are particularly vulnerable to health "shocks". The various dimensions of poverty can become mutually reinforcing over time, e.g. ill-health often undermines income earning capacity, leading to undernutrition, inability to afford access to healthcare, and further health deterioration.

How do chronically poor people exit poverty?

Just as there are many drivers of chronic poverty, so other processes can interrupt chronic poverty. People have found a variety of routes to avail themselves of economic opportunities and exit poverty. Analysis of panel data on rural households highlights a few key themes:

- Owning land: those poor households who have managed to retain some land are more likely to exit poverty (in urban areas, other assets - perhaps housing security or education - may be more important);
- Migration is more often of member(s) of a household rather than the whole household, to urban areas for better employment opportunities, especially where prior information and contacts can reduce costs and increase benefits;
- Greater village level infrastructure and district urbanisation, is associated with a higher rate of household exits from poverty, through greater connection to economic opportunity (especially labour markets).

POLICY ON CHRONIC POVERTY

Government Approaches

There has been a vast array of Government of India anti-poverty policies since independence. Policymaking has been informed by three main views of the causes of, and best approaches to combating poverty. Structuralist theories have suggested efforts to redistribute productive resources and break down social barriers; another approach views this as problematic, and focuses on extending growth into marginalised areas and population sectors. A third highlights the multi-dimensional deprivations of poverty and calls for social security measures, both to address these deprivations themselves and support poor people's participation in growth.

The major anti-poverty programmes represent a mix of all these approaches. They can be grouped into six categories:

1. Land distribution and land reforms;
2. Area-based approaches for community and rural development, focusing on marginal and small farmers, and areas with particular problems e.g. those that are drought-prone;
3. Individual-based targeted approaches, providing access to productive capital and skills among the poor, including vulnerable groups like women, SC, ST and the landless;
4. Social security or safety-net programmes, comprising the National Social Assistance Programme (which includes the National Old Age Pension Scheme (NOAPS)), employment and self-employment programmes and relief works, distribution of commodities like food (Public Distribution System (PDS) and others), clothing, housing for the poor and the vulnerable groups;
5. Special schemes for education among socially marginalised groups such as Scheduled Castes and Tribes, subsidised primary education, midday meals in school and special nutrition and health care programmes for women and children;
6. Reservation policies, in employment, education and political representation, for particular groups.

Policies in Action

India's anti-poverty programmes in total amount to some 6-7 per cent of total Government of India budgetary expenditure, or 1 per cent of GDP (IBRD, 2000). Poverty rates have declined and there have been notable successes – e.g. the building of a social contract around famine prevention. Despite this, there remains a chasm between official policies on the one hand, and the experience of the poor on the other. In terms of technical policy design, while all the policy approaches outlined earlier contain useful insights, a disaggregated and dynamic analysis is generally lacking in all of them: weakening their effectiveness at engaging with the specific processes that drive people into poverty, or enable them to escape, in particular contexts.

Policy on poverty has tended to become part of a political economy that proliferates 'doles', which often exist more to allow political power bases to be consolidated than to help the poor. Thus, while there has been poverty reduction, anti-poverty budget increases have not made the contribution that was hoped for; and the targeting of anti-poverty programmes is poorly handled, producing both errors of inclusion and exclusion.

State level implementation of programmes and the performance of Panchayati Raj institutions, has also been variable. In some cases, alliances that include some chronically poor groups have had success, in others lack of financial resources or patronage politics have weakened and distorted implementation. Structural maintainers of chronic poverty, especially unequal distribution of land and social hierarchies, remain powerful. State and sub-state political economy also often leads to poor performance of rural development schemes which are notoriously prone to "leakage" into a bureaucrat-contractor-village leader nexus, restricting their potential to boost agricultural growth.

However, some progress on these problems can be observed. Electoral competition has driven government to focus on poverty more recently. And movements at the grassroots, such as the Mazdoor Kisan Shakti Sanghathan (MKSS) in Rajasthan and other "right to information" campaigns, have played a part in extending and deepening democratic politics beyond urban and literate classes. In some areas they have exposed the corruption and inefficiency of poorly-performing schemes, even to the point of seeing corrupt officials pay back embezzled funds. At state and national level, anti-poverty programmes have been subject to redesign and change in recent years. For example, even in Orissa, which remains one of the poorest states in monetary terms, improvements in human development indicators such as child malnutrition, infant mortality and literacy have been achieved. Several schemes have undergone reforms, rationalisation and better targeting with a greater role for local government in implementation and for beneficiary selection and monitoring, a stress on transparency, making information available at the village level, and on social audits. This points to the tremendous positive potential of better central-local cooperation and the mobilisation of poorer people.

However, while these reforms are very welcome, there is still a long way to go. Structural factors constrain government's ability to bring about any rapid change, despite repeated attempts to implement land reform, anti-discrimination policies, etc. In several districts conflicts have erupted over land issues along caste-class lines.

Tenancy reform has helped poverty reduction in West Bengal, and tensions (generally) remain lower than in neighbouring Bihar. Across the country, poor people seeking to claim their rights and improve their situation – a key factor for poverty reduction – face great dangers. Violent reactions to political awakening and activity among sections of the poor continue to cause many tragedies.

Meanwhile, at the level of national policy debate, growth, while important, has perhaps sometimes been over-emphasised at the expense of specific policies for poverty reduction. Yet this is not inevitable. There are a number of promising policies and policy areas that government should consider, to stop the operation of the processes that drive people into poverty and maintain them there by blocking exit routes, and to increase the opportunities to exit. These are explored in several papers in the CPRC-IIPA working paper series and in the final section of CPRC Policy Brief 4, "Chronic poverty in India: policy responses".

The CPRC's Work in India

CPRC's Indian partners maintain a focus on measuring and understanding chronic poverty in the Indian context and providing a range of multi-dimensional solutions. Their work therefore covers a wide range of issues, including:

- Producing estimates of the extent of chronic poverty in India over the last several decades – the numbers of people in persistent poverty, and the incidence of entries into and exits from poverty - using panel data.

- Attempting to identify the factors driving impoverishment and maintaining people in poverty, and those facilitating exit
- Policy responses to chronic poverty and evaluating lessons from programmes and schemes.
- Understanding the characteristics and determinants of the uneven geographical distribution of poverty, with particular attention to remote rural areas, forested and tribal areas (notably in Orissa), and dryland areas, and work on potential policy responses
- Work on conceptualising 'multi-dimensional poverty' in an Indian context, Chronic poverty and agriculture in India, in particular casual labour, and the impact of technological change;
- Chronic poverty and conflict especially in Bihar and Manipur.
- Chronic Poverty and Socially Disadvantaged Groups especially the Scheduled Castes and Scheduled Tribes.
- Casual Labourers in Rural Areas and Changes in Wages
- Ill Health and entry into poverty, especially in the context of HIV/AIDS and its gendered impact.
- Best Practice in Escaping Poverty.
- Urban Poverty
- Economic Growth and Chronic Poverty
- Production of working papers, books and briefings covering all of these issues and more

10

Growth and Poverty in India—An Analysis of Interstate Differences

INTRODUCTION

The object of this paper is to analyse differences in poverty across states overtime in India. In doing so, it seeks to focus on inter-state differences in economic growth as an explanation. But it also considers other factors that might explain inter-state differences in the incidence of,or reduction in poverty overtime. Reduction of poverty has been the major goal of development planning in India since independence. But, with more than a quarter of India's population still living below the official poverty line (GOI 2001), ensuring a minimum standard of living for all its citizens still remains the greatest challenge before the nation.

The scope of the study is related to both rural and urban poverty across Indian States during the period from 1991 to 2001. Reducing poverty has been the prime focus of the Indian government and has received a great deal of attention in the country's economic agenda, beginning with the first five year plan adopted in 1951. However, progress has been highly uneven over time and space.

The structure of the paper is as follows. Section-II explain various measures of poverty and defines poverty line in India. Section III provides a brief review of the literature on the subject. Section IV sets out an analytical frame work and Section V draws results and finally, conclusions are discussed in Section VI.

Poverty: Concepts and Measures

In order to ascertain the determinants of poverty, it is imperative to explain how poverty is measured. In estimating poverty levels, defining a poverty line is the first step. A poverty line demarcates the poor from the non poor. It is identified as the minimum required consumption level of food, clothing, shelter, transport and healthcare. According to latest estimates of poverty released by government state specific poverty lines in 2004-05 are as given in Table 1.

Table-I:

State / UT's	Poverty lines (Rs per capita per month) 2004-05
Andhra Pradesh	542.89
Assam	378.84
Bihar	435.00
Chhatisgarh	560.00
Delhi	612.91
Goa	665.90
Gujarat	541.16
Haryana	504.49
Himachal Pradesh	504.49
Jammu & Kashmir	553.77
Jharkhand	451.24
Karnataka	599.66
Kerela	559.39
Madhya Pradesh	570.15
Maharashtra	665.90
Orrisa	528.49
Punjab	466.16
Rajasthan	559.63
Tamil Nadu	547.42
Uttar Pradesh	483.26
Uttarakhand	637.67
West Bengal	449.32
Dadra and Nagar Haveli	665.90
All India	538.60

Source: Economic Times ,22 March,07

The poverty ratio was 27.5 percent in 2004-05 as compared to 36 percent in 1993-94. The statistics of 2004-05 in comparison with that of 1999-2000 and 1993-94 are based on different consumer expenditure patterns.

Although, different measures of poverty are available we use headcount index which is defined as the percentage of population living in households with a per capita consumption below the poverty line.

Review of Literature

In the literature, there has been substantive discussion and debate on the determinants of poverty. Traditional focus in development thinking has been on how economic growth leads to poverty – reduction, as it increases per-capita real income levels to increase incomes of the poor. This is referred to as the "trickle down" effect of growth, which simply implies a vertical flow of income from the rich to the poor at a given rate (Kakwani and Pernia, 2000). In this process, the benefits of economic growth are reaped first by the rich, and subsequently by the poor once the rich starts spending their gains.

We can identify three mechanisms through which economic growth leads to poverty reduction. First, there is 'income effect' of growth, where the average income of the poor increases with growth. Second, economic growth leads to employment creation, which yields incomes for the poor to sustain their private consumption. Third, rapid growth has multiplier effects, which raise the returns to income –earning assets of the poor and sustain their consumption. (TN Srinivasan, 2000).

Yet, we may also consider the view that more rapid growth may possibly be associated with increases in poverty levels, atleast in the short run. This is best explained by simple arithmetic of poverty, inequality, and growth (Bourguignon, 2004).

In the recent times, there has been a significant shift in focus in the poverty literature away from the 'trickle down' concept of growth towards the idea of 'pro-poor' growth (Kakwani and Pernia, 2000). They define pro-poor growth as "growth that enables the poor to actively participate in, and significantly benefit from, economic activity". The ideal outcome of such a growth process should be that no person in society is deprived of the basic minimum needs.

At the macro level, the linkages between growth and poverty can be conceptualized in terms of the average productivity of the employed workforce, which gets reflected in the level of real wage or earning in self employment.

From these discussions it becomes necessary to identify and control factors which can reduce poverty directly, even if growth does not increase or which can improve the mapping of growth onto poverty.

(a) Public Expenditure

Public spending in India is divided into development and non-development spending with the former being important from the view point of poverty-reduction. (Fan, Hazell and Thorat, 1999).

Public development expenditure aids in poverty-reduction in two ways. First, public expenditure on poverty-alleviation programmes and social services could directly reduce poverty by raising private consumption. As table 2 shows expenditure for major employment programmes.

Table 2: Expenditure for Major Employment Programmes (Rs crores)

Year	Wage Employment					Self Employment				
	JRY	EAS	MWS	IAY	Total	IRDP	PMRY	KVIC	Total	Grand Total
1990-91	258.9	--	28	21.3	308.1	80.9	4.5	18.6	104	412.8
2000-01	220.6	126.1	213.2	243.2	803.1	46.5	20.2	--	66.7	869.8

Source : Planning Commission, 2001

Thus, including both wage employment and self employment programmes total expenditure went up from Rs. 412.1 crores to Rs. 869.763 crorers over the period, possibly contributing to the declining poverty ratio.

Note

JRY : Jawahar Rojgar Yojana; EAS: Employment Assurance Scheme; IAY : Indira Awas Yojna; IRDP : Integrated Rural Development Programme; PMRY: Prime Minister Rojgar Yojna; KVIC : Khadi and Village Industries Commission

(b) Human Resource Development

There is a need to combine human – resource development along with other growth promoting policies to formulate an effective anti-poverty strategy. Hence, in recent years, poverty has come to be viewed not only in terms of lack of adequate income, but as a state of deprivation of the poor, which prevents their effective participation in the growth process (UNDP, 2001). This has resulted in the renewed focus on development indicators in the area of education and health attainments. Dreze and Sen (2002) highlight the instrumental role of education in enabling people to make use of economic opportunities created by the growth process. The best example of this is Kerela where an extremely high literacy rate of about 90 percent has underlined India's most successful performance in rural poverty-reduction. On the other hand, Bihar, the largest Indian State in terms of long term where poverty reduction is also characterized by low literacy rate. Datt and Ravallion (1998) showed that initial levels of education affect the poverty reduction impact on growth.

(c) Infrastructure Development

Investment in physical infrastructure contributes significantly to the pursuit of socially inclusive development (Ali and Pernia, 2003). Physical infrastructure is directly concerned with the needs of such production sectors as industry, trade, agriculture etc and these services are used as inputs for production in the directly productive sectors. Physical infrastructure services such as irrigation, power, transport, telecommunication etc pave the way for higher economic growth of country.

(d) Socio –Political determinants

There is an increasing acceptance of the view that social institutions influence poverty–alleviation. Moreover, these factors could reinforce the transmission of economic growth to poverty reduction. It is argued that a reduction of gender disparity leads to an increase in the rate of economic growth, which, in turn, is poverty reducing. This is because greater gender equality enables women to take up income –earning opportunities, and participate in the growth process. Further more, gender inequality in access to education may hinder a reduction in fertility and infant mortality.

In sum, governments in India over the years have relied on 2 basic approaches to reduce poverty. The first is based on the expectation that the effects of economic growth would spread to all sections of society such that poverty –reduction is achieved alongside increases in economic growth. The second has relied on specific anti-poverty programmes. However, very few attempts have been made so far to test the impact of these programmes to check poverty levels.

Data Base and Methodology

The study is conducted at two points of the time (1991 and 2001), for the 14 major States in India. Our choice of years is defined by NSSO surveys from which we obtain estimates of poverty headcount ratio. During this period almost all the major states have seen a trend decline in poverty levels. In order to establish a relationship between poverty, reduction and various variables relating to infrastructure and human development, (the two prime factors of growth) an effort has been made to club these variables by taking the indexes of infrastructure and human development as developed by CMIE and Economic Survey of India. In our study we will analyse the relationship between poverty, infrastructure index, and human development index.

Table 3: Headcount Ratio of Poverty Levels by Major States

State	1990-91	2000-01
Andhra Pradesh	23.86	14.90
Bihar	53.52	40.83
Gujarat	27.63	12.85
Haryana	20.41	7.33
Karnatka	35.27	18.43
Kerela	28.43	11.33
Madhya Pradesh	42.79	36.64
Maharashtra	38.59	23.46
Orrisa	51.59	46.92
Punjab	12.46	5.53
Rajasthan	29.40	13.86
Tamil Nadu	38.98	19.41
Uttar Pradesh	41.15	29.77

West Bengal	39.93	25.80
All India	37.38	24.74
CV	32.25	55.67

Source: CSO (Different rounds of NSS survey) and Planning Commission, Govt of India, New Delhi

Table-4: Infrastructure Index for Different States

States	**1990-91**	**2001-01**
Andhra Pradesh	98	105.01
Bihar	97	86.85
Gujarat	124	88.76
Haryana	156	116.59
Karnatka	93	116.10
Kerela	138	188.43
Madhya Pradesh	72	100.18
Maharashtra	111	102.70
Orrisa	86	115.64
Punjab	211	144.18
Rajasthan	85	95.20
Tamil Nadu	139	154.08
Uttar Pradesh	117	115.16
West Bengal	115	111.14
All India	100	100
CV	29.60	22.89

Source: CMIE Basic Statistics, States, Sept 1994

Table-5: Human Development Index for different States of India

States	**1990-91**	**200-01**
Andhra Pradesh	98.95	88.14
Bihar	80.84	77.75
Gujarat	113.12	101.48
Haryana	116.27	107.84
Karnatka	108.14	101.27
Kerela	155.12	135.17
Madhya Pradesh	86.09	83.47

Maharashtra	118.64	110.81
Orrisa	90.55	85.59
Punjab	124.67	113.77
Rajasthan	91.08	89.83
Tamil Nadu	122.31	111.25
Uttar Pradesh	82.41	82.20
West Bengal	106.04	100
All India	100	100
CV	18.46	15.39

Source : Economic Survey of India, 2003-04 Govt of India, New Delhi

Table-6: Results of Regression Analysis

Equation 1		**P=f(IDI)**	
	Constant	Regression Coefficient	R^2
1990-91	P=60.448**(7.334)	- .221*(3.274)	.472
2000-01	P=41.487*(2.823)	-.167 N.S.(-1.365)	.134
Equation 2		**P=f(HDI)**	
	Constant	Regression Coefficient	R^2
1990-91	P=67.761*(4.574)	- .371*(2.218)	.302
2000-01	P=74.846*(4.336)	-.533*(-3.102)	.445

Equation 3		**P= (IDI, HDI)**		
	Constant	**Regression Coefficient**		**R^2**
		IDI	**HDI**	
1990-91	P=67.230*(5.095)	-.183*(-2.032)	-.106 NS(-.669)	.492
2000-01	78.186*(4.528)	+.178 NS(1.157)	-.778*(-2.871)	.505

* means significant at 5 percent level

** means significant at 1 percent level

N.S. means non significant

SECTION-V: RESULTS AND DISCUSSIONS

It became clear from table 3 that over the years poverty ratio which was found to be 37.38 percent in 1990-91 came down to 24.74 percent in 2000-01 at all India level. In case of states, in 1990-91, there were seven states which were having poverty ratio more than the national average. There were only five states in 2000-01 which has higher poverty ratio than the national average of (24.74 percent). Between 1990-91 and 2000-01, some states reduced poverty much faster than others. The coefficient of variation over these two time periods, however, signifies the fact that interstate differences in poverty ratio has increased overtime. The coefficient of variation which was 32.25 in 1990-91 increased to 55.67 in 2000-01. This increase in CV shows that inter-state differences in poverty reduction has increased overtime. Some progressive states have been able to reduce poverty more successfully as compared to the backward states. Table 4 shows the inter-state infrastructure index and it becomes clear from the table that this index was found to be highest in Punjab in 1990-91 (211) but in 2000-01, Kerela had the highest value of this index (188.43) followed by Tamil Nadu (154.08) and Punjab's position has gone down to third place (144.18). However, the lowest value of this index was found to be in case of the state of the M.P. in 1990-91 (72) whereas this value was minimum for the state of Bihar in the year 2000-01. The coefficient of variation for these two periods has declined from 29.60 in 1990-91 to 22.89 in 2000-01 showing that the inter-state differences in infrastructure index have been narrowing down overtime.

Similarly, Table 5 shows the inter-state human development index for two time periods 1990-91 and 2000-01. Kerela maintained the top position in both the periods with HDI value of 155.12 and 135.17 respectively. The coefficient of variation has fallen from 18.46 percent in 1990-91 to 15.39 percent in 2000-01, again indicating narrowing down of the inter-state differences in human resource development index among the various states in India.

The relationship between these three variables has been studied with the help of regression analysis.

The regression results for these three variables are shown in the table 6. In 1990-91, 47 percent of the variations in poverty are explained by infrastructure index and the coefficients of regression were found to be significant at 5 percent level. But in year 2000-01 the importance of infrastructure index in explaining variations in poverty has come down and the coefficient of regressions was found to be non-significant whereas, in case of second equation i.e. poverty and human development index the value of R^2 has improved from 0.302 in 1990-91 to 0.445 in 2000-01.

Moreover, the value of regression coefficient has also increased overtime and was also found to be significant. The results of multiple regressions also corroborate the same findings that in 1990-91 the role of infrastructure index was found to be more important in reducing poverty whereas afterwards it is human resource development index which has been playing a significant role in explaining variations in poverty. This notion acquired greater importance and thus there was a shift in contemporary economic analysis, from seeing capital accumulation in largely physical terms to viewing it as a process in which the productive quality of human beings is integrally involved. Now, emphasis is on capital formation through which people can become much more productive, and this can contribute to the process of economic growth.

CONCLUSIONS

Two main approaches to reducing poverty can be identified from India's experience. One is through economic growth which when combined with good initial conditions in physical infrastructure, produced significant reductions in poverty in states such as Punjab and Haryana. The second approach relied on human resource development. This has allowed for instance Kerela to reduce its poverty incidence- through increased exports of relatively skilled labour and the resulting inflow of remittance despite modest economic performance. However, Bihar, failed on both counts; there was too little growth and human resources were underdeveloped. The study concludes that no state effectively combined both approaches.

Thus, India should reduce poverty in the future, faster and in more effective way than it has done in the past. Higher inclusive growth should be there that increases growth of all sectors and which further leads to faster reduction in poverty. Thus human development and infrastructure development should be followed simultaneously to reduce poverty alleviation. So, the lessons for the future are clear; promote growth and invest in human capital and infrastructure.

11

Poverty Eradication and Democracy in the Developing World

INTRODUCTION

In the most meticulous and comprehensive statistical examination yet of the relationship between democracy and development, Przeworski et al (2000) have provided compelling evidence for a hunch long held by observers of development. "The lists of miracles and disasters", they argue, "are populated almost exclusively by dictatorships... The tigers may be dictatorships, but dictatorships are no tigers" (p. 178). Indeed, Przeworski et al could explicitly have taken another analytic step, a step that can be logically derived as a syllogism from what they say. Moving beyond a bi-modal distribution – miracles and diasters — they could have also constructed a third, in-between category. They would have found that democracies tend to fall almost exclusively in the unspectacular but undisastrous middle. No long-lasting democracy in the developing world has seen the developmental horrors of a Mobutu's Zaire, but none has scaled the heights of a South Korea, Taiwan or Singapore.

Can this argument be extended from economic growth, which is the focus of Przeworski et al, to the poverty-eradicating record of democracies in the developing world? Would it be true to say that while no democracies have attacked poverty as successfully as Singapore, South Korea or Taiwan, none has made economic life as awful for its poor people as a Guatemala, a Honduras, or an Ethiopia? I argue below that, indeed, the poverty-eradicating record of democracies in the developing world is neither extraordinary nor abysmal. Democracies have succeeded in preempting the worst-case scenarios, such as famines (Sen, 1989) and a consistent or dramatic deterioration in the welfare of the poor, but they have not achieved the best results, which for the purposes of this paper means removal of mass poverty. The performance of dictatorships, in comparison, covers the whole range of outcomes: the best, the worst, and the moderate. Some dictatorial regimes have successfully eradicated poverty; in others the problem has worsened, or no significant change in mass poverty is observable; and in still others, like democracies, the progress has been slow but steady.

Why are democracies stuck in the middle? Two arguments can be made. First, if we draw a standard distinction between the direct and indirect methods of poverty-alleviation, it is possible to show that in the developing world, democracies find it politically easier to subscribe to the direct methods of poverty alleviation, despite the by now widely recognized economic inferiority of such methods. Contrariwise, indirect methods have little political appeal in democracies, even though their greater long-term effectiveness is clear in economic thinking.

Direct methods consist of public provision of income (e.g., food-for-work programs, and credit and producer subsidies for small farmers) or a transfer of assets to the poor (e.g., through land reforms). Indirect methods are essentially growth-mediated — not any kind of growth, but one that aims at enhancing opportunities for an increase in the incomes of the poor. Over the last two decades, the conventional wisdom in economics has moved towards the superiority of the indirect method, suggesting that it is more productive (how resources are used) and also more sustainable in the long-run (how long the provision of public resources can be financed, without impairing the capacity to provide them further)? The political logic, however, goes in the opposite direction in democracies. Due to electoral and mass pressures, democracies tend to have an elective affinity with direct methods of poverty alleviation. Not given to electoral renewal of mandates, this problem is avoidable in authoritarian polities. If indirect methods are better at eradicating poverty, it follows that authoritarian countries – some, not all, as argued later – would have greater success with poverty eradication.

My second argument has to do with the distinction between class and ethnicity. At its core, class is an economic category, but ethnicity is defined in terms of a birth-based (ascriptive) group identity, imagined or real. Ethnic politics of subaltern groups is typically not couched in terms of poverty, but in the language of dignity and social justice, in which poverty is typically only a component, incorporated in a larger theme emphasizing self-respect, equality of treatment, and an end to everyday degradation — in schools, fields, places of work and worship, and on roads and public transport. If the poor, irrespective of the ethnic group they come from, were to vote or mobilize strictly on economic grounds, they would also press the decision-makers to attack poverty a great deal more forcefully. However, at least in multiethnic democracies, it is not only easier to mobilize the poor as members of identity-based communities, but that is also how they often vote – via ethnicity, not via class. Both poverty and denial of dignity together constitute a more serious force in democratic politics than poverty alone.

That being so, even with direct methods, a democratic polity is better able to attack poverty a) if ethnicity and class roughly coincide for the poor, not if they clash, and b) if the subaltern ethnic group(s) are also relatively large in size. If the poor belong to very different ethnic groups (defined by caste, language, race or religion), the pressure on the political elite to remove poverty significantly decreases.

In short, my argument is that no democracy in the developing world has successfully eliminated poverty because a) direct methods of poverty-alleviation have greater political salience in democracies, and b) because the poor are typically not from the same ethnic group. The former hurts the poor because it can be shown that the indirect, market-based methods of poverty alleviation are both more sustainable and more effective; and the latter goes against them because a split between ethnicity and class militates against the mobilization (and voting) of the poor as a class and dilutes the exertion of a pro-poor political pressure on governments.

DEFINITIONS, STATISTICS, MEASUREMENTS

In what sense am I using the key terms proposed above — "dignity" "poverty", "democracy"? Are all of them measurable, and if not, how does one think about them? Dignity. Of the three, the term "dignity" is by far the most straightforward. Scholars of modernity tell us that dignity is a modern notion, to be separated from and contrasted with the medieval notion of "honor". Honor, argues Berger in an influential essay, is "associated with a hierarchical order of society... honor is a direct expression of status, a source of solidarity among social equals and a demarcation line against social inferiors" (Berger, 1983, p. 174). "For some to have honor in this sense", contends Taylor, "it is essential that not everyone have it" (Taylor, 1992, p. 27). In medieval times, some — those high on the social scale — had honor; others — those low on the social scale — did not.

Dignity, in contrast, " pertains to the... individual regardless of his position in society" (Berger, 1983, p. 176). If only some have honor, all have dignity; if birth is central to honor, being a person, regardless of ascriptive location, is critical to dignity; if honor is hierarchical, dignity is egalitarian; and if "in the world of honor the individual discovers his true identity in his roles", he does so "in a world of dignity... by emancipating himself from social imposed roles" (Berger, 1983, p. 177).

There are two senses in which this distinction is relevant for our purposes. First, "this concept of dignity is the only one compatible with a democracy" (Taylor, 1992, p. 27). A democracy begins to undermine ascriptive hierarchies in the public realm. Second, according to the recent developments in the theories of ethnicity and nationalism, one can visualize ethnic movements in two ways. Some ethnic movements, typically those led by the dominant groups, are movements of exclusion; others, typically those led by subaltern groups, are movements of resistance. The former rely on the notion of honor, resisting the struggle for equality; the latter rely on the notion of dignity, challenging historically inherited social hierarchy and seeking equality.

It follows that if dignity and respect are denied in modern times to an ethnic group that is also poor, the struggle of the subaltern groups, ipso facto, becomes a struggle against both ethnic prejudice and poverty. If the poor do not come from an ethnic group but are constituted by many ethnic groups, then the struggle of the subaltern is either against prejudice, or against poverty, but not against both. This, as I will show later, has serious implications for the politics of poverty alleviation.

POVERTY

By now, as we know, the term "poverty" is used in two ways. The conventional usage of the term is consumption-inked, focusing primarily, though not exclusively, on a caloric floor that the human body, on average, minimally needs to function "normally". In this narrower sense, hunger and endemic malnourishment more or less define poverty. In the richer parts of the world, we typically try to reduce the number of calories our bodies consume every day. In the developing world, the first challenge is not to reduce, but to provide a minimum of, calories to millions of people. The $1/day yardstick used in PPP terms by the World Bank conforms to this, hunger-base definition of poverty.

The term "poverty" is also used more broadly. If we go by the human development arguments, the term would include education and health, in addition to consumption (hence income). I will not use the term "poverty" in this sense. The reason is not that education and health are not valuable. It is simply that I am clearer about the relationship between democracy and what is sometimes called income poverty, to be distinguished from human poverty. It will be interesting to speculate whether the former relationship also extends to the latter. Democracy. In the seminal works on democratic theory (Dahl, 1989 and 1971), democracy is defined in terms of two basic criteria: contestation and participation. The first principle inquires how freely the political opposition contests the rulers, and the second asks whether all groups, irrespective of social and economic criteria, or only some groups, participate in politics and determine who the rulers should be. The first principle is also called political liberalization; and the second political inclusiveness (Dahl 1971).

Democracies may have an identifiable impact on poverty, but it should be noted that poverty itself does not enter the definition of democracy. The best we can say is that if poverty, despite democratic institutions, obstructs the free expression of political preferences, it makes a polity less democratic, but it does not make it undemocratic. So long as contestation and participation obtain, democracy is a continuous variable, not a discrete or dichotomous variable. Variations in degree and dichotomies need to be distinguished. As Dahl famously put it, before the civil rights revolution of the mid-1960s the United States was less democratic than it is today, and America's future can be even more democratic if there is greater reduction in economic inequalities (Dahl, 1971, p. 29).3 In the presence of contestation and participation, an absence of poverty certainly makes a polity more democratic, but elimination of poverty by itself does not constitute democracy. There is no democracy without elections.

Another important conceptual issue should be clarified. In the first world, democracy is a stock variable, but in the developing world, it is a flow variable. In the poorer countries, a military coup or a wanton suspension of the legislature by the executive can dramatically alter the democratic score of a country, as it were. That is to say, on a 0-1 scale, the values of democracy in poorer countries can easily fluctuate between 1.0 and 0, but richer countries typically don't have coups and their governments don't normally suspend legislatures. This difference in the institutionalization of political structures has a serious implication for how we go about measuring the impact of democracy on poverty. For analytical tractability, it is necessary, first, to identify which countries have been relatively stable democracies - i.e., democracies for a long enough period – in the developing world. An exercise like this is not necessary in the first world, where democratic stability can be assumed.

It is difficult, though not impossible, to analyze the impact of democracy on poverty if democracy itself is not stable. If we construe "long enough" to mean more than half of the period since the late 1940s, or since independence, then, countries that would meet the criterion of longevity are few and far between: India, Sri Lanka, Botswana, the former British colonies in the Caribbean, Costa Rica, the Philippines between the late 1940s and 1960s and after the mid-1980s, Venezuela since 1959, and some other very small states, smaller than even Botswana and Trinidad4

(Huntington, 1983; Weiner, 1989). Some would add Malaysia to this list as well, but it should be noted Malaysia is by now seen as a long-lasting, consociational-type democracy, where participation may be high but contestation is limited between political parties by consensus, and political competition, by agreement, is designed around ethnic groups, not individuals (Lijphart, 1977).5 Malaysia, in other words, is a particular kind of democracy, not one in the standard sense. For our purposes here, we can count it as a democracy, given that universal-franchise elections are regularly held, so long as we remember the specific nature of electoral competition and consider its economic implications.

In short, it is the countries above that are critical for analyzing the relationship between democracy and poverty. Democracy has come to many more countries since the late 1970s than ever before (Huntington, 1991), but if we enlarge the canvas to include the entire post-1945 period,6 it will be hard to add many more countries to the small list above. In contrast, the number of countries, which remained authoritarian for long periods after 1945, is very large.

This asymmetry means that we only have a small number of observations about long-lasting democracies. If the n were larger, we could have a robust statistical analysis of their economic consequences for the poor. Until the post-1980s wave of democracies — the third wave (Huntington, 1991) — has produced many more democratic observations for inclusion, rigorous qualitative reasoning is our best analytic option (King, Keohane and Verba, 1994).

Poverty Eradication: How Much? Where?

Whether democratic systems have reduced poverty, it should be clear, is not a crosssectional question. We need least two sufficiently distanced periods for analysis, if not an entire time-series. Such data on an inter-country basis do not exist. Based on an international poverty line of $1/day in PPP terms, global figures for poverty were first calculated for 1985 (The World Bank, 1990). Though doubts remain as to the authenticity of such large-n, inter-country statistics, the World Bank are now customarily used for discussion of world poverty. Note, however, that even if we agree with the World Bank, all we can say is that between 1987-93, about 30 per cent of the world population remained more or less consistently below the $1/day poverty line. Whether the proportion has gone down since remains unclear.

We simply do not know the numbers of the poor, either globally or countrywise, for the 1950s or 1960s in any systematic sense. If, to gather such statistics, we rely on the reports available for each country, we find that the criteria used by different countries to define and measure poverty either do not match, or often the criteria have not been consistently used within the same country. A methodologically tight time-series on poverty for the entire developing world is not available, nor it is easy to create it for the pre-1985 period.

Luckily, some broad conclusions can nonetheless be presented, for they do not depend on statistical accuracy but on statistical reasonableness. Complete data sets would be necessary if we were to make finer judgments – for example, if we were asked to rank order all developing countries on poverty eradication, just as Human Development Reports rank all countries on HDI. Since, instead of a comprehensive rank ordering, all we need is categorical judgments, the available statistics, despite being incomplete, do permit some fairly robust conclusions. On poverty-alleviation, there is a huge variation in the record of authoritarian countries. Spectacular authoritarian successes at attacking poverty (South Korea, Taiwan and Singapore) coexist with miserable failures (in much of Sub-Saharan Africa and Latin America).

And many countries also fall in the middle of the two extremes. All developing countries, where close to, or more than half, of the population was still below the poverty line in the early 1990s, have in the last four to five decades been mostly authoritarian: Guinea-Bissau, El Salvador, Gambia, Guatemala, Haiti, Malawi, Lesotho, Madagascar, Niger, Peru, Rwanda, Senegal, Sierra Leone, Uganda, Zambia.

It bears repeating that until we have a better data set on poverty, we don't have a uniquely acceptable way of identifying these countries. We have to work with the second best. Thus, for inclusion in the list above, I have chosen a method, which gives us working and approximate but not precise figures. The method relies on a comparison of national and World Bank poverty estimates. A country is included in the above list: a) if both the national and World Bank poverty estimates more or less coincide around 50 per cent; b) if one of the two estimates is available and is significantly above 50 per cent. In cases where there is a serious divergence between the two estimates, I have not included that country in the list. But even if we include the third category, it is significant that all of them come from the set of countries, which have been mostly authoritarian: Honduras, Kenya, Mauritania, Nepal, Nicaragua. In comparison, long-lasting democracies are neither the biggest successes, nor the greatest failures.

The proportions of population below the poverty line in relatively stable poor democracies for the latest single year in the period between 1992-97 (unless otherwise noted) are: India (35%), Jamaica (34.2%), Botswana (33% in 1985/6), Venezuela (33% in 1990), the Philippines (37.5%), Sri Lanka (25%), Costa Rica (22% in 1990), and Trinidad and Tobago (21%).8 In the early 1960s, South Korea, Taiwan and Singapore were roughly as poor, or poorer, than these countries (Morris and Adelman, 1973), but by now they have wiped out mass poverty, and some have become developed economies. Economically speaking (though not politically), Singapore today is a first world country, considerably richer than the UK and without the obvious signs of poverty one often sees in parts of Britain. In short, the violent authoritarian fluctuations contrast sharply with a certain middling democratic consistency. Democracies may not be necessarily pro-poor, but authoritarian systems can be viciously anti-poor. Democratic attacks on poverty have simply been slow but steady.

UNSPECTACULAR BUT UNDISASTROUS: WHY?

Direct versus Indirect Measures

As is often noted in economic literature, direct methods of poverty alleviation represent income transfers to the poor (producer and credit subsidies, or poor-based employment programs) and at a more radical level, asset transfers (land reforms). The indirect methods are growth mediated. Since economic growth, according to mainstream economic wisdom today, is best achieved through trade liberalization and a generally more market-oriented economic strategy than was typically adopted in the developing world till the late 1970s, these trade- and market oriented policies have also, by implication, become the indirect methods of poverty-eradication in economic thinking.

Two clarifications, however, must be added. First, the emphasis on a growth-mediated strategy does not imply that all growth strategies are good for poverty-alleviation. A labor intensive growth strategy is better then one that is capital-intensive. Since trade-oriented growth is, by definition, more labor-intensive for poor countries than import-substituting growth, which tended to rely on the domestic production of capital goods, the former can qualify as an indirect method of poverty alleviation, but the latter may not. Stated another way, there is a difference between South Korea and Brazil. Both relied heavily on high growth, but the former has been trade-oriented since the late 1960s and the latter only since 1991 (Sachs and Warner, 1995, p. 23).

South Korea has more or less eradicated mass poverty; Brazil has not. Second, a growth-based strategy of poverty-alleviation does not entail a full-blown external liberalization of the economy, nor does it imply a complete absence of reliance on direct methods. Trade liberalization can be argued to be infinitely superior to the liberalization of capital markets (Bhagwati, 1998; Krugman, ; Sachs, Varshney and Bajpai, 1999; Stiglitz,), and so long as growth is generating enough resources, it may even be possible for public authorities to allocate more for direct measures, such as food-for-work programs. Therefore, even the sustenance of some direct methods, if not all, is heavily reliant on growth-generating policies, but the reverse may not be true. Direct measures can often be more effectively run in the framework of growth-enhancing, trade-oriented policies. In democratic politics, however, these arguments have a very different meaning.

Whether their impact on poverty is lasting or not, direct methods have clearly comprehensible and demonstrable short-run linkages with the well-being of the poor. The impact of indirect methods — exchange rate devaluations, tariff reductions, privatization of public enterprises and, generally, a market-oriented economic strategy — on poverty is not so clear-cut, short-run, and intuitively obvious. This has serious political consequences in democratic politics. To illustrate the point, let us consider the politics and economics of trade liberalization and currency devaluations. Under what conditions would their link with mass welfare be clear and direct? If a country's economy were heavily dependent on foreign trade, a bringing down of tariff walls, a lowering of quantitative trade restrictions and a devaluation of the currency would potentially be of great concern to the masses. In 1996, trade constituted more than fifty per cent of the GDP of Singapore, Malaysia, Thailand, the Philippines, Mexico, Hungary, South Korea, Poland and Venezuela, and between forty to fifty percent of the GDP of Israel, Chile, China and Indonesia. Dramatic changes in the trade and exchange rate regimes of these countries thus have a clear potential for mass politics and welfare.

However, if external trade is a small part of the economy, changes in trade and exchange rate regimes will be of peripheral importance to the masses. Thus, in order for trade and exchange rate regimes to become part of democratic mass politics, economies must become more trade-dependent in the future. If globalization does proceed further, this scenario is quite possible. But it is important to recall that in the ISI era that lasted right until the late 1970s and early 1980s, such political potential simply did not exist. One can, of course, suggest that even if trade-dependence of an economy is small, overvalued exchange rates or relatively closed trade regimes will have a negative effect on mass welfare. Anne Krueger (1991), for example, has argued that an ISI-type trade and exchange rate regime made "import competing" industrial goods dearer for the countryside and also discouraged exports, thus systematically discriminating against the countryside all over the developing world.

A majority, or large plurality, of a developing country's population was thus hurt, even when trade was a small part of the economy. This is exactly where the politics and economics of development strategies dramatically begin to diverge. Rural politicians have long been prominent in developing countries, but they have never mobilized the rural masses in favor of an open foreign trade regime, concentrating instead on the absence of land reforms in some cases, or on the unfavorable urban-rural trade in others. These latter policies may indeed have, as Krueger argues, caused less overall damage than exchange rate and trade regimes, yet they have been politically more salient. It should, of course, be noted that such indirect links between trade and exchange rate policies on the one hand and rural welfare on the other were not clear to the economists earlier. By and large they continued, until the 1970s, to look at rural welfare primarily in term of internal terms of trade and direct benefits to the countryside. If the economists were not aware until recently, can we expect democratic politicians to mobilize peasants over the relatively unclear, though hugely important, links between foreign trade and rural, or mass, welfare in a poor country? Long-run and indirect links do not work well in democratic politics: the effect has to be simple, intuitively graspable, clearly visible, and capable of arousing mass action.

Direct evidence on how the masses look at market- oriented economic reforms is also available. In a large survey of mass political attitudes in India conducted between April-July 1996, about five years after reforms were initiated there, it was found that 32 per cent of the urban voters knew of reforms, but only 12 per cent of the rural electorate had heard of them (Yadav and Singh, 1996), even though a change in trade-regime implied that the protection offered to manufacturing relative to agriculture had gone down significantly and agriculture's terms of trade had improved. Further, nearly 66 per cent of the graduates were aware of the dramatic changes in economic policy, compared to only 7 per cent of the poor, who are illiterate and mostly residents of the countryside. Thus, India economic reforms, toasted enthusiastically in the domestic and international economic community, had barely made an impression on the rural folk and the poor.

An equally dramatic direct attack on poverty, however economically unsound, would almost certainly have registered more prominently. Consider now some evidence from Latin America. After the emergence of third wave democracies in Latin America, politicians during the Presidential campaigns have not on the whole made market-oriented reforms the central plank of their electoral strategies, but have joined the reform bandwagon only after coming to power. Susan Stokes (1999) analyzes such "policy switches" at length and concludes that since the early

1980s, mandates have been "widely and severely violated" in Latin American democracies (p. 126). Democratic campaigns are not hospitable to discussions of indirect links between macroeconomic reforms and poverty. Such an elective affinity between democracy and direct methods has on the whole — and so far — limited the ability of democracies to eradicate poverty. This problem also suggests what the outer limits of democratic political action could be. For, even if we could mobilize the poor as a cohesive force, and their pressure led to something as dramatic as land reforms, the consequent effect on poverty, though positive, would not be as substantial, or as long-lasting and sustainable, as has been customarily imagined.

Land reforms are commonly seen as the most effective direct method of attacking poverty. But for land reforms to remove poverty, two other conditions must be met: a) there should be enough land to go around, making sure that a suboptimal distribution of small plots does not inhibit the post-reform productivity of the poor; and b) new agricultural technology, which is relatively expensive and therefore not easily affordable by the poor, is provided to the poor at a subsidized price by government (Varshney, 1995). A better utilization of labor inputs, possible and likely after the tenant is more secure or people work on their own lands, will by itself not bring about sustained increases in productivity and therefore income (Herring, 1989). If plots end up being suboptimal or new technology — irrigation, HYV seeds and chemical fertilizers — can not be bought by the beneficiaries, land reforms may introduce a measure of justice, but they can also leave most beneficiaries at a low-level economic equilibrium, instead of leading to a sustained increase in their incomes. That is why security to tenants and allocation of land to the tiller do not necessarily raise them above the threshold of poverty line. The questions of productivity and access to new technology continue to be relevant.

This, I should emphasize, is not an argument against land reform or asset redistribution per se. It is simply a call for pushing the inquiry towards asking how it compares with other methods and whether other methods are more productive and sustainable, while also being poverty-alleviating simultaneously. Land reforms are defensible, if one can show that they promote productivity and can be a source of sustained increases in income. In Latin America, where the Gini coefficients of land distribution are considerably higher than elsewhere, the land/man ratio is not entirely unfavorable, and there is enough land to go around, a case can still be made for land reforms.

By contrast, where landlessness is not typically high (for example, Sub-Saharan Africa), the poor will not gain much from land redistribution. Other methods of raising productivity may be more relevant, including public investments in irrigation on a continent not known for high irrigation/total acreage ratios, or scientific research on seeds that are less water-using and therefore more usable in semi-arid conditions. If land distribution to the poor, or security of tenancy, cannot always guarantee an end to poverty, the effectiveness of income transfers — though credit or producer subsidies — to the poor is even more open to question. The fiscal sustainability of such direct transfers to the poor, when a large plurality of the population is below the poverty line, can be highly dependent on whether economic growth is generating enough public revenue for the programs to be large-scale and long-lasting. To conclude this part of the discussion, the direct methods are less economically effective but politically more attractive in democracies, and the indirect methods are more economically effective but harder to sell politically. A better alignment of the political and economic may be possible in authoritarian countries, where politicians do not have to carry the masses with them in election campaigns and the long-run and indirect methods of poverty removal can simply be implemented by decree (if a political elite is committed to the poor, which may or may not be true). Unless the trade-dependence of an economy qualitatively changes, making more and more people dependent on trade for their welfare, a trade-oriented strategy will not arouse political passions in a democracy, and the economically desirable methods will continue to have a mismatch with the likely forms of democratic politics.

Class versus Ethnicity

The argument above underlines why direct methods of poverty-alleviation, even though politically attractive in poor democracies, are not well-equipped to end mass poverty. The argument does not imply that direct methods will have no impact. To repeat, both methods can make a dent; one is simply more productive and sustainable.

Within the parameters of direct action, however, the best results are obtained when class and ethnicity coincide for the poor, not when class and ethnicity clash. The former are called ranked ethnic systems in the literature, and the latter unranked ethnic systems (Horowitz, 1985). If ranked ethnic systems are also democratic, the poor can exert more effective pressure on governments and the effect on poverty is greater than is normally possible in unranked ethnic systems. Why should this be so? And what kind of evidence do we have to support the claim? In generating collective action, the greater power of ethnicity vis-à-vis class can be explained in three ways. Two of them treat all kinds of ethnic mobilization together, contrasting them with class mobilization. The third separates ethnic mobilization of the dominant groups from that of the subaltern. All three are relevant, the third most especially so.

First, developments in collective action theory seek to show why ethnicity solves the collective action problem better than class does. Class action is bedeviled by free-riding (or, what would be analogous, by problems encountered in a prisoner's dilemma), but the main strategic problem in ethnic collective action is one of coordination, not free-riding (Hardin, 1995). Coordination games are different from the prisoner's dilemma game. They rely on "focal points" to facilitate convergence of individual expectations; hence they show how collective mobilization becomes possible. Ethnicity can serve as a focal point; class can not, at least easily.

The idea of "focal points" comes from Schelling's seminal treatment of the coordination problem in bargaining. In the famous Schelling example: Schelling goes on to suggest that without having an intrinsic value for the couple, the "lost and found" section of the department store could be one such place. It will, however, not be a focal point if there are too many "lost and found" sections in the store. A focal point is distinguished by its "prominence" or "uniqueness": it has the instrumental power of facilitating the "formation of mutually consistent expectations" (Schelling, p. 84).

Ethnicity can be viewed as one such focal point for mobilization. There is no equivalent in class action. The second line of reasoning, not deployed in the political economy literature as the reasoning above typically is, has emerged from the theories of ethnicity and nation-building. Though the primary purpose of these theories is to show that ethnic and national groups are imagined communities (Anderson, 1983), they have serious implications for the concept of class.

Any collectivity that is larger than a village, a neighborhood or a small organization is an imagined community for it does not allow face-to-face intimacy. Thus, classes, like ethnic groups and nations, are also imagined communities. An individual does not "naturally" feel his class; such consciousness depends on political mobilization, public policy, or other people's behavior towards that individual.

Why, then, is caste/religion/nation more powerful than class? Because compared to class, caste, ethnicity and religion are more likely to form a historically enduring bond and provide common histories, heroes and villains. Moreover, the poor as a class rarely have leaders from among the poor. In contrast, a poor ethnic community can witness the emergence of a small middle class, and thereby generate its own leaders.

A third explanation also comes from the field of ethnicity and nationalism, focusing especially on the distinction between the ethnic politics of exclusion, which typically expresses the interests of dominant groups, and the ethnic politics of resistance, which reflects the interests of the subaltern. In subaltern ethnic politics, economic issues, dealing with the poverty of the group, are typically woven into a larger template emphasizing equality of treatment and an end to quotidian insults and humiliation in public spaces — in schools, fields, places of work and worship, and on roads and public transport. In contemporary times, the political equality of democracy clashes with a historically inherited world where group-based hierarchy, humiliation and degradation continue to exist (Taylor, 1992). The denial of basic human dignity and practice of discrimination on grounds of one's birth, when added to poverty, constitutes a much more powerful foundation of resistance than poverty alone.

Clearly, such a distinction between ethnicity and class may not be present everywhere. It will certainly not mark the politics of monoethnic societies (such as South Korea, Taiwan and many, though not all, Latin American countries); or societies where the subaltern ethnic group is not only poor but small in size and yet to develop a middle class. For all of these reasons, in the literature on ethnicity, Latin America (Dominguez, 1996) and East Asia (Horowitz, 1985) are normally considered outliers. They have seen a lot of class politics, but not enough ethnic politics, at least not yet. In comparison, in South and Southeast Asia, Sub-Saharan Africa, Eastern and Central Europe, ethnicity has often trumped class.

Ranked Ethnic Systems and Poverty: Examples

Let me now turn from theoretical reasoning to the empirical world. What examples can be cited for the claim that unless poverty is linked to identity politics, it does not necessarily become a force in democratic politics? While we know a great deal about the ethnic profiles of most poor democracies, intercountry comparisons on poverty, as already stated, are rendered difficult by the absence of a time series and lack of consistency in measurement criteria. Still, from what we know, of all poor democracies – consociational or adversarial — Malaysia has shown by far the best results on poverty-reduction. The proportion of population below the poverty line has declined in Malaysia from 49.3 per cent in 1970 to 9.6 per cent in 1995 (IMF 1998). We must, however, note two special features of Malaysian political economy. First, when democracy was instituted, the majority ethnic group - the Malays — was vastly more rural and poor than the major minority group, the Chinese. Once inaugurated, democratic politics got ethnically structured (Milne, 1967).

The majority ethnic group, led by its small upper and middle class, came to power and once in power, the elite undertook a large number of direct measures, both in the countryside and cities, to increase the incomes of their ethnic group (Jomo, 1990). Second, the direct measures were undertaken within the larger framework of a trade-oriented economic policy. Right since 1963, Malaysia has been an open economy, reducing its average tariff to less than 40 per cent, not allowing not-tariff barriers to cover more than 40 per cent of trade and not letting its currency overvalued by more than 20 per cent (Sachs and Warner, 1995, p. 21).

By comparison, it may be noted that Sri Lanka, often compared to Malaysia both for its size and potential (and, one might add, considerably more literate and peaceful in the 1950s and 1960s), used direct poverty alleviation measures only. It was able to alleviate poverty significantly, but not as much, or successfully, as Malaysia. Unlike Malaysia, open since 1963, Sri Lanka remained a closed economy until 1978.13 By the late 1970s, the fiscal ability of Sri Lanka to run its direct antipoverty programs were clearly in doubt (Bruton et al, 1992) Though indicative, these inter-country comparisons may not be as methodologically tight as intra-country comparisons, where a great many factors other than ethnicity can be controlled for and the effect of ethnicity on poverty identifiEd with greater certitude. In India, detailed and disaggregated statistics on statewise poverty, going back to the 1960s, are available. Patterns of state politics and policy can thus be clearly linked to the outcomes for poverty.

The states of Punjab and Kerala have shown the best results.15 In Punjab, the green revolution, an indirect and growth-based method, has been key to poverty alleviation. In Kerala, the method was direct. Land reforms and extensive job reservations in government employment were the twin strategies. Was the emphasis on direct methods in Kerala a result of the poor organizing themselves as a class? On the face of it, this would appear to be the case, primarily because a Communist party, repeatedly elected to power after 1957, led the campaign for land reforms and social justice.

Its rhetoric was based on class. However, both social history as well as electoral data make it clear that there was a remarkable merging of caste and class in Kerala, the former defined ethnically, the latter economically. At the center of this coincidence is the Ezhava caste, estimated to constitute a little over 20 per cent of the state's population. The Ezhavas traditionally engaged in "toddy tapping" (production of fermented liquor) and were therefore considered "polluting" by the upper castes. They were not only considered "untouchable" but also "unseeable". The catalogue of everyday humiliations for the Ezhavas was painfully long : At the turn of the century, experiencing some mobility and developing a small middle class, the Ezhavas rebelled against the indignities of Hindu social order and started fighting for their civil rights. Led by a famous Ezhava saint, Sri Narain Guru, sometimes called the Gandhi of Kerala, their protest movement aimed at self-respect and education. Self-respect entailed withdrawal from toddy tapping, a movement into modern trades and professions, and a nonviolent attack on the symbolic order. Since they were denied entry to temples and were only allowed to worship "lower gods and spirits", the Ezhavas, the Guru said, would have their own temples, in which they would worship "higher gods" to whom they would offer flowers and sweets, not animals and liquor reserved for the "lower gods". Meanwhile, to improve their economic and social status, they would educate themselves. And to facilitate all of these activities, they would set up an organization. "Strengthen through organization, liberate by education" was the motto.

These issues, all caste-based, decisively restructured the politics of Kerala in the 1930s. Entry into temples, an attack on the social deference system concerning dress and access to public roads and a more equal access to education drove the civil rights campaign. It is only subsequently that tenancy rights and land reforms spurred the mobilization for economic rights; it is only in 1940 that the Communist Party of Kerala was born. If the fit between the Ezhava caste and the rural poor had not been so good between the 1930s and 1940s, class mobilization would have made little headway. Class politics was inserted into the campaign for caste-based social justice.18 To this day, the Ezhava caste continues to be the principal base of the CPM. People of similar class-positions, if Nair, have gone on the whole with the Congress; if Christian, with Kerala Congress; if Muslim, with the Muslim League (Nossiter, 1982, pp. 345-375).

POLICY IMPLICATIONS

Instead of summarizing the argument in this concluding section, let me draw out its policy implications. First, while democracy in the developing world does not have the best record in alleviating poverty, it does not have the worst record either. Some authoritarian countries have done extremely well, eliminating poverty; others, like democracy, have done moderately well, reducing poverty but not eliminating it; but a large number of authoritarian countries have been viciously anti-poor, caring little for the conditions of the poor.

No stable democracy in the developing world falls in this, last category. The implications should be obvious. When it comes to poverty-eradication, authoritarian polities have a "going for broke" quality. They can do very well, but the odds that they can worsen the conditions of the poor, instead of improving them, are also highly significant. Moreover, once the anti-poor turn sets in, there are no checks on authoritarian countries either. Democracies remain the best bets, for they do not allow the conditions of the poor to decline consistently or dramatically, and almost always, do moderately well in alleviating poverty. The concern of the policy community should be on improving the performance of democracies through the pressure of public criticism. To bet on dictatorships is to take a huge risk.

Second, the argument about dignity also suggests a policy reformulation of the poverty debate. If it is true, as I have argued, that the impact of a polity on poverty-alleviation is greater, when the politics of poverty-alleviation is conducted in the framework of dignity and social justice, then redesigning the politics of poverty in the language of self-respect, equality of treatment, and an end to everyday degradation — in schools, fields, places of work and worship, and on roads and public transport – may go farther in mobilizing the poor as a political force than if they were mobilized only as an economic group of the poor. At least in multiethnic polities, where it is politically easier to mobilize the poor as members of identity-based communities, this path deserves greater policy attention. Both poverty and denial of dignity, taken together, make for a more potent force in politics than poverty alone.

Finally, some implications for globalization are also worth noting. As an instance of the indirect strategy of poverty-alleviation, economic globalization has been implicitly present in the paper, not explicitly analyzed. The context of poverty-alleviation has remarkably changed in the last decade, as more and more countries have adopted a market-based and trade-oriented economic strategy (Sachs and Warner, 1995). In what ways are the arguments about poverty above, summarizing on the whole the post-1945 development experience, relevant to the era of economic reforms, if at all?

To begin with, not all aspects of globalization are desirable, even in a purely economic sense. The arguments about the ill-effects of the liberalization of capital markets, especially for the poor, in the developing countries are compelling (Bhagwati, 1998). Trade liberalization and liberalization of investment and regulatory regimes may be more welfare-enchancing than a fullblooded liberalization of capital markets.

The political issue, however, is different. Whether or not, in a purely economic sense, de-regulation, and trade and investment liberalization are in the medium to long run better for the entire society, including for the poor, politically speaking, globalization in the developing world has thus far not emerged from below, which is where the masses, and therefore the poor, are located. Reforms have emerged from above — through economic bureaucracies, both national and international such as the World Bank — in moments of economic crisis that have demonstrated the exhaustion of statist and inward-looking economic strategies.

The masses may have felt an acute dissatisfaction against the excessive and abusive powers of the state, especially in the former Communist world, but a desire for lesser state interference in everyday life does not necessarily translate into a support for economic reforms. Reliance on markets has simply emerged from the ruins of a discredited statist ideology of economic development, whose capacity to deliver mass welfare had seriously declined and which had resulted in a widespread abuse of authority by state officials as well. This diversion may cease to be an indirect source of support for reforms, if markets fail to deliver mass welfare. In short, as of now, democratic politics and globalization are quite awkwardly aligned. It is not a happy and permanent marriage.

The key question is how to make markets – domestic and global — work for the poor. Unless economic reformers produce a political language for their arguments that can be understood

make development assistance more effective. Many low-income countries are taking charge of their own future and recognizing the importance of instituting and maintaining sound policies and their own efforts. In adopting the PRSP process, low-income countries are putting poverty reduction at the center of their development strategies. For many countries, the development and implementation of broad based national poverty reduction strategies is a process of "learning by doing." But, in doing so, PRSPs are leading to better informed decision-making and more effective use of public resources, and serving as a framework for better coordination of the support from development partners.

Complementing the greater poverty focus of public resources is a growing emphasis on the policies that will accelerate growth and thus make this reduction in poverty sustainable over the long haul. National poverty reduction strategies recognize that sound growth requires investment, not least in human capital and infrastructure, as well as the right macroeconomic and structural policies, good governance, and healthy institutions. Countries are seeking to build an improved investment climate, to compete in world markets, and to foster development that is less dependent upon official financing in the long-term. But the process is not a one-way street.

The international community, too, has a critical role to play by increasing aid, opening its markets to developing country exports, and phasing out trade-distorting subsidies. These are essential complements to the efforts of those countries that are implementing effective poverty reduction strategies and to the alignment of development assistance with national strategies. It is only through such concerted actions by rich and poor countries alike that the fight against poverty can be effectively sustained and the challenge of meeting the Millennium Development Goals (MDGs) for 2015 can be met.

It is clear, however, that the development of PRSPs is a major challenge for low-income countries, both in terms of analysis and organization. Besides managing a complex policy dialogue with development partners, low-income country governments have to put together an integrated medium-term economic and poverty reduction strategy, complete with short- and long-term goals and monitoring systems; these are a set of tasks that few industrial countries could systematically do well. And, in many countries, these tasks must be managed with limited technical and institutional capacity and in ways that reinforce—rather than undermine—existing national institutions, processes, and governance systems. Thus, there is a need to have realistic expectations about the PRSPs that are being developed.

More importantly, strategies alone are not sufficient—they must be followed up by actions. Countries must follow through on the policy commitments laid out in the PRSPs. Donors must provide the promised technical and financial support in a timely fashion and in a way that does not impose undue administrative costs on the recipient country. Civil society organizations must cooperate with governments and coordinate their actions to achieve the commonly shared poverty reduction objectives set out in the PRSPs. And all involved must realize that the challenges facing many of the PRSP countries are difficult and complex and the links between actions and outcomes are sometimes imprecise. For this reason, attainable short-term targets are needed and monitoring procedures must be developed, so that all partners know whether the country is moving along the right track. The Bank and the Fund will play a catalytic role in launching PRSPs, but ultimately the success of countries' poverty reduction strategies will depend on the action of countries themselves and the concerted aide of all their development partners.

HOW THE JOINT STAFF REVIEW WAS CONDUCTED

This review has been open and inclusive, with a concerted effort to elicit the views of low-income country governments, development partners, and other stakeholders. The focus of the review has been on countries' experience to date in developing, implementing, and monitoring their PRSPs, recognizing that most countries are still at the early stages of the process. In carrying out the review, Bank and Fund staff drew on four main inputs:

- country contributions from PRSP teams and national civil society organizations (CSOs), including at four regional PRSP events which brought together countries in Africa, Europe and Central Asia, East Asia, and Latin America;

- external views from development partners and other stakeholders (including civil society groups) regarding their experience with the PRSP approach, communicated through some 50 papers and a series of seminars and outreach activities;
- Bank/Fund staff contributions, including thematic reviews of key aspects of the approach (participatory processes, poverty diagnostics, human development, rural and infrastructure, and cross-cutting issues such as gender, environment, and conflict), summaries of Executive Directors' views of the approach and of individual country experiences, and an issues paper prepared as background for the international conference; and
- an international conference on the PRSP approach in January 2002, which brought together representatives from 60 low-income countries, their external development partners, and representatives from civil society to discuss their views about how to strengthen the developmental impact of the approach.

Since 1999, ten countries have completed their first full PRSP and three countries have completed their first annual PRSP implementation progress reports. Some 42 countries have also completed their interim poverty reduction strategy papers (I-PRSP) and 7 countries have subsequently submitted their PRSP preparation status reports for consideration. Although the pace of completing full PRSPs has been slower than initially expected, there is now a sufficient basis to begin learning and to apply the lessons of this emerging experience, recognizing that it is still in its early stages.

This paper highlights the main findings and recommendations of the review. A more detailed account of the early experience with I-PRSPs and full PRSPs is presented in a companion paper. The next section presents the main messages. Section IV discusses various emerging good practices from the early experience of countries and development partners which can serve to enhance the process and content of other country-owned strategies, as well as to help ensure that assistance activities are appropriately aligned behind these strategies. Section V reviews priorities for knowledge and capacity building in low-income countries. The paper concludes with issues for discussion by Executive Directors on actions that the Bank and Fund can take to enhance the impact of the PRSP approach.

MAIN MESSAGES

The central message emerging from this review is that there is broad agreement among low-income countries, civil society organizations and their development partners that the objectives of the PRSP approach remain valid and that the PRSP process can improve joint efforts aimed at poverty reduction. Moreover, it is generally recognized that there have been improvements over time in both process and content as countries have moved ahead with preparation and then implementation. This has been the case for countries that started at very different points, indicating that the PRSP process has been quite adaptable to different country circumstances.

There is also widespread agreement on four key achievements of the PRSP approach to date:

- a growing sense of ownership among most governments of their poverty reduction strategies, and both government representatives and many civil society organizations from diverse settings have voiced their commitments to this process and its objectives;
- a more open dialogue within governments and with at least some parts of civil society than had previously existed. Some CSOs are increasingly mobilized and have gained capacity to participate in the preparation and monitoring of the implementation of the PRSP, and favorable "second round" effects may be anticipated;
- a more prominent place for poverty reduction in policy debates, extending beyond social sector interventions with data collection, analysis, and monitoring becoming more systematic; and
- an acceptance by the donor community of the principles of the PRSP approach, from major UN organizations (for example, UNDP and WHO) to bilateral donors (including the Canada, Denmark, France, The Netherlands, and the

United Kingdom), and the prospects are good that PRSPs will lead to stronger partnerships with countries and better donor coordination.

This consensus is underpinned by several main themes which were most recently reinforced at the international conference on the PRSP approach:

- the importance of country ownership as a guiding principle;
- a recognition that the focus should now shift beyond process to content and implementation, and the importance of improving the understanding of the linkages between policies and poverty outcomes;
- the importance of utilizing and building local capacity in core areas needed for effective poverty reduction strategies;
- the need for realism in the setting of goals and targets, as well as in managing expectations, both within countries and among their development partners;
- the importance of openness and transparency, both within each country and in international development partnerships;
- the importance of flexibility to allow for different country starting points;
- the desirability of debate about alternative policy choices; and
- the importance of patience and perseverance with implementation.

There is substantial scope for countries to improve both the preparatory process and the content of their national strategies. In order to lay stronger foundations for the PRSP approach over the medium- to long-term, the Review suggests that good practice at the country level would include a high, near-term priority to: (a) improving public expenditure management (PEM) systems; (b) placing greater emphasis on, and building capacities for, monitoring and evaluation; and (c) strengthening and institutionalizing participatory processes with respect to a broad range of domestic stakeholders, as well as development partners.

For the Bank and the Fund, a key consideration is how to strike the right balance between pushing for more rapid achievement of the full potential of the PRSP approach and ensuring realism in light of country capacity constraints and the need for the process to be country driven. As a general proposition, the staffs' view is that, given the primary importance of country ownership, the PRSP approach requires flexibility so that both the process and the content of poverty reduction strategies can vary across countries in light of national circumstances. Therefore, any measures that would set more specific and rigid guidelines should be considered with caution.

PRSP DESIGN AND IMPLEMENTATION: KEY FINDINGS

While it is premature to draw any firm conclusions about the development impact of the PRSP approach, there are nonetheless a range of good practices by countries and their development partners. This section reviews the key findings of the review, and highlights instances of good practice which are summarized in bullet form at the end of each section. In reality, there are only a few concrete cases where such practices are in place and the staff does not expect that these examples could be generalized across all countries in the short- to medium-term for the reasons outlined above. They will be of varying relevance for different countries depending on specific circumstances. The aim here is to provide useful illustrations and directions for countries and partners and not to establish further guidelines on requirements for PRSPs. The examples of good practice are typically accompanied by recommendations for the Bank and Fund that indicate specific actions that could be undertaken by the two institutions.

INTERIM PRSPs

At the outset, the Boards recognized preparing a full PRSP could take more than one year. In such cases, countries were requested to prepare an I-PRSP, which the Boards would consider together with a joint staff assessment. I-PRSPs were intended to be short documents that described a country's current poverty situation and policies, and presented a plan for preparing a full PRSP.

The shift away from Bank/Fund staff authored policy framework papers (PFPs) to country-authored I-PRSPs has been a major achievement. While the quality of I-PRSPs has varied, the preparation of I-PRSPs has served a useful purpose by encouraging countries to take stock of existing data and policies, to launch a broader process of rethinking current strategies, and to produce time-bound roadmaps for the preparation of their first full PRSP. In many cases (e.g., Mongolia and Nicaragua), I-PRSPs were longer than expected, as countries put forward quite comprehensive documents. At the same time, however, the roadmaps were sometimes relatively weak with respect to plans for participatory processes (e.g., Senegal); plans to fill data gaps (e.g., Sierra Leone) and the proposed institutional arrangements for the PRSP (e.g., Moldova and Tajikistan). This appears to have been due to both an unclear understanding about the intended nature of an I-PRSP, coupled with pressures imposed by HIPC and/or PRGF timetables.

Although I-PRSPs were initially viewed as a transitional device, they may still be useful in many of the nearly three dozen low-income countries that will need to prepare PRSPs for access to Bank/Fund concessional lending and/or debt relief. For future I-PRSPs, the following good practices and recommendations are relevant:

Good practices for countries

- Preparing an I-PRSP which focuses on establishing a good roadmap and realistic timetable for preparation of the full PRSP; and
- including key agencies, sectoral ministries and civil society in I-PRSP preparation. Good practices for development partners (including the Bank and the Fund)
- Encouraging countries to keep their I-PRSPs short and well focused; and
- during I-PRSP preparation, clarifying expected support in preparing for the full PRSPs.

Actions by the Bank and the Fund

- Retain the option for countries to prepare I-PRSPs as the basis for access to Bank/Fund concessional assistance for countries not immediately in a position to prepare a full PRSP.

PRSP Participatory Processes

The open and participatory nature of the PRSP approach is regarded by many as its defining characteristic and its most significant achievement. PRSPs have often led to an improved dialogue within the various parts of governments and between governments and domestic stakeholders. There is some evidence that the active involvement of civil society has influenced PRSP content, particularly in drawing attention to social exclusion, the impoverishing effects of poor governance, and specific policy issues, such as the elimination of school fees in Tanzania and health fees in Uganda. The challenge for most countries is to move away from ad hoc consultations to more institutionalized forms of dialogue.

The role of Parliaments in the preparation, approval, and monitoring of country strategies has generally been limited, and is a concern that has been expressed by a number of development partners (including the Utstein Group of bilateral donors and the E.C.). There is however some good practice: where individual parliamentarians have been involved (e.g., Honduras and Nicaragua), or where progress in implementation will be reported to parliament along with the budget, as in Mozambique, for example.

Various concerns have been expressed about the lack of involvement of specific groups in the participatory process. While the patterns differ across countries, CSOs that were out of favor with the government; local government officials; private sector representatives; trade unions; women's groups; and direct representatives of the poor are among the groups that have not always been fully involved in the PRSP process. Concerns have also been expressed by civil society groups as to whether governments are limiting participation to information sharing and consultation, and whether civil society can extend its role in the decision making process beyond targeted poverty reduction programs to the macroeconomic policy and the structural reform agenda, especially trade liberalization and privatization.

The PRSP process is also intended to promote stronger partnerships between countries and donors. Although a number of donors were frustrated by their initial lack of involvement, by mid- to late 2001 most donors indicated that they have been able to engage in PRSP preparation at the country level. Some donors, however, feel that the PRSP process has been dominated by the Bank and the Fund, in part because they were unable to engage jointly in the dialogue with government during Bank and Fund missions, as well as because they felt that Joint Staff Assessments (JSAs) drew the government's attention away from alternative views. Others have been concerned about the lack of commonly-accepted modalities for formal donor consideration of PRSPs outside of the discussions of the Bank and Fund Boards.

Some observers have suggested the need for clear and strict standards for participation (for example, on the role of parliaments) in order to ensure that the goals of broader country ownership and increased government accountability could be met. On the other hand, many governments have stressed that the PRSP process should not involve "political conditionalities," and that the donor and the CSO community are ill-equipped to make judgments in this domain. Others have noted that the circumstances among countries vary so greatly that global standards or guidelines are neither desirable nor feasible. Based on experience to date, the following good practices could usefully be pursued to improve the quality of the participatory processes being undertaken in countries:

Good Practices for Countries

- Sustaining key aspects of participation, including information sharing and openness of decision-making and debate about alternative policy choices, so that dialogue with non-governmental stakeholders can be routinely conducted by governmental institutions;
- linking to and building on existing processes and institutions, including the involvement of parliaments, cabinets, and sectoral ministries in PRSP preparation at appropriate stages;
- involving all significant stakeholder groups in the participatory process, such as civil society, including the private sector, and donors, and making particular efforts to reach out to traditionally marginalized groups;

- making PRSPs and related information available and understandable to local civil society;
- improving mechanisms for feedback to local participants in the PRSP process, as well as reporting in PRSPs concerns expressed by key stakeholders; and
- presenting draft PRSPs to donor round tables or Consultative Group meetings before transmission to the Bank and Fund Boards.

Good practices for development partners (including the Bank and Fund)

- Providing timely and constructive feedback to PRSP teams, both early in the process and when the PRSP is completed, but resisting extensive comments on drafts that could undermine ownership; and
- supporting capacity building of civil society to engage substantively in the process.

Actions by the Bank and Fund

- Make the whole country team operationally relevant to the PRSP, with dialogue on the PRSP being undertaken on most missions, not only "PRSP missions;"
- provide advance notice of mission timing and purpose to stakeholders and other development partners; and
- indicate in Joint Staff Assessments whether staff have received views from civil society and/or donors on a country's PRSP, including on the participatory process.

Conflict-Affected Countries

A number of low-income countries are currently, or have recently been, affected by conflict. Several, including Armenia, Azerbaijan, Bosnia-Herzegovina, Cambodia, Guinea Bissau, Rwanda, and Sierra Leone have prepared I-PRSPs and are working on their full PRSPs. In all of these countries, adequate progress towards cementing the peace and establishing security is necessary prior to embarking on the PRSP process with meaningful participation from all stakeholders. However, since poverty, exclusion, and poor governance underlay many conflicts, the PRSP process itself can make an important contribution to furthering peace and preventing future conflict. Countries emerging from conflict frequently face particularly acute poverty that is complicated by internally displaced populations, war-wounded and demobilization of combatants, disrupted production and social infrastructure, and a weak security situation.

While countries may be able to prepare an I-PRSP shortly after conflict has subsided, they face additional constraints in preparing a full PRSP: a weak administrative capacity, including poor data; a continued weak security situation, and a fractured social and political environment. As they emerge from conflict, these countries often face a high degree of political and economic uncertainty that can impede preparation of a full PRSP. In such cases, it may be necessary to delay the PRSP until conditions are more settled. Nonetheless, reconstruction priorities and strategies need to remain flexible, so as to ensure that they do not subsequently constrain or clash with the priorities and strategies outlined in the full PRSP.

A key issue for the review was whether the existing PRSP framework is sufficiently flexible for the special needs of conflict-affected countries. Where a country is still embroiled in an intense conflict it is obviously difficult to see how the PRSP process can be undertaken. More generally, however, the emerging consensus of key stakeholders is that the framework was adequate and in several cases to date has been quite valuable, but that special emphasis is needed in certain areas to ensure its effective implementation in conflict-affected countries. In addition to those mentioned elsewhere, good practices for conflict-affected countries and their development partners include the following:

Good Practices for Countries

- Describing in PRSPs as to how conflict-related problems and constraints are being addressed; and
- focusing on the public actions and institutions most urgently needed to rebuild core government systems and trust in public institutions. Good practices for development partners (including the Bank and Fund)
- Improving donor coordination and timeliness of external support for conflict-affected countries; and

- supporting country efforts in formulating strategies for conflict analysis, prevention and peace building.

Actions by the Bank and the Fund

- Sensitize Bank and Fund country teams to the special needs of conflict-affected countries, offering to pilot promising post-conflict analysis when requested; and
- flexibly apply the JSA Guidelines in conflict-affected countries, especially in terms of the expected extent of participation, the quality of poverty diagnostics, and degree of detailed articulation of priority public policies.

Improving Poverty Diagnostics, Targets and Indicators, and Monitoring and Evaluation

In most countries, the preparation of PRSPs has involved useful steps toward better poverty data and diagnostics, helped to clarify national targets and indicators for poverty reduction, and increased attention to monitoring and evaluation. Many countries have identified and started to fill important gaps in their data about poverty and inequality, and have begun to strengthen the institutional arrangements for on-going data collection and analysis. All the PRSPs have included short-term and longer-term targets for economic growth, for reductions in the number of poor (in terms of income poverty measures), and for improvements in education and health. And all have included plans to improve monitoring and evaluation capacities, although these are seldom detailed. Despite this progress, the experience to date has also highlighted a number of weaknesses in poverty data and analysis, and in target setting. Quantitative survey data are sometimes out dated and/or not sufficiently frequent and comparable to permit analysis of trends. While many PRSPs set long-term targets for poverty reduction, these are sometimes overly ambitious. Some stakeholders have argued that the MDGs should be uniformly included in PRSPs as national goals, whereas others stress the need for national goals to be set against the MDG backdrop, but be realistic in light of country circumstances.

Poverty and social impact analysis (PSIA) of major policies and programs has typically not been undertaken as part of PRSPs, for reasons to do with national capacity constraints and its inherent technical difficulties. The data and capacity needs are formidable and serious methodological issues remain unresolved, despite some analytical advances in this area. Nevertheless, as reiterated by both civil society groups and donors during the Review, there is a need for development partners to assist countries in being more systematic in undertaking analysis of poverty and social impacts of major policy choices.

This is likely, for example, to enhance the focus on equity concerns related to the distribution of assets as well as differences in access to services. Given variations in data availability and capacity among countries, undertaking such analyses will necessarily involve adopting a flexible approach with a variety of instruments and techniques that take account of country circumstances, data and time constraints, and the specific policy issues being considered. Progress in this area will also necessarily be gradual and involves using existing techniques more systematically with respect to analyzing the impacts of major policy reforms, developing ways to improve the applicability of new analytical techniques, and improving the information base.

Work in the Bank is quite advanced on summarizing knowledge on PSIA methodology and its application to the analysis of policy reforms, and providing practical guidance to staff. A preliminary version of this guidance material is expected to be available for public comment by the time of the 2002 Spring meetings. A staff learning program will be designed based on the approaches described. At the same time, the Bank's Research Group has been working on identifying the relevance and practicality of a number of new approaches, including extending existing models to analyze distributional issues. That work will be integrated over time into the guidance material and learning programs. The Bank is supporting specific applications of PSIA in collaboration with development partners.

Vis-à-vis the Fund, the Bank is the lead agency on PSIA since these analyses focus on structural and social issues which are within the Bank's core areas of expertise.5 The Bank provides upstream advice and analysis to countries through its economic and sector work, such as poverty assessments, and through its

but then went on to propose an array of measures in each area. Others have imposing lists of measures with little sequencing or ranking. While there are numerous positive examples of specificity of priority public actions, many of the PRSPs had little or no information about what was to be done, by whom, and when. The key to effective prioritization is for countries to fully cost their proposed actions within a medium-term expenditure framework (MTEF) that takes into account the existing fiscal constraint and that is consistent with the overarching need for macroeconomic stability and fiscal and debt sustainability. Weak prioritization thus reflects limited country capacity to cost programs and policies, and limited public expenditure management capacity. It is also partly the product of the demands generated by donors and by domestic constituencies through the participatory process.

In all of the early PRSPs, countries recognized the paramount importance of macroeconomic stability to growth and poverty reduction and put forward macroeconomic frameworks that were consistent with these twin objectives. There were also examples of fiscal flexibility (e.g., Mauritania) where a relaxation in the fiscal stance would be accommodated in the event that additional concessional assistance was forthcoming. In several cases, countries put forward macroeconomic and structural policies that were similar to those of the recent past, since their PRSPs were building on existing policy frameworks that continued to be the most effective way of ensuring sustained growth and poverty reduction.

There were, nonetheless, various shortcomings in the macroeconomic frameworks put forward in the early PRSPs, both in terms of presentation and content. Some countries (e.g., Albania and Burkina Faso) included only a limited discussion of their macroeconomic frameworks, while others (e.g., Mozambique, Tanzania, and Uganda) could have elaborated more on the linkages between their macroeconomic and structural policies and poverty reduction.

All of the early PRSPs included ambitious growth targets and could have benefited from a sharper analysis of the likely sources and levels of growth. Given the importance of vulnerability to external shocks in several of these countries (e.g., Bolivia, Mauritania, and Uganda), their PRSPs could have usefully put forward an appropriate set of macroeconomic policies to reduce the risks of these shocks and/or to ensure debt sustainability. Finally, sound alternative macroeconomic scenarios and related structural policy choices and trade-offs could have also been made more explicit, including the ex ante specification of contingency spending plans in the event of higher/lower than expected resource flows.

An important aspect of prioritizing public actions for poverty reduction is increasing the allocation of public spending for poverty-reducing activities while reducing unproductive expenditures. Recent Fund staff analysis indicates that full PRSPs are associated with an increased emphasis on sectors important for reducing poverty, including social sectors, rural infrastructure, and water supply (although exact definitions vary by country). For example, spending on health and education is projected to increase significantly as a share of GDP and total government spending and in real per-capita terms in PRSP countries.6 However, few PRSPs adequately define poverty–reducing spending, fully cost priority public actions and targets, and discuss the impact of alternative fiscal policy choices on the poor. Mobilizing domestic resources in support of countries' poverty reduction strategies has been recognized by countries and partners as a priority, both to augment support for priority spending and to reduce aid dependency. The early PRSPs, however, were generally revenue neutral and, with the exception of Mozambique, typically did not discuss revenue measures.

Key cross cutting issues—such as gender, HIV/AIDS, good governance, and rural development—have been addressed, to varying extents across countries. The coverage of gender issues was generally good in education and health, but tended to be much lower in other sectors. Attention to gender issues also tended to decline as countries moved from diagnosis to actions and from actions to monitoring. The treatment of HIV/AIDS pandemic, which has grown from being a health issue to a serious challenge to development, has tended to be weak in most PRSPs, although some countries (including Madagascar and Mozambique) are making good progress in developing poverty-AIDS analyses. All the early PRSPs highlighted governance concerns, often as a result of public consultations. Several countries, including Burkina Faso and Mozambique, have highlighted good governance as a principal PRSP objective. All the PRSPs also explicitly discussed the problem of corruption and included strategies to address some dimensions of this problem. Most PRSPs, however, did not present a systematic diagnosis of the key governance challenges, and failed to set out intermediate indicators to monitor progress on governance reform. Rural development has been incorporated in PRSPs as a cross-cutting thematic issue, with interventions frequently targeted towards increasing access to and the productivity of natural assets (like land and water), to complement efforts to improve rural education and health. However, the discussion of rural issues tends to be generic and brief, and the institutional framework for their implementation is generally vague, so that it is difficult to assess the specific content or the poverty focus of the actions proposed.

All the PRSPs to date have emphasized that access to services are a key concern for the poor. Improving access to education, especially at basic levels and in rural areas, has been a key priority, and the PRSPs reflect a range of measures to improve efficiency and quality of schooling. Similarly, there is a consistent focus on health outcomes, and on diseases of the poor, alongside efforts to improve access to health services. For example, all the African PRSPs to date have indicated an increased emphasis on primary health care, with efforts to balance the objective of improved quality of services against distributional concerns motivating fee exemptions for certain services (e.g., for immunizations in Mauritania). The degree of focus on social protection programs varies, and is largest in the ECA region and in Latin America, where countries have clearly diagnosed the sources of household risk, and the PRSPs address a broad range of social protection issues as a coherent part of their overall poverty reduction strategy.

In general, PRSPs have acknowledged the primacy of the private sector for growth, and thus for poverty reduction, although the extent of treatment of related structural issues varies across countries. They also generally recognize that the private sector, often through small and medium enterprises, and rural based production, will be critical for income generation. Significant attention has been given to marketing issues, with Mozambique and Uganda's PRSPs seeking improved market information systems, improved access to markets and strengthened marketing channels and infrastructure.

Several PRSPs have discussed intended privatization of public utilities, including Burkina Faso, Mauritania, and Nicaragua, although the depth of discussion varies considerably. Several PRSPs include a focus on improving the environment for small and medium enterprise development, and a number also have an explicit focus on the expansion of credit and savings opportunities for the poor. All the PRSPs include interventions to improve access to rural credit. An important element in the growth strategies of PRSPs has been the development of infrastructure, through expanded public provision and/or structural reforms. Mozambique's PRSP, for example, gives priority to the most densely populated and poorest regions in planned investments to improve the road network and expand access to energy and water. In general, the focus on infrastructure is concentrated in rural areas.

While all full PRSPs have supported the desirability of trade openness in broad terms, the majority has dealt with the underlying issues in a fairly limited way. None of the PRSPs have dealt systematically with past experience of trade reforms, but several PRSPs (including Albania, Honduras, and Mozambique) have included specific measures in support of trade promotion and liberalization. Only in Honduras and Mozambique was there an attempt to clarify the link between these reforms, and growth and poverty reduction. Based on country experience to date, the following could be considered as good practices to assist countries on the policy front:

Good practices for countries

- Discussing in detail in PRSPs the macroeconomic framework (including a comprehensive set of tables) and reviewing the sources of pro-poor growth underpinning projections;
- developing alternative macroeconomic scenarios in PRSPs, including contingency spending plans and measures

supporting alternative revenue paths, in light of uncertainty regarding growth projections, and projected revenue paths;

- including policies to reduce the risks from external shocks and/or to ensure debt sustainability;
- exploring options to improve the efficiency of services that are of key relevance to the poor;
- improving prioritization of policies and including appropriate levels of specificity about proposed actions;
- analyzing and considering the links between sectoral issues (e.g., the impact of education on health outcomes) and cross-cutting issues (e.g., gender and the environment) in developing priority public policies;
- undertaking an upstream review of governance and institutional development problems early in the PRSP process, with inputs from donors and civil society, in order to build consensus among various stakeholders on the main governance challenges to poverty reduction; and
- developing institutional capacity of sectoral ministries in core PRSP skills including public expenditure management, poverty diagnostics and monitoring and indicators).

Good practices for development partners (including the Bank and Fund)

- Fostering civil society capacities for establishing priorities, benchmarking, and monitoring progress on governance;
- continuing to invest in tools about sectoral and governance-poverty links, and support adaptation to specific country settings, and support dissemination of good practice;
- providing support—particularly to line agencies—to prepare sectoral strategies based on the PRSP approach; and
- deepening current efforts to understand more fully the linkages between policy actions and pro-poor growth. This needs to take place at the country level, through economic and sector work, complemented and supported by relevant international research efforts, including at the Bank and the Fund.

Actions by the Bank and the Fund

- Bank/Fund will devote sufficient resources to support training, economic sector work, and technical assistance in key areas, including costing poverty measures and in developing methodologies for assessing intersectoral trade-offs between policies and in analyzing the sources and patterns of growth.

Public Expenditure Management

In many countries, current PEM systems are too weak to support a meaningful presentation of the overall public expenditure program in the PRSP and to monitor implementation. For HIPCs, these common weaknesses in current PEM systems have been confirmed most recently by a Fund-Bank study of their capacities to track poverty-reducing spending, though, of course, HIPCs (or low-income countries more generally) are not the only countries with weaknesses in their PEM systems.7 Government budgets in low-income countries typically lack comprehensiveness and meaningful functional classifications of expenditures, and seldom provide sufficient detail about allocations to programs that are targeted toward poverty reduction. Budget data often exclude donor-financed projects (even when they are a large component of expenditures) and typically exclude extra-budgetary activities and sub-national spending. Budget execution often differs significantly from budget allocations.

Auditing systems are extremely weak. And medium-term expenditure frameworks (MTEFs) are the exception rather than the rule. Yet, PRSPs to date have sometimes included only broad references to the need to improve PEM systems, generally without sets of specific measures for doing so. And, even where improvement plans have been enunciated, they may not be embraced broadly throughout government, or the capacity to implement programs may be weak. Expectations should, therefore, be realistic about the time needed to develop institutional capacity for PEM systems in PRSP countries.

While recognizing that improvements in PEM systems will take time, the importance of improving PEM systems and presentation of the public expenditure program has been highlighted by both domestic stakeholders and donors, who regard these as essential for improving the overall effectiveness of development policies and programs and as an important entry point for improving governance in general. Increasing importance is being attached to developing and implementing detailed plans for improving PEM systems, such as those being developed by HIPC governments with Fund and Bank assistance. Also, many donors have stressed PEM as a means to increase accountability for external assistance, including debt relief, and to justify shifting to budget support. Based on country experience to date, the following could be considered as good practices to strengthen PEM systems:

Good practices for countries

- Outlining in PRSPs an assessment of the current state of PEM systems and realistic plans for improving them. Looking ahead, for HIPCs, these plans could be derived from the Assessments and Action Plans for tracking poverty-reducing spending as these become available; and
- where a medium-term budget instrument/process does not exist, outlining plans for how MTEFs are being developed. Good practices for development partners, including the Bank and Fund
- Providing sufficient resources for technical assistance in support of capacity building for PEM in ways that are responsive to country needs and constraints, supportive of national capacity, and coordinated across donors.

Improving the Integration of PRSPs into Other Decision-Making Processes

In general, there is commitment and involvement in preparing the PRSP at the highest levels of government. There has also been a tendency to shift the responsibility for poverty reduction to Ministries of Finance so that such policies are more closely linked to national budget decisions. This, together with greater emphasis on the link between growth and poverty reduction, has been an important trend associated with the PRSP approach. In some countries, however, the extent to which the PRSP is integrated within existing decision-making processes has been problematic. Initially, this was because the I-PRSP timetables were driven primarily by HIPC and PRGF schedules. In some countries, there was uncertainty about how the PRSP exercise should be related to previously established government planning or national strategic exercises. In many countries, sectoral ministries have been less fully involved in PRSP preparation than would have been expected, and this may have implications for implementation.

Given the diversity of country circumstances and institutional arrangements and the importance of country leadership, a specific approach to better integration cannot be prescribed. However, it may be useful for governments to reassess the timing and linkage of their PRSPs to enhance the likelihood of effective integration and mainstreaming with other government processes. Based on country experience to date, the following could be considered as good practices to improve the integration of PRSPs with existing decision making processes:

Good practices for countries

- Integrating PRSPs (and annual PRSP implementation progress reports) with other government decision making processes, especially with the budget; and
- including in PRSPs information about the institutional arrangements for preparing and implementing strategies, including the role of parliament.

Good practices for development partners, including the Bank and Fund

- Respecting and aligning assistance with national cycles for government decision making, particularly annual budget cycles.

Improving Donor Alignment and Harmonization

Donor alignment and harmonization of donor processes are crucial to sustaining the PRSP approach. In part, the approach has been designed to overcome long-standing problems of poor donor coordination, weak country ownership of donor-financed programs, and the fragmentation of governmental programs and institutions caused by multiple, and often inconsistent, donor aid delivery and management policies and procedures. To overcome these problems, donors must take very seriously the challenge of aligning their programs with countries' PRSPs. If this challenge can be met, PRSPs will become effective instruments for countries to gain better control over external assistance. This will help reduce the administrative burden on recipient countries, reduce the transaction costs of development assistance and enhance development effectiveness, and streamline their documentation and reporting requirements.

Nearly all donors have agreed in principle to align their programs with PRSPs, but much remains to be done to achieve this objective. The dominant view among governments in low-income countries at the recent international conference was that they should take the lead in donor coordination and alignment and that donors need to accept and defer to such government leadership. They recognized that donor alignment would be facilitated if PRSPs provided greater prioritization and specificity of public policies, but asked donors to exercise self-discipline and not force their own agendas on countries. Programmatic lending (including Sector-Wide Approaches and general budget support) is potentially an important instrument for alignment which should be actively used when circumstances warrant. However, many donors remain cautious about such support given weak public expenditure and fiduciary management systems. There is considerable scope for alignment with PRSPs even without programmatic lending.

Although achieving donor alignment and harmonization around countries' PRSPs is a challenge for the entire donor community, the Bank and the Fund have a special responsibility to demonstrate their own willingness and ability to do so. For the Bank, the key step is to align its Country Assistance Strategies (CASs)—in timing and in substance—with PRSPs.8 This has already been adopted as Bank policy and is being put into practice as full PRSPs are finalized. The Bank has decided that, beginning July 2002, it will normally not prepare a new CAS until an IDA country has completed its PRSP. The principle that CASs in IDA countries will normally be based on PRSPs is explicitly set out in the new draft CAS guidelines for staff.

The challenge now is to ensure that in future CASs the Bank's program is aligned with the PRSP, to strengthen, in combination with other donors, the Bank's support to the government's poverty reduction efforts. A second challenge is to align lending operations' conditionalities and the policies they support transparently in line with PRSP priorities. The Poverty Reduction Support Credit (PRSC) is a Bank instrument designed (specifically) for supporting PRSP implementation. Although there are only two new CASs that have been prepared building on PRSPs (Uganda and Burkina Faso) and PRSCs have been approved for only three countries (Uganda, Vietnam, and Burkina Faso), early indications are that the CAS can be effectively built on countries' PRSPs and that, within the CAS framework, the PRSC will become an effective complement to other IDA instruments in supporting the implementation of a country's poverty reduction strategy. Reports to the Boards on PRSP progress in implementation will include information concerning the alignment of CASs with PRSPs in countries that have completed their full PRSPs.

For the IMF, the key challenge is aligning the PRGF with countries' PRSPs, which is the focus of the PRGF review. While a good start has been made in incorporating the key features of PRGF into program design, there is scope for deeper implementation and for clarifying the linkages between PRGF arrangements and PRSPs. The Bank and the Fund have made important strides in inter-agency coordination. At the operational level, this includes joint or parallel PRSP-related missions and the preparation of Joint Staff Assessments (JSAs), and streamlining conditionality in lending instruments, complemented by the operations of a Joint Implementation Committee (JIC) at the central level.

Based on experience to date, the following good practices could be pursued to improve donor alignment behind countries' poverty reduction strategies:

Good practices for countries

- Involving donors in PRSP preparation through, for example, including donor representatives on PRSP working groups;

- actively leading coordination and alignment of the local donor community; and
- disclosing lending and granting documents associated with the PRSP approach (i.e., PRGF, PRSC, and SAC for the Bank and Fund, and similar operational documents for other donors).

Good practices for development partners, including the Bank and Fund

- Aligning donor "business plans" with PRSPs, including performance triggers and conditionality, and justifying the choice of instruments against PRSP objectives;
- using Consultative Groups and similar fora, as well as DAC "peer reviews," to identify alignment issues;
- developing lending operations' conditionalities and policy support transparently and encouraging governments to open up discussions on lending instruments to broader consultations with domestic stakeholders, as well as other branches of government, including parliament;
- actively seek to reduce the heavy burden on countries of accessing donor aid, through eliminating duplicative and overlapping reports, harmonizing and simplifying procedures at both the country and international level, and strengthening countries' capacities and systems around a framework of commonly-agreed standards;
- exploring the expanded use of programmatic lending, including Sector wide Approaches (SWAps), when country circumstances warrant; and
- providing country authorities with information on a timely basis about medium-term aid commitments and debt relief, and improving the predictability and timing of aid flows.

Actions by the Bank and the Fund

- Build on recent progress in aligning the Fund's PRGF with countries' poverty reduction strategies;
- align the Bank CAS to a country's PRSP once the PRSP is completed;

- use PRSCs as a key complement to other Bank instruments to support PRSP implementation within the CAS framework;
- publish country documents in the language that the document was transmitted;
- enhance transparency by allowing authorities to voluntarily disclose their documents in support of Bank/Fund lending (i.e., letters of intent and associated memoranda of economic and financial policies for the PRGF at the Fund, and letters of development policies for the PRSC at the Bank) immediately after they are circulated to Executive Directors (EDs), but before EDs discuss the lending operation. Directors will discuss this issue and its broader implications in the context of the upcoming transparency review at the Fund, with parallel discussions at the Bank (in the context of the first progress report on disclosure implementation in FY 2003).
- strengthen internal review of lending programs to ensure that policies and conditionalities are derived from the PRSP; and streamline conditionality.

Balance Between Speed and Quality for HIPCs

One of the most common criticisms of the PRSP approach is that governments, especially HIPCs, are induced to prepare their strategies too quickly and that this has compromised the quality of the strategies with respect to both technical content and the breadth of country ownership. Some governments and NGOs have urged the Bank and the Fund to delink decisions under the Enhanced HIPC Initiative from PRSPs so that there is no delay in receiving debt relief and/or making it irrevocable, whereas other PRSP countries, some donors and CSOs view delinking as reducing the likelihood that debt relief would be well used and excessively weakening the incentive to complete and begin implementing a PRSP.

For HIPCs that begin to receive interim debt relief from the Decision Point on the basis of I-PRSPs, the key question is whether or not to eliminate or change the current requirement of one year's satisfactory implementation of a full PRSP in order to receive the irrevocable debt relief at the Completion Point.10 In this connection, it should be recognized that, for many HIPCs, the annual debt relief received during the interim period between the Decision and Completion Points is a substantial share of the annual debt relief after the Completion Point. Hence, these countries do not need to rush completion of their PRSP, thus compromising the quality of their strategies, for the sake of increasing flows of debt relief. However, this is not true for some countries (Chad, the Gambia, Mauritania, and Niger) for which a large part of the debt is held by creditors that do not provide any interim debt relief, or for which the debt service profile is lower right after the Decision Point than 2-3 years later.

The Bank and Fund will retain the presumption of a one-year period of satisfactory PRSP implementation before the Completion Point. Should there be a future country case which merits some flexibility in timing, prior to that Completion Point, the staffs will prepare a separate note laying out the conditions under which such flexibility would be applicable.

Future Monitoring

Effective implementation of countries' PRSPs is more likely to occur when there is regular monitoring, evaluation, and revision of the strategy. With this in mind, the current PRSP guidelines envisage that governments—through a participatory process¾would prepare annual implementation progress reports and then, every third year, a full revision of the PRSP. Only three countries (Burkina Faso, Tanzania, and Uganda) have implemented their PRSPs for at least one year and have prepared annual implementation progress reports. No country has yet faced the task of updating its full PRSP.

The value of regular monitoring of PRSPs at the country level is widely accepted by countries, CSOs, and development partners, and the annual reports to date have been useful and informative for both the governments as well as partners. Yet, concerns have been raised about progress reports and periodic updating of strategies, most notably that requiring annual progress reports would impose an excessive burden on governments. Others have expressed concern that the three-year cycle for updating a PRSP may be difficult in some cases in light of national capacity constraints and/or traditional planning cycles.

Also, in cases where there is a change in government, there is at present no clear procedure about how a new government should indicate its intentions with respect to an existing PRSP. Questions of relevance and updating may also arise in the wake of major changes in country circumstances—such as a large change in its terms of trade or a large-scale natural disaster—although the inclusion of contingency spending plans in PRSPs in the event of likely shocks would seem most appropriate.

Bibliography

Angel, Bradley: Toxic Threat to Indian Lands: A Greenpeace Report, San Francisco, Greenpeace, 1991.

Balchin, P., & Kieve, L.: Urban Land Economics, London, MacMillan Press, 1977.

Dahiya, L.N.: Dynamics of Economic Life in Rural India, Delhi, Gian, 1991.

Damon, William: Social and Rural Development in Indian Villages, New York, Norton, 1983.

J.H. Dully, and R. Jolly: Redistribution with Growth, London, Oxford University Press, 2001.

John Ehrenberg: Civil Society: The Critical History of Anti-Poverty Development, New York, New York University Press, 1998.

Kenneth, R.: Social, Poverty, and Rural Development, New York, Wiley, 1998.

Koontz, H.: Anti Povery Development: A Global Perspective, New York, McGraw Hill, 1993.

Meyer, Art: Earth Keepers: Environmental Perspectives on Hunger, Poverty, and Injustice, Scottsdale, Herald Press, 1991.

Peter Willetts: Pressure Groups in the Global System in India, London, Francis Pinter, 1982

Thomas Carroll: Intermediary NGOs: Rural Development in India, West Hartford, CT: Kumarian Press, 1992.

Thomas Princen and Matthias Finger: Environmental NGOs in World Politics, London, Routledge, 1994.

Varian, H. R.: Intermediate Microeconomics, New York, W W Norton and Company, 1987.

William, D.: Social and Poverty Development, New York, Norton, 1983.

Index

♦♦♦